Politics & Apocalypse

Studies in Violence, Mimesis, and Culture

SERIES EDITOR
William A. Johnsen

The Studies in Violence, Mimesis, and Culture book series examines issues related to the nexus of violence and religion in the genesis and maintenance of culture. It furthers the agenda of the Colloquium on Violence and Religion, an international association that draws inspiration from René Girard's mimetic hypothesis on the relationship between violence and religion, elaborated in a stunning series of books he has written over the last 40 years. Readers interested in this area of research can also look to the association's journal, *Contagion: Journal of Violence, Mimesis, and Culture.*

Plans for future books in this series include *Encounters in Friendship and Truth*, a series of essays on René Girard, and the English translation of Giuseppe Fornari's *Da Dioniso a Cristo: Conoscenza e sacrifizio nel mondo greco e nella civilità occidentale.*

The publication of Politics and Apocalypse *was assisted by a special Incentive Allocation from the College of Arts and Letters at Michigan State University. The conference that produced these essays and their publication in the Studies in Violence, Mimesis, and Culture series has been generously underwritten by Peter Thiel, president of Clarium Capital Management. Thiel has given the kind of patronage that Yeats approved in* Duke Ercole, Guidobaldo, and Cosimo: "*. . . della vera città almen le torre.*"

Politics & Apocalypse

Robert Hamerton-Kelly, *Editor*

Michigan State University Press · *East Lansing*

♾ The paper used in this publication meets the minimum requirements of ANSI/NISO Z39.48-1992 (R 1997) (Permanence of Paper).

Michigan State University Press
East Lansing, Michigan 48823-5245

Printed and bound in the United States of America.

13 12 11 10 09 08 07 1 2 3 4 5 6 7 8 9 10

LIBRARY OF CONGRESS CATALOGING-IN-PUBLICATION DATA
Politics & apocalypse / Robert Hamerton-Kelly, editor.
p. cm. — (Studies in violence, mimesis, and culture)
Includes bibliographical references.
ISBN 978-0-87013-811-9 (pbk. : alk. paper) 1. End of the world. 2. Religion and politics. 3. History—Religious aspects. I. Hamerton-Kelly, Robert. II. Title: Politics and apocalypse.
BL503.P65 2007
901—dc22
2007035887

Cover and book design by Sharp Des!gns, Inc., Lansing, Michigan

green press INITIATIVE Michigan State University Press is a member of the Green Press Initiative and is committed to developing and encouraging ecologically responsible publishing practices. For more information about the Green Press Initiative and the use of recycled paper in book publishing, please visit *www.greenpressinitiative.org*.

Visit Michigan State University Press on the World Wide Web at *www.msupress.msu.edu*

Table of Contents

An Introductory Essay

Robert Hamerton-Kelly
Stanford University (retired)

Where the corpse is, there will the vultures flock.
—Matthew 24:28/Luke 17:37

Leave the dead to bury the dead. "Come! Follow me!"
—Matthew 8:22/Luke 9:60

The conference that produced these articles was planned by Peter Thiel and myself and held at Stanford, California, in the week of 12 July 2004. We wanted to discuss current affairs with René Girard in a leisurely way and so invited only eight participants and scheduled the meeting for six full days. As his essay shows, Thiel believes the event of 9/11 reveals that our Western political philosophy can no longer cope with our world of global violence—"the brute facts of September 11 demand a reexamination of the foundations of modern politics."[1] In refining the topic we consulted Wolfgang Palaver, who, not surprisingly suggested the title "Politics and Apocalyptic," not surprisingly because Palaver is the clearest of us all on the apocalyptic nature of Girard's thought in general, and mimetic theory in particular.[2] I changed the title to "Politics and Apocalypse" because "apocalyptic" is an adjective, and to use an adjective as a substantive is still a solecism in English. The change did not, however, solve all the problems, because the substantive, "Apocalypse," is a piece of literature, as the book of Revelation in the New Testament—from which nineteenth-century scholars borrowed the term "apocalypse" in the first place to classify a type of literature—describes itself: "The apocalypse of Jesus Christ which God gave him, to show to his servants what must soon take place" (Rev. 1:1). However, since the documents called apocalypses are classified by their content more than by their form, we might use the term to describe the type of visionary material they contain, and then by further extension the whole apocalyptic phenomenon—thought, method, form, imagery.

There are three major items in our discussion—politics, mimetic theory, and apocalypse—and we must, of course, understand each one. However, rather than offer an introductory description of each, I propose to leave their meanings to unfold as our essayists use them and the context of the discussion demands. For instance, I shall not offer an introductory definition of politics but leave the discussion for our essays that deal with the thought of Carl Schmitt. Likewise, mimetic theory will unfold as we all apply, criticize, and defend it, and in any case we assume that most of our readers are already conversant with it. Apocalypse, however, seems to me to need an introduction, because it is currently so widely and loosely used and is the category that orients our attention to the other two. It is the interpreting background of all we say here.

What Is an Apocalypse?[3]

The root meaning of the Greek term *apokalypsis* is "unveiling" or "disclosure"; and the background of all the articles here is the assumption that something is being revealed about our world's order, whether by divine grace or human reason, and that the revelation not only documents the threat to order but also causes order's increasing instability. How does Girard's theory help us to interpret the apocalypse of world history in general, and the period after 9/11 in particular? We can only suggest an approach to an answer, but in any case we must be clear about how the term "apocalypse" is currently used and what its trajectory or line of meaning through history has been and will be.[4]

Some Current Examples

Gillian Hanna, the English actress, recently described the last public performance of actor and playwright Harold Pinter as an apocalypse. The cancer-stricken Pinter had just performed his friend Samuel Beckett's *Krapp's Last Tape,* and Hanna, speaking to Alan Cowell the critic said, "It is beyond acting. There is something about the coming together of this particular piece and this performance that took me somewhere else." Cowell continues: "That place, [Hanna] said, with a bleakness that might be expected, was 'an icy steppe' or an apocalypse."[5] So an apocalypse is a bleak and ravaged place, where death reigns; an after-the-battle scene of cold corpses, dead horses, and splintered guns.

Paul Krugman, the economist and Bush nemesis—I have read him closely for the last six years and can testify that he has called the president a liar early and often—upon hearing former Speaker of the House Hastert blame George Soros for the public revulsion at Representative Mark Foley's sexually driven misuse of public office, recalled a 1964 essay by Richard Hofstadter, itself provoked by the Goldwater movement, whose heirs have controlled the federal government in all its branches for the last decade, and entitled "The Paranoid Style in American Politics." Hofstadter describes political paranoia as "the sense of heated exaggeration, suspiciousness, and conspiratorial fantasy." (Compare Hastert on Soros: "You know I don't know where George Soros gets his money. I don't know where . . . if it comes from overseas or from drug groups or where it comes from.") Hofstadter continues: the "paranoid spokesman" sees things "in apocalyptic terms. . . . He is always manning the barricades of civilization. . . . what is at stake is always a conflict between absolute good and absolute evil. . . . the enemy is thought of as being totally evil and totally unappeasable, he must be totally eliminated. . . . The demand for total triumph leads to the formulation of hopelessly unrealistic goals . . . and since these goals are not even remotely attainable, failure constantly heightens the paranoid's sense of frustration." Krugman adds that this facet of apocalyptic paranoia easily leads to the conclusion that the failure to achieve goals is the result not of poor planning and execution but of treachery and the "stab in the back." One need hardly quote the president and vice president here to document the paranoid style of their rhetoric: documentation is on every newspaper's front page and can in any case be found in Krugman's article.[6] So apocalypse is an attitude of paranoid grandiosity.

David Brooks, the conservative columnist, has recently traveled widely in the country asking for opinions on the current scene. He reports that the U.S. "street" thinks the Pope raised precisely the right question when he asked whether or not Islam encourages irrationality and violence. "What these Americans see is fanatical violence, a rampant culture of victimology and grievance, a tendency by many Arabs to blame anyone other than themselves for the problems they create. . . . The Muslim millenarians possess a habit of mind that causes them to escalate conflicts. They seem confident they can prevail, owing to their willingness to die for their truth. They don't seem marginalized, but look down on us as weak, and doubt our ability to strike back." So the Muslims too have a paranoid style of politics, millenarians who think they can take over the world because of their willingness to die.[7] One might also note that the atmosphere of Brooks's article is "responsibly alarmist," hinting that we must take the threat seriously and act accordingly, an attitude that itself can slip easily into "responsible paranoia." So apocalypse is an attitude of quasi-paranoid self-righteousness.

Tim LaHaye, a Christian fundamentalist, has written a series of novels, some with Jerry Jenkins, called the "Left Behind" novels.[8] This refers to the Bible's apocalyptic expectation that the believers in Jesus will be snatched from the earth and taken to heaven—"raptured" is the jargon word—while those left behind will incur horrible torture, which God will bring to unbelievers when He wraps up the world. Reading the final volume of the series, one can only conclude that this text was written by sadists for masochists. It paints a pornography of resentful violence. One might dismiss this phenomenon with a murmured *de gustibus,* but the novels have sold in the scores of millions and spawned games, workbooks, kiddies' books, conferences, clubs, periodicals, and websites. The website's monthly newsletter is called "Interpreting the Signs," and currently frets that avian influenza might be a harbinger of the end. Its practitioners call this mode of interpretation "prophecy," and contrast it with the "historical" interpretation of more mainline churches.[9] So the Muslims and the politicians are not the only groups infected with apocalyptic contagion; religious circles too include millions of sufferers. Apocalypse to them is a worldview that sees into the future and prophesies the glorious vindication of the in-group and the cruel punishment of those outside.

Michael Ley of the University of Vienna[10] provides compelling evidence that the medieval apocalypticist Joachim of Floris influenced Adolf Hitler, especially by the prophecy that when the Messiah comes to bring in the third kingdom he will exterminate all the enemies of God. According to Joachim, history unfolds as three dispensations or divine kingdoms, the first of the Father (Israel), the second of the Son (Jesus), and the third of the Holy Spirit (soon to come). The third is to be inaugurated by the Messiah, and the propaganda of the Third Reich implied that the Fuehrer was this Messiah and thus obliged to exterminate God's special enemies, the Jews. More important in this regard than the claims of the propaganda was the fact that Hitler believed the claims of the drama and accepted his role in it. Apocalypse has been the ideology of extreme historical actors and catastrophic historical action.

War is a staple of apocalypse, expressing a dominant feature of the genre, the deep dichotomy between the two major protagonists. In the Bible's apocalyptic world, the final battle between Good and Evil, God and the Devil, or Michael archangel and Satan archfiend is the battle of Armageddon. The name comes from the Hebrew for "the mountain [*har*] of Megiddo," in Greek, "Armageddon" (Rev. 16:16; 2 Chron. 35:22; 2 Kings 9:27, 23:28–30, Judg. 5:19). Megiddo was a fortress city of the kings of Israel, in the vicinity of present-day Haifa, and significant battles, most notably the one with Pharaoh Neco in 609 B.C.E., in which Josiah the monotheistic reformer king of Judah died, to the embarrassment of the biblical authors of his history, for whom good monotheists were not supposed to perish prematurely, were fought before its gates. Today, pilgrimages of fundamentalist Christians go to stand on the mound of the excavated city and look over the valley that runs before it from Haifa to Galilee, while their preachers tell them that this will be the place of the final battle. It requires imagination to fit so huge an event into the limited space of this charming valley, more suited to placid hiking than war. It is well known that the term Armageddon has slipped in and out of U.S. presidential rhetoric ever since the days of Ronald Reagan. So apocalypse is fixated on the final solution of the problems of the group, and the final solution must be war and extermination.

The Biblical Roots

The term "apocalypse" comes from the Bible (Rev. 1:1). Biblical thinking is historical rather than metaphysical, in the sense that its dominant mode is narrative. From the Bible we learn that apocalypse and politics are intimately connected from the start; indeed, in most cases *apocalypse is an interpretation of politics in the form of a coded narrative.* This definition of apocalypse shows its close relevance to politics and goes a long way to explaining the rationale of our project. The commentary in a typical apocalypse is a seamless union of prophecy and politics, and once we appreciate how Jewish apocalypse and its worldview came into being as political commentary and propaganda, we shall be able to move freely between politics and apocalypse in our reflections on the present world situation. We shall be following the procedure of the first apocalypse, the biblical book of Daniel.

The inaugurator of the apocalyptic worldview is the book of Daniel.[11] All of the four apocalypses we shall be looking at here—the Dead Sea Scrolls, the Synoptic Gospels, Paul's second letter to the Thessalonians, and the book of Revelation—are based on Daniel and some actually quote him. Written in a situation of political stress, probably the Greek oppression of Jewish religious culture in the early second century B.C.E., when in 163 Antiochus IV Epiphanes king of Antioch, scion of one of Alexander's successor generals, took

Jerusalem and, by conservative Jewish standards, desecrated the temple, the book of Daniel encourages the "resistance" by means of an encoded political commentary.

The Jewish "resistance" to Greek oppression took at least two forms. The quietists retreated from the political sphere into closed communities, living together in cities and villages and probably also in a mother house by the Dead Sea, although the identification of the ruins in the Wadi Qumran as a "monastery" is continuously contested. (Most recently they have been seen as a commercial establishment.) In any case the scrolls found at Qumran contain a high level of apocalyptic content, and include a scroll that calls itself "The War of the Sons of Light against the Sons of Darkness," which provides a prophetic vision of that final military denouement in which the angels participate and the Messiah of David—there were two messiahs for these folk, one of David and one of Aaron, that is, of palace and temple respectively—leads to victory the armies of God.

The activists, on the other hand, rushed to arms, and John, Simon, Judah, Eleazar, and Jonathan, the five sons of Mattathias, a priest of the lineage of Hasmon, became the "Hammers of God," the Maccabees. They turned out to be gifted generals whose military successes broke the political control of the Syrian Greeks and in 142 B.C. put in office a high priest of their own Hasmonean lineage. The traditional account of the exploits of these heroes of Hannukah is in the three books of the Maccabees, in the collection that Catholics include in the canon and Protestants marginalize as apocrypha.

This change of the ruling high priestly family from Zadokite to Hasmonean did perhaps more damage to the Jewish polity than did the Greeks, because for the old-guard followers of Zadok it compromised the temple and invalidated its ritual. The Hasmoneans were not the true high priesthood. The people we have called quietists are also known, following the contemporary historian Josephus, as Essenes, but their name for themselves is "Sons of Zadok," and in their commentary on Hosea (4QpHosea), they mention a "wicked priest" who persecuted their "Righteous Teacher." This reference is best interpreted as a description of the origin of the sect in the resistance of Zadokite loyalists to the new Hasmonean high priest, and the price they paid in power and relevance.

So there were two reactions to the Greek assault on Jewish polity and culture, both of which were religious, namely, the quietist and the activist, the Zadokites and the Maccabees. It is of special importance for our theme that the more apocalyptic of the two were the quietists, warranting the speculation that apocalypse is the literature of the resentful, in Nietzsche's sense, of those whose revenge has failed. For Nietzsche the best way to deal with wounding is immediate retaliation, absent which the sting of insult sours to self-righteousness and poisons the system, until, growing ever more self-justifying, the victim projects the poison like the cobra onto real or imagined foes. Those who, like the Maccabees, acted successfully to avenge themselves did not produce apocalypses; they had no marinating vengeance to be served (cold?) and no humiliation to be rectified at some future time.

The Sons of Zadok were compensated for their temporary humiliation by two gifts: the gift of the *pesher* interpretation, and the knowledge of the heavenly secrets (*razim*). *Pesher* exegesis is based on the conviction that these are the last days and those who know this also know that the biblical text describes the present final age rather than the past time in which it was written. The biblical writers were prophets who in code wrote of our time rather than their own and of our group's founding and future. The characteristic phrase of the *pesher* is "The meaning of this is [*peshro*]," a way of citing the Old Testament that is well known from the New Testament. For these apocalyptic interpreters the Old Testament text was, therefore, a long prophecy in code describing their current historical situation, assumed to be the end of history, and interpreting the signs of the end.[12] In order to know the deeper meaning of the biblical text, one had also to be privy to the celestial secrets (*razim*) hidden from the foundation of the world. The "right teacher" of Qumran demonstrates this necessity as he closely combines the two components of revelation, disclosing the secrets by means of the exegesis and guiding the exegesis by means of the secrets. Thus we see that apocalyptic activity was mainly the literary activity of "scribes," the writers and interpreters of texts, and thus warrants, if that is at all needed, our mimetic method, which emerged from literary interpretation and rose to become a principle of historical intelligibility and a revealer of hidden things.

The secrets were units of special knowledge of God's plan for history, also called in the New Testament the "wisdom of God." In 1 Corinthians 2:7–9, we see a good example of how Paul the Apostle uses this concept. He writes: "yet among the mature we do impart a wisdom, although it is not a wisdom of this age or of the rulers of this age, who are doomed to pass away. But we impart a secret and hidden wisdom of God, which God decreed before the ages for our glorification. None of the rulers of this age understood this; for if they had, they would not have crucified the Lord of Glory." Girard makes much of this Pauline text as showing how the powers of this age destroyed themselves when they crucified Christ, because the Cross revealed their violence and showed this world to be a structure of sacred violence. Had the powers known the secret wisdom, they would not have served God's plan so well by disclosing their own surrogate victim ruse. In their ignorance they gave away the secret of their power, which is covert violence, and damaged themselves irreparably.

We turn now to the contents of some representative biblical apocalypses to illustrate the nature of the original apocalypses in the Western tradition, and we begin with the seventh chapter of Daniel. The original is in Aramaic rather than Hebrew, indicating that it is relatively late in the canon, stemming, as we have already remarked, from the second century B.C.E. It is the product of people in circumstances of crisis, who deal with their situation by locating themselves in history by means of an apocalyptic historiography that makes them the goal of an unfolding divine providence on the way to post-history and transcendence.

Chapter 7 of Daniel is set in the first year of the reign of Belshazzar of Babylon, 554 B.C.E., but this dating is fictional, since the whole work is pseudepigraphical and was actually written about 400 years later. Daniel dreams of four great beasts that symbolize four great empires: the first is "like a lion" with eagle's wings, the second is "like a bear" with three ribs in its mouth, the third is "like a leopard" with four wings and four heads, and the fourth is not compared to anything else but simply described as unlike the previous three—"terrible, dreadful and exceedingly strong," having "great iron teeth," with which it chewed up most everything in sight, and what it missed with its teeth it stomped with its feet. Its most remarkable feature, however, is its ten horns, in the midst of which, as he watched, Daniel saw a little horn sprout and lay low three of its predecessors. It had human eyes and a mouth "speaking great things."[13]

The climax of this procession of horrors is the appearance of an old man whose hair and garment are dazzlingly white, seated on a throne in the midst of a glorious court. Books are opened and judgment is pronounced on the basis of the records they contain. The last-appearing beast is slaughtered and burned while the prior four are deprived of dominion but allowed to live. Then appears "one like a human being ("son of man" in Aramaic idiom) who approaches the throne of the glittering old man (the "ancient of days"), who in turn gives him "dominion, glory and royal power, that all peoples, nations, and languages should serve him; his dominion is an everlasting dominion, which shall not pass away, and his kingdom one that shall not be destroyed" (7:14).

Daniel the dreamer now asks one of the courtiers to explain the meaning of all that has transpired, and the courtier tells him that the four beasts represent four kingdoms—which we know to be, respectively, the Chaldeans

(Babylonians), the Medes, the Persians, and the Greeks of Alexander, precisely the empires that impinged on the Jews from the Babylonian exile of 586 B.C.E. to the desecration of Jerusalem in 163 B.C.E. Thus we know that this is prophecy *ex eventu,* the wisdom of hindsight tricked out as foresight, but in any case the wisdom of insight, in narrative guise. The "human being" ("Son of Man") represents "the Kingdom of the Saints of the Most High," clearly the name of a religious group like the "Sons of Zadok," a sect perhaps also at odds with the Hasmonean priesthood of the temple.

From this account we glean all the formal characteristics of the content of apocalypse, as well as its general significance as the origin of the concept of a universal history. The stable elements of the content are the heavenly world, the interpreting angel, the special group, the books of secret records, the war and final judgment, and the seer or, as the Mormons would say, "revelator," who is the earthly counterpart of the angelic interpreter. Enoch is the archetype of the revelator; in Genesis 5, deep in one of those numbing recitations of "begats," we read that Jared begat Enoch, that Enoch begat Methuselah, and that "Enoch walked with God; and he was not, because God took him" (Gen. 5:24). The apocalyptic tradition interpreted this enigmatic statement to mean that God hoisted Enoch bodily to the realm of the angels, to the heavenly archives, and even to the outskirts of the holy place where stands the throne of God Himself. Since Enoch had been elevated bodily he could later return to earth and record what he had seen for our edification and warning. From Enoch's records, extant in three books, we learn, among other marvelous things, that there are seven heavens, five archangels, and a *massa damnata* of fallen angels in the third heaven.

Universal history ends in universal judgment, and at that trial of trials the litigants, both prosecution and defense, consult the books of record, which describe not only the deeds of individuals but also those of nations, and thus present an account of the history of the world to the end of time. Whoever gains access to those records can foretell, and this is the priceless knowledge a Daniel or an Enoch brings to us. Here, then, we have a universal history of the world from beginning to end, with the "human being" at the climax.

Because the purpose or end of universal history is human, apocalypse emphatically uses the principle of moral responsibility to interpret its trajectory. The final judgment is a moral rectification of the order of history. Rectification is the best translation of the term used so much by the Apostle Paul, namely, "justification." The rectification or justification achieved in Daniel 7 is the restoration of human beings to their original hegemony over the beasts. In Genesis, God made Adam ruler of the beasts (Gen. 1:26–29), but as a result of his sin, Adam became subject to the beasts and endured a long and humiliating servitude. When the "Son of Man" comes with his "Kingdom of the Saints of the Most High," humanity returns to mastery of the beasts and the disorder of the creation is rectified. "The authentic human being" ("Son of Man") is the vanguard of this rectification, and at this point it is worth noting that of all the titles the Gospel traditions use to describe Jesus's status, "Son of Man" is the only one Jesus seems historically to have accepted.

Thus Jesus is the inaugurator of the New Creation, which is a world of equal status for all human beings and the theme that the Apostle Paul makes central to his own understanding of the significance of Jesus. Universalism is the dominant note of earliest Christianity; Paul celebrates it when he realizes that his narrow religiosity had made him a persecutor (Gal. 2:19–21), and eventually proclaims, "There is neither Jew nor Greek, bond nor free, male nor female, for you are all one and the same in Christ Jesus" (Gal. 3:28). At the Colloquium on Violence & Religion (COV&R) meeting of 2004 held at Ghost Ranch, New Mexico, Michel Serres claimed that Paul is the thinker for our time because he participated uniquely and knowingly in the death of one culture and the birth of another, and we are currently again at such a hinge of history. Serres' address on that occasion might itself be taken as an apocalypse in the sense of a disclosure of the meaning of the signs of the times.[14] Paul could do what he did because he thought in apocalyptic terms of a universal history and an event of universal significance, the Resurrection of Jesus, in that history. The end of all history, the Resurrection of the dead and the New Creation, has happened in the course of human history, so "then at the end" has become "now in the midst."

This identification of the center of history with the end is the identification of a spatial with a temporal concept, "here and now" with "then and there." For most of us the promise of "then and there" is enough. Time attests our human frailty with respect to the appropriation of reality. We must, because of that frailty, be content to receive reality in "coffee spoonfuls," as T. S. Eliot puts it, dribs and drabs from time to time, because we cannot bear too much. We are time bound and reality comes to us along the trajectory of that bondage. Ultimately when the timeline ends, we go "face to face" (1 Cor. 13:12), but in the meantime we, like the old-time remittance man, receive our periodic allowance. The mystic, or revelator, or prophet, on the other hand, has episodes of direct contact with the really real, and is thus able to keep the rest of us informed and encouraged. The Incarnation of God as the authentically human gives us all a glimpse of the real, enables us to anticipate and enjoy it, and therefore is the apocalyptic event par excellence, the end of history. Since it has occurred in the midst of time, it has the proleptic status of the "already but not yet," already in substance but not yet in durance.

The effect of compounding the symbolism of time and space, the "then" and the "there," in the portrayal of transcendence might be most clearly seen in the Gospel of John. "Truly, truly, I say to you, the hour is coming and now is when the dead shall hear the voice of the Son of God, and those who hear will live" (John 5:25). The future consummation of all earthly things is already present in the heavenly realm, says John, and then he adds the revolutionary and essential Christian claim that they are present also on earth, in the midst of time, as the person of Jesus himself ("I am the Resurrection and the Life": 11:25). The final judgment takes place now as we judge ourselves in the choice we make to accept or reject Jesus (5:21–24; 3:16–21). So the Incarnation of God is the entry of "there" into "now," and the time of this is the eschatological moment.[15] In Jesus we encounter the end of the world, in both senses of end, namely, the purpose and the finish.

Reading the signs of the times is prominent in the apocalyptic sayings attributed to Jesus in the Synoptic Gospels (Matthew, Mark, and Luke). In turning to the Jesus of the Synoptics, we begin with one of the epigraphs to this essay: "Where the corpse is, there will the vultures flock." In Matthew it is the climax of that gospel's apocalyptic discourse, while in Luke it is part of the build up to the apocalypse. To be sure, it is a sinister injunction full of the negative freight of catastrophe, evoking the scene of evening on a battlefield. Could Jesus be as sardonic as this? Let's assume that he could, and that this aphorism, hardly to be remembered for its cheerfulness, is from him. It suggests a weary reluctance to enter into the eager discussion of the signs of the time, beyond urging wakefulness and attention. "Don't be so eager to walk with the vultures among corpses," he says to those who wish the day of their vindication would make haste to come.

The so-called "Synoptic Apocalypse" is in Mark 13:1–37; it is the basis on which Matthew and Luke built their apocalypses by adding to it from the hypothetical source Q. The narrative begins with Jesus prophesying the destruction of the temple, and the disciples asking when this will happen and what will be the signs of its imminence. Jesus refuses to specify signs, but rather warns of persecution and general tribulation, urging discrimination and sobriety. When he does advert to signs, the prophecy has already been fulfilled, the "desolating sacrilege" is already there in the Holy of Holies of the temple, and the reader is prodded to interpret correctly. ("But when you see the desolating sacrilege set up where it ought not to be [let the reader understand], then let those who are in Judea flee to the mountains" [Mark 13:14/

Matthew 24:15; Daniel 9:27, 11:31, 12:11; 1 Maccabees 1:57].) The phrase "desolating sacrilege" is quoted from Daniel, and the little hint to the reader confirms that we are reading an encoded history, probably of the actual rape of the temple by the Romans under Titus in 70 C.E., and shows not only that the apocalyptic type of historiography from Daniel is operating but also that the writer is interpreting the actual text of Daniel by means of the *pesher* exegesis. The evangelists use the method and the actual imagery of Daniel to tell us that the desecration of the temple by the Romans is prophesied in a document that presents itself as a sixth-century B.C.E. message from Babylon but in fact is a second-century account of Antiochus's defiling of the temple, now presented as if it were a 70 C.E. account of Titus's atrocity in the first Jewish war. Thus they discover and reapply the constant elements in their history, saying that Daniel wrote of our times, even in Babylon. The "desolating sacrilege" set up in the temple is probably the standards of the legion that captured Jerusalem.[16] So the synoptic apocalypse is like Daniel a prophecy after the event, attributed to Jesus, who by the time of these happenings had been gone from this world for more than 30 years.

The master message that emerges from these synoptic apocalypses is that since no one knows when these final events will come to pass, the proper attitude is not curiosity but sobriety and attentiveness (Mark 10:32–33: "But of that day or that hour no one knows, not even the angels in heaven, nor the Son, but only the Father. Take heed, watch; for you do not know when the time will come").

The last book of the Bible, known as the Revelation, calls itself "The Apocalypse of Jesus Christ" (Rev. 1:1), and since it is the archetypal apocalypse in literary history we must take a brief look at it. We need not dwell on it, because we have already seen in Daniel all the characteristics of the apocalyptic genre in both thought and technique. Written some time during the reign of Roman Emperor Domitian (81–96 C.E.), who had persecuted Christians and confined the author of the book to a labor camp on the island of Patmos, the Apocalypse of John bears the marks of its provenance in crisis and suffering. It is for the most part an account of happenings in heaven that impinge upon earth at the end of history, relayed through a revelator to those still here. Chapter 13 begins as a paraphrase of Daniel 7 and goes on to become a new composition as the beastly visions receive a new and extended interpretation. The beast from the sea combines the powers of the four beasts of Daniel and represents the Roman Empire.[17] From this apocalypse we also get most of the conventional components of popular apocalyptic eschatology, like the millennium or thousand years of joy when Satan is locked up, the fire in which the devil and his angels, and all the humans who served them, will burn eternally, the tribulations of the end times, and the reward of the righteous.

One important feature of apocalyptic historiography that we have not yet emphasized is the principle "as in heaven so on earth," the parallel course of events and the parallel existence of institutions in heaven and on earth.[18] For example, war in heaven becomes war on earth (Rev. 12:7–9), the rituals of heaven are archetypes of the ritual in the temple on earth, and the heavenly Jerusalem is an archetype of the earthly (Rev. 21:1ff; cf. Galatians 4:25–27). At the climax of history the heavenly city descends to earth and replaces the earthly city. There is no temple in this city, because God himself is present in all its districts; that is, the heavenly liturgy, so lovingly described, replaces its erstwhile earthly approximation but need no longer be confined to a temple, because the temple and the city have become one, and heaven itself, of which the temple was a sign and an anticipation, is now with us on earth.

Finally we turn to a Pauline apocalypse in 2 Thessalonians 2:1–12, which is the background of Carl Schmitt's important figure of the *katechon*. Some members of the Thessalonian congregation believe the "Day of the Lord" has already come and are stirred up. Paul explains why the day has not come and why they should settle down. He sets out his understanding of what must happen, and as in all the other examples we have seen, the apocalypse he writes draws on Daniel. He might indeed be reciting an already existing piece rather than composing *de novo*, which if true would show that this apocalypse was a general property of the early church and not a composition of the apostle. It plays an important role in Schmitt's thought and Palaver's essay.

First must come "the apostasy," then the appearance of the man of lawlessness,[19] the son of perdition, who opposes and exalts himself against every so-called god or object of worship, so that he takes his seat in the temple of God, proclaiming himself to be God; but now you know what is holding him back (the *katechon* = "the thing that restrains") until he is revealed in his proper time. "For the mystery of lawlessness is working now, only he who now restrains him (the *katechon*) will continue to do so until he disappears from the scene and the lawless man is revealed whom the Lord Jesus shall destroy with the breath of his mouth when he comes" (2 Thess. 2: 4–8; cf. Rev. 19:15). The man of lawlessness (*anthropos tes anomias*) is in mimetic terms the symbol of the sacrificial crisis, the chaos in which all distinctions disappear.

The lawless man in this drama acts with the power of Satan and works fraudulent miracles; he is the "mystery of lawlessness, the opponent of the will of God" (2 Thess. 2:9). In the letters of John this is the antichrist (1 John

2:18–25). As the "Son of Man" (Christ) is the representative human being, so "the man of lawlessness" is the representative enemy of human being (antichrist). He is not Satan but the son of Satan, so to speak, as Jesus is the Son of God. Antichrist in our apocalypse resembles Antiochus IV Epiphanes in Daniel, and so this element is probably a literary reference rather than a symbolic presentation of a current historical figure. Nevertheless, the idea that it might refer symbolically to Emperor Gaius Caligula is worth attention. Josephus tells us that Gaius, in the winter of C.E. 39/40, believing himself to have been insulted by the inhabitants of the Judean village of Jamnia, ordered a statue of himself to be set up in the temple in Jerusalem. The statue came by sea from Sidon and landed at Ptolemais, where the governor of Syria, Petronius, delayed the offloading again and again because of massive public protests. During this delay, Caligula was murdered and the crisis passed. Decoding our apocalypse by the light of this history, we might read that the wicked man who thought he was God and sat in the temple is Caligula, and the restraining force or *katechon* is the power behind the wisdom of Petronius and the murderers of Gaius.[20] In any case, on a mimetic reading, the man and the mystery of lawlessness in our apocalypse refer to the sacrificial crisis of the erasure of distinctions, the chaos of undifferentiation whence violence comes.

Be that as it may, the action here is controlled by the apocalyptic idea of the "right time," and the restraining historical power is there to keep events from happening prematurely. It does not prevent them from happening at all but serves only to ensure that the apocalyptic calendar is kept. To the Thessalonians who thought the day of the Lord had already come, Paul says that the *katechon* will assure that the end will come "at its proper time" (2 Thess. 2:6).

Let these apocalypses serve to give content to the term "apocalypse" and to illustrate its details. Apocalypse describes what "is" eternally and what "shall be" temporally when the history of this world ends and becomes the eternity of that world. We have cataloged some current uses of the term: the "icy steppe" of "somewhere else" where the dying actor plays the dying character and death kisses death; the paranoid politician's intolerably grandiose self-justification of the in-group and reckless damnation of the "outs"; the violent imaginings of the condign punishment of opponents, as seen in the Bible through the lens of sadistic novelists. "Apocalypse" today has all its traditional meaning: the final justification of the precious group by means of a final cataclysmic act of universal punishment, as well as a newer secular meaning of simple catastrophe. Apocalypse is the lens through which we view international politics because it is the *fons et origo* of the concept of history and historiography. Were it not for apocalypse, we would not have the categories of mind with which to ask the questions of meaning and adequacy of interpretation.

Mimetic Theory as Apocalypse

Girard's contribution to our volume is a good example of the apocalyptic nature of mimetic theory. Here in a hitherto unpublished work from what he calls "my creative period," we encounter the basic insights of the double guile that bests the guile of sacred violence, still with the freshness of discovery on them. Mimetic theory is ironically apocalyptic because it is in fact the opposite of what normally passes for that genre. It is nonviolent, while the vulgar apocalypse is violent, it decodes while the vulgar encodes; nevertheless, it is apocalyptic because it deals with universal history and human nature and assumes that historiography is possible and the human story is not "a tale told by an idiot." It is apocalyptic because it decodes the encryption of violence in the vulgar apocalypse, in symbols such as the divine judgment and the torture of the guilty.

From the first, Girard's mimetic theory was an apocalyptic theory. He entitles the penultimate chapter of his early work, *Deceit, Desire, and the Novel* (1965),[21] "The Dostoyevskian Apocalypse," and in it summarizes the achievement of Dostoyevsky in disclosing what at that time Girard was calling "metaphysical desire." At this early stage of the idea of mimetic desire, Girard was concerned to expound how the great novelists reveal the way desire imitates desire and operates as a triangle of "desire, desired, and model or mediator of desire." He called this desire "metaphysical," because it is essentially a desire to gain being from the other. I feel deprived of being and in my need I think that the model has a fullness of being that I, the desirer, might acquire by desiring the same objects as the model, and eventually the being itself of the model. Desire's dearth of being is the result of its deviation from the true source of being, in the divine, to the human other, by way of pride. Pride claims self-sufficiency for the desirer, who in fact, all unawares, is being humiliated rather than exalted because he depends now for being on the equally exiguous other. Desire has deviated and down this detour the blind lead the blind into the empty mimetic ditch.[22]

The master revelator of deviated desire and the Romantic myth of self-sufficiency is Dostoyevsky, initially in *Notes from the Underground* and climactically in *The Demons* (earlier translated as *The Possessed*). The penultimate chapter of the latter describes the death of Stepan Trofimovich Verkhovensky, who "constantly played a certain special and so to speak civic role among us."[23] In this role he instigated the metaphysical rivalry of the young men around Nikolai Vsevolodovich Stavrogin, his protector's only son, and now lies on his deathbed confessing to a stranger, a woman seller of Bibles. She reads to him three biblical passages that are crucial to an understanding of the novel as a whole and especially its proper novelistic ending in conversion. The three passages are chosen in three different ways, a fact that is of importance to the interpretation. The Bible lady chooses first and reads the Sermon on the Mount; second, he asks her to open the Bible at random and read the first thing she sees, and she reads the letter to the church in Laodicea from the third chapter of the Apocalypse (Rev. 3:14–22), which warns the congregation that because they are neither hot nor cold, but lukewarm, God will spit them out of his mouth like stale coffee. Thus the Apocalypse discloses Stepan Trofimovich's lifelong lack of seriousness.[24] The third and final passage she reads is at his request; it is the account of the Gadarene demoniac in Luke 8:32–36, which, the narrator reminds us, is one of the epigraphs of the whole novel.[25] So while the two gospel passages are deliberately chosen, the one from the Apocalypse presents itself at random; apocalypse is always there, under the surface, ready to pop out when least expected.

Placed at the beginning of the novel and at its end, the story of the madman and the swine is the key to the novel as a recovery of the proper goal of desire in God enabling the journey from madness to sanity, from deviated desire to divine fulfillment, from the emptiness of being to the plenitude of love, from sin to grace, from hell to heaven by way of revelation and conversion. The conversion includes the two classic elements, confession and turning to God.

Thus he confesses his sin: "My friend, when I understood . . . that turned cheek, I . . . right then also understood something else. . . . *J'ai menti toute ma vie* [I have lied all my life], all my life!"[26]

Thus he turns to God: "My immortality is necessary if only because God will not want to do an injustice and utterly extinguish the fire of love for him once kindled in my heart. And what is more precious than love? Love is higher than being, love is the crown of being, and is it possible for being not to bow before it? If I have come to love him and rejoice in my love—is it possible that he should extinguish both me, and my joy, and turn us to naught? If there is a God, then I am immortal! *Voila, ma profession de foi* [There is my profession of faith]."[27] (Thus we see the transformation of the goal of life from being to love, for "God is Love"—1 John 4:8.)

Conversion is metaphorically an exorcism, but empirically it is an apocalypse, and in 1961 Girard proposed that it also describes the experience of the great novelist who eventually gains insight into the mimetic dynamics of himself and his narrative characters and then rewrites the narrative from the point of view of the unveiled. Every great novel is written twice, once as concealment and once as apocalypse. Recently Milan Kundera wrote: "If you imagine the genesis of a novelist in the form of an exemplary tale, a myth, that genesis looks to me like a *conversion story* [his italics]; Saul becoming Paul; the novelist being born from the ruins of his lyrical ["romantic"—in Girard's sense] world." Did Kundera get this insight from Girard? I do not know. He and Girard are acquainted and have had conversations. In any case Kundera might have discovered this important part of the mimetic truth himself, because he is a great novelist.[28]

A "Legion" of demons leaves the demoniac and goes into a group of swine, which rushes over a cliff and drowns in the lake. The man sits at Jesus's feet, restored to life and peace. This is the individual experience, but there is a group experience too. Girard points out that the demons are both one and many, Legion and legion, and Stepan Trofimovich compares the demoniac to Russia as a whole, possessed but soon to be purified. Girard made a similar move in his thinking; farther along his intellectual trajectory he turned from Legion to legion, from the individual to the group.

The dying man says, "it's exactly like our Russia. These demons who come out of a sick man and enter into swine—it's all the sores, all the miasmas, all the uncleanness, all the big and little demons accumulated in our great, dear, sick man, Russia, for centuries and centuries! . . . but the sick man will be healed and sit at the feet of Jesus . . . and everyone will look in amazement."[29] Since this sick man is Russia as a whole, we might use the image as a segue from mimetic theory as a theory of the individual in the group to a theory of groups in relationship with each other and of the institutions that give stability to groups.

In *Violence and the Sacred*[30] and *Things Hidden since the Foundation of the World*,[31] Girard discerned how mimetic desire gives structure to groups and maintains public order. At this stage the theory becomes an apocalyptic anthropology. As apocalypse entails a universal historiography, so mimetic theory entails a universal anthropology. The analysis by means of mimetic rivalry and the scapegoat leads to the vision of this world as a structure of Sacred Violence, erected by the three powers of the surrogate victim, namely, ritual, myth, and prohibition. Ritual makes institutions, myth makes identity, and prohibition makes law. The sacred structure of "this world" thus emanates from the surrogate victims as a series of differences whose first and foundational difference is the gap between the profane and the sacred, that is, the difference between the lynch mob and its victim. The victim—which conducts violence out of the social system—founds the sacred structure on the far side of the gap between itself and its victimizers, by being the catalyst for the solidarity of the lynch mob. Thus the surrogate victim mechanism gives stability to the group normally wracked by mimetic rivalry and competing violence, but this stability is unstable.

Ritual sacrifice renews the stability, myth hides it, and law enforces it, but each of these agents is disingenuous. The ruse's effectiveness depends on its being hidden from view and immune from understanding, and if this is so, then the last thing the ruse can tolerate is an apocalypse, or unveiling of the hidden secrets. Inasmuch as the Crucifixion of Jesus unveils the victim slain from the foundation of the world (Rev. 13:8), it is the decisive apocalypse, nothing less than the arrival of the end of time in the midst of history. Therefore, the Crucified is the "Son of Man," our liberator from the sacrificial crisis in which Daniel's monsters appear. When Daniel dreams of monsters and links them to imperial structures of violence, he begins the unveiling (apocalypse) that culminates in the revelation of the Son of Man as the victim slain from the foundation of the world. In this sense the mimetic theory shows how the Cross demythifies the world, that is, tells the truth about the world's origin and survival as an ever renewed structure of sacred violence dependent on the rituals of sacrifice, the myths of origins, and the laws of prohibition and enforcement. "World" in this usage, then, is the world of human beings organized by the ruse of the surrogate, around the mound of the idolized victim. The foundation of this world is the moment of the first successful surrogate ruse, when life was made possible by death and the two natural states were distinguished culturally and symbolically.

The effect of the preaching of the Gospel in Western culture has been to unveil the secret of society's survival through the ritual of the victim and thus to put that survival in jeopardy. The better we know the ruse, the worse it works to sustain the structures of the sacred within which we secure ourselves somewhat from violent disorder. Currently, globalization is eroding cultural distinctions, self-victimization is becoming a cultural industry, and most significant of all, violence is erasing even the existential distinction between life and death. In the cults of the suicide killers, the desire for mass destruction, contained during the Cold War in the sacred structure of deterrence, is now leaking to more and more minor players. The suicide fighter erases the lines of deterrence that map a common world in which everyone concerned values his/her life. Suicidal antagonists cannot be deterred on the old assumptions; the distinction crucial to the cultural control of violence, between the mob and the victim (the living and the dead), is finally eroding entirely and the sacrificial crisis is conjuring monsters once again.

Suicidal murder is an advanced symptom of the collapse of the surrogate victim system and it is now a component of our global culture. The surrogate victim ruse operates by killing someone else; suicidal murder operates by killing the self as well as someone else, and thus erases the distinction between killer and victim and confuses the principal distinction in the culture, namely, the one between the sacred and the profane, between the dead victim on the one hand and the live perpetrators on the other, out of which ritual, myth, and law emerge as generators of further distinctions and stabilizers of all the other cultural distinctions. The Muslim radicals probably believe that their deaths enable others of their group to live, and they strengthen this belief by underlining the distinctions between insiders and outsiders, but in fact they break out of the system of distinctions, which rests on the difference between life and death, and reenter the world of monsters, the world of the living dead and the undead, and the demoniac who lives among the tombs.

Ironically, the sacred violence of jihadist Islam, which believes it is strengthening its sacral foundation, is in fact sawing at the branch on which the religion sits. Suicidal violence no longer confirms the fundamental distinction but rather erases it, and deals crippling blows to the system of good violence that is supposed to control bad violence. The violence that no longer heeds the distinction between life and death might indeed be fatal to the sacrificial mechanism, which like an ancient automobile is shaking itself to bits on rocky roads. The beginning of the apocalyptic end might be upon us, and a gigantic sacrificial crisis breaking out.

So mimetic theory leaves us with a vision of a long-lasting, universal social and cultural structure of sacred violence, based on the working of the surrogate victim ruse, now reentering the great sacrificial crisis of the original period and thus disintegrating into confusion and increasing uncontrolled violence. The fact that Islam is the current vanguard of this crackup can be no surprise, since monotheism is the first and most effective blow against the pagan sacrificial order, and every great religion is great to the extent that it decodes its own mythology of sacred violence. In doing this the great religions disclose the ruse and render it progressively ineffectual, thus weakening the traditional religious control of violence. Islam has reached a new extreme of this process and by destroying itself as a religion is ultimately saving itself as a faith, if indeed it is the true faith. If not, it is simply destroying itself.

Islam is in the throes of an advancing sacrificial crisis, indicated by the emergence in it of suicide as a virtue where it has traditionally been a sin, making the world wait in vain for a representative and authoritative Islamic condemnation of murder by suicide. When will the leadership, however fragmented, emphatically and repeatedly announce that those who do such things are not Muslims but pagans and are going not to paradise but to hell? We wait in vain for such transparency and cannot shake the suspicion that Islam does not speak out because it affirms the violence of the sacred and is by mimetic standards nothing but a mode of pagan sacrifice, blaming the scapegoat and purchasing internal unity with the blood of the external enemy. This last, desperate attempt to make the mechanism work is already uniquely undermined by the suicidal, self-sacrificial erasure of the first distinction between the mob and the victim, between life and death. Where the mob kills itself for the sake of itself, the logic of the ruse has entered a stage of terminal decay, and sacrificial structure will soon be utterly unable to control violence. This is the sign that the latter days of the present world are upon us.

I do not mean that soon the stars will fall from the night sky and the moon be washed in blood, the dragon arise from the lake of fire, and the wicked be tortured by God; no, I mean simply that the present global order is in a process of deep transformation and the outcome is uncertain. The old order is collapsing, and sacrifice can no longer stop the crisis of disorder or hold it up. The United States with all its military power, which I regard as a prime instance of good violence, cannot bring order in Iraq, which is a sign of this historical stage of advanced sacrificial failure, an apocalypse indeed.

Reading the Signs of the Times

The conference of which these papers are a record convened to assess the competence of mimetic theory to disclose the structure and dynamics of human history and by this theoretic light to "read the signs" of our especially violent times, that is, to spot the vultures and find the corpse. One can test a theory only by application; mimetic theory's success at interpreting events attests its adequacy as a theory, but there is another, less useful to be sure, way of testing a theory, and that is by comparing it with other comparably significant theories. Our competence and interest led us to three twentieth-century savants, Carl Schmitt, Leo Strauss, and Eric Voegelin, and to the further question of whether philosophy as such can be a reliable guide to the human situation or whether mimetic theory should replace it. Our participants deal with these topics, and I do not intend by way of introduction to summarize their work; rather, I shall take up only some salient features of their arguments that dovetail with the apocalyptic background of the reflection as a whole.[32] If mimetic theory is an apocalyptic theory, then how do the theories of these major twentieth-century thinkers, themselves apocalyptic in significant ways, impinge on it, and how does it fare in comparison with them?

Carl Schmitt

Schmitt serves to introduce the other pole of our title, namely, politics, and along with politics he introduces war. Clausewitz famously said that war is politics by other means, while Schmitt reverses direction and holds that politics is war by other means. The distinction between friend and enemy and the struggle for power between these two antagonists are the essence of politics. One might compare this with the opening paragraph of Clausewitz's *On War,* in which he says that war is essentially a combat between two antagonists (*ein Zweikampf,* usually translated as "a duel") and that the *Zweikampf* is more like a wrestling match (*ringen*) than pistols for two at dawn. Schmitt's marvelously clarifying definition is an apocalyptic description of politics, using the characteristic theme of the dichotomy. The ur-dichotomy is that between the surrogate victim and the mob, and classic apocalypse is structured by this distinction. The very fact that the definition is so clarifying shows that the friend/foe distinction is mimetic and apocalyptic, and incidentally, that mimetic theory and apocalyptic theory are in this regard barely distinguishable.[33]

Palaver shows clearly that Schmitt's idea of politics and his social vision are based on the surrogate victim mechanism. In it the structure of sacred violence exercises the power that restrains history (*katechon*) in its accelerating drift toward world revolution (sacrificial crisis). The *katechon* is Schmitt's apocalyptic term, taken, as we have seen, from the Bible, to name a phenomenon very like Girard's order of the Sacred in its effect of holding back history and warding off chaos. To the extent that Schmitt's thought is a theology, as in *Political Theology,* the title of one of his better-known books, it is a pagan version of Christianity, an adaptation of Christian theology to the service of sacred violence. So despite his confusion of theology with mythology, Schmitt is a reader of the signs whose reading confirms the insight of mimetic theory.

Palaver calls him anti-apocalyptic, ranking him with Strauss and Voegelin as thinkers who fear the potential for chaos in Christianity's vision and energy. For this reason one must suppose that Schmitt's use of *katechon* is ironic, in the sense that it is an apocalyptic idea used against the apocalypse. One might ask whether Schmitt does not misuse the idea because he misreads the text. The text says that the *katechon* is a temporary phenomenon serving the apocalyptic calendar, concerned only that the antichrist appears at his proper time and not before, not something that can forever hold back history hurtling to its end. Palaver's discussion of the *katechon* is nicely nuanced, pointing out how it resembles the Sacred in having two valences, chaos on the one hand and order on the other, bad violence and good violence, and referring to Bonhoeffer's view of it as the force within history that sets limits to violence. In any case, Schmitt compares it to the Roman Empire and in so doing shares the Apostle Paul's view of the empire's service to the divine will as set out in the little apocalypse of Romans 13.

Leo Strauss

Strauss had early contact with Schmitt and found him compatible. Strauss might be seen as another anti-apocalyptic thinker, but as a segue from Schmitt we would like to ask whether the two of them do not in fact use some apocalyptic ideas to nullify others, and so might be called semi-apocalyptic thinkers. Following Ranieri's excellent reading of Strauss's links to Nietzsche, it seems that Schmitt and Strauss have two important apocalyptic ideas in common, one negation and one affirmation; that is, on the one hand they oppose the messianic, universal side of apocalypse and on the other hand they cherish the centrality of the chosen group, like "the Saints of the Most High" or the "Sons of Zadok," for Schmitt the German people and their homeland, and for Strauss the Jewish people and Zion. Thus in the Bible, Strauss favors the kings of Israel and Judah who struggled to manage history in the present, above the prophets who railed at them in the name of a future judgment and a final utopia; and he counsels the Jews, scions of these kings, to find their dignity and significance not in a messianic hope but in the dignified endurance of their present humiliation.

Another apocalyptic and mimetic point they have in common is that since the opposition from outside strengthens the centripetal forces inside the group, it is not altogether negative. The group needs its enemies for the sake of its coherence.

Strauss, however, is thoroughly apocalyptic in his contention that the wise man conceals rather than reveals his wisdom. He points to a tradition of such occlusion in the Greek philosophers, and practices it himself. For this reason he is famously difficult to read, reserving his hidden wisdom for those who have the energy to search and struggle. The apocalypse, as we have seen, is a hidden wisdom, now revealed, but revealed in code and demanding effort to understand. ("Let the reader understand.")

Eric Voegelin

It is particularly important to consult Fred Lawrence for a balanced treatment of Voegelin, because the point that captivates me is the one made by Rossbach, in his brilliant but narrowly focused investigation as to whether Voegelin became a Christian in the end.

Voegelin shares the apocalyptic view of a universal history and the exegesis by which the symbols that history throws up are made to open like windows onto its meaning and direction. He leaves his work unfinished because his projects run into insoluble difficulties and he is too honest to force the interpretation, and because, as Rossbach argues, he is prevented by his stance as a philosopher from ever reaching a conclusion or end. Voegelin shares with Schmitt and Strauss the negative attitude toward messianic or utopian expectation. He calls the messianic stance gnostic insofar as it claims to be privy to the divine secrets and so to have "secret knowledge," and thus to be able to act with a certainty that belies arrogance and risks nemesis. Such enthusiasm is both gnostic and apocalyptic, insofar as secret wisdom is an organizing principle in the composition of both kinds of view.

Rossbach wisely refuses to accept Gnosticism as a stable historical category and calls it rather a "line of meaning."[34] I welcome this maneuver, which holds, of course, for many other classifying categories of traditional scholarship as well. For instance, it has always been difficult formally to distinguish the categories of apocalypse and gnosis from one another, and now it is no longer necessary, since they are both positions plotted on a trajectory and moving toward and away from each other as different positions are entered on the graph of history. Distinctions between the two may now be ad hoc and provisional.

Apocalypse is much concerned with "ending," that is, with the end of history or the end of this world. Rossbach meditates on Voegelin's late statements in the light of Girard's early insight into the ending of a great novel.[35] The hero of the novel and the author of the book are both enslaved to metaphysical desire; the author portrays the hero in such a way as to exempt himself from the desire he represents, until the moment when he sees himself in his hero and owns his own enslavement to desire. At this point he can begin to break free, and thus sees the hero anew, rewrites him accordingly, and lifts his narrative from mediocrity to greatness. The moment of this insight is the moment of conversion. According to Rossbach, Voegelin did not attain it; like Stavrogin he merely died.

Mimetic Theory and Philosophy

So we arrive at a concluding unscientific postscript, having to do with philosophy and theology, reason and revelation, observation and apocalypse. For Girard the philosopher is the author who never repents and so can never end. I recall at this point the saying of that third-century Patristic extremist, Tertullian, to the effect that the Greeks make a virtue of ceaseless seeking, which is silly, because the sensible man stops, contented, when he has found what he has been looking for. Philosophers make a virtue of seeking, and no one more than Voegelin, who was allergic to dogma of any kind. For him the truth is in the honest and endless search for the light whose shadows alone we can see in the cave of this world. For him conversion is the Platonic turning from the shadows on the back wall to the luminescence that causes them, and eventually to the light itself.

When asked what the mimetic objection to philosophy is, Girard, in one of the conference sessions, said that the philosopher never includes himself in his analyses but stands outside in the place of the self-sufficient observer. At this point it is only fair to refer again to Lawrence, our professional philosopher, to take note of how elegant and helpful philosophic discourse can be. He compares Girard and the others in the traditional terms of "Jerusalem and Athens," while nuancing the comparison in light of Strauss's emotional link to the Jews and Voegelin's strenuous attempts to penetrate the Bible philosophically. He criticizes Girard for neglect of the category Nature, which he believes would paradoxically help denaturalize the apparent naturalization of sin in Girard's schema. This is a helpful philosophical criticism, but I think Girard already has answered it in the idea of being and the loss of being through pride that he adumbrates in his earliest work.

In terms of the ending of *The Demons*, the philosopher is Stavrogin, who simply dies, while Stepan Trofimovich, who had been, to be sure, a bad philosopher all his empty, lying life, goes from earth to heaven on the wings of apocalyptic angels and his own late-won truth that he had been a liar all his life.

So we end with the second epigraph of this essay, which is a summons to the good apocalypse in the midst of the accelerating shudder of the bad:

> *Leave the dead to bury the dead. "Come! Follow me!"*
>
> —Matthew 8:22/Luke 9:60

NOTES

All translations of Greek texts are the author's own. Hebrew texts follow the Revised Standard Version of the Bible (New York: Oxford University Press, 1962).

1. Cf. Francis Fukuyama, *After the Neocons: America at the Crossroads* (New York: Profile, 2006). Fukuyama continues to think within the boundaries of received international relations theory and proposes a policy of "realistic Wilsonianism." Such a proposal is merely tactical, while what we need is strategic, that is, a new master paradigm to govern tactical positions such as realism, Wilsonianism, and "realistic Wilsonianism." C.f. George Soros, *The Age of Fallibility: The Consequences of the War on Terror* (New York: Public Affairs, 2006). Soros, with characteristic insight, sees that millennialist beliefs have shaped the present administration's thinking in well-known apocalyptic ways. The central misconception due to this inspiration is to have turned terrorism into the apocalyptic "Universal Adversary," followed closely by the failure, because of faith-based decision making, to correct errors and adjust practice, that is, a failure of prudence. Soros refers to the classic source, Norman Cohn, *The Pursuit of the Millennium: Revolutionary Millenarians and Mystical Anarchists of the Middle Ages* (New York: Oxford University, 1970), and to Kevin P. Philips, *American Theocracy, The Peril and Politics of Radical Religions, Oil, and Borrowed Money in the 21st Century* (New York: Viking, 2006).
2. Wolfgang Palaver, *René Girards mimetische Theorie: Im Kontext kulturtheoretischer und gesellschaftspolitischer Fragen* (Münster, Germany: Lit Verlag, 2003, 315–18 and passim). Cf. Chris Fleming, *René Girard: Violence and Mimesis* (Cambridge: Polity Press, 2004).
3. The most accessible and conventional short answer to this question is given by J. J. Collins in *Harper's Bible Dictionary*, ed. Paul J. Achtemeier (San Francisco: Harper and Row, 1985), 35–36. Collins writes: "The apocalyptic books report mysterious revelations that are mediated by angels and disclose a supernatural world. They are characterized by a focus on eschatology (*teaching about the last times and the last things*), which often entails cosmic transformation and always involves the judgment of the dead. The apocalypses are usually pseudonymous—the revelations are attributed to ancient heroes such as Enoch or Abraham, not to the real authors" (35; italics added).
4. I take the phrase "line of meaning" from Stefan Rossbach, *Gnostic Wars: The Cold War in the Context of a History of Western Spirituality* (Edinburgh: Edinburgh University Press, 1999). I prefer the term "trajectory," which although more metaphorical is less clunky than "line of meaning."

5. *New York Times*, 26 October 2006, A15.

6. *New York Times*, 9 October 2006, A17.

7. *New York Times*, 30 September 2006, A14. For more information on this Muslim frame of mind, see Lawrence Wright, *The Looming Tower: Al-Qaeda and the Road to 9/11* (New York: Knopf, 2006), and Gregory M. Davis, *Religion of Peace? Islam's War against the World* (Los Angeles: World Ahead Publishing, 2006).

8. See *LeftBehind.com*, and Chris Hedges, *American Fascists: The Christian Right and the War on America* (New York: Free Press, 2007).

9. Face to face with such extreme fundamentalist interpretation, we do well to heed Niewiadomski's warning not to throw out the baby with the bathwater and turn away from apocalypse, as he says the main church has in fact already done. This book, we hope, is a small attempt to correct that wrong turn and deal responsibly with apocalypse, that is, to read the signs of the times in the light of the divine revelation.

10. *Kleine Geschichte des Anti-Semitismus* (Stuttgart: Utb, 2003). Rossbach (*Gnostic Wars*) gives a rich account of the history of Joachim and his influence in the context of Voegelin's political theory.

11. Collins, in *Harper's Bible Dictionary*, says there are two types of apocalypse, the historical apocalypse that deals with events in this world, and another type that describes the "other" world (pp. 35–36). Daniel is the chief example of the former and Enoch of the latter. This is a very general and possibly misleading distinction, since history and heaven are so tightly interwoven in both types.

12. This method of interpretation is alive today as the prophetic interpretation of Scripture by millenarian groups, as against the historical interpretation of the mainline churches.

13. Mimetically speaking, the incomparable appearance of the last apparition shows that the sacrificial crisis has arrived and monsters, technically speaking, appear, that is, unprecedented combinations of body parts, hitherto integrated in stable shapes, now chaotically combining. The first three are "like a lion, like a bear, like a leopard," and the last one is like nothing on earth. This one symbolizes the actual makers of the author's mayhem, the Antiochian Greeks, who are defiling the temple and murdering the saints.

14. Michel Serres, "Ego Credo," *Contagion: Journal of Violence, Mimesis, and Culture* 12–13 (2006): 1–11. One cannot recommend this article too highly; it is inspired.

15. We might here distinguish between the terms "eschatology" and "apocalypse." Eschatology is the general term for the description of the presence of the transcendent. It literally means the doctrine of the last things, without specific form or content. Apocalypse is one form of eschatology, defined by its focus on the catastrophic ending and deployed in literary works called apocalypses. "Eschatological" is the term most used by biblical scholars to refer to the transcendent in general and to the Incarnation in particular. The Incarnation of God is "the eschatological event." So while current secular usage takes "apocalyptic" to mean simple catastrophe, Christian thought takes it to mean the "eu-catastrophe" of the New Creation, the revelation of Jesus as the creator and re-creator of our world (John 1:1–3).

16. Titus had four legions for the siege of Jerusalem, the 5th, 10th, and 15th, which were left behind by his father Vespasian when he returned to Rome in 69 CE to be proclaimed emperor, and his own 12th legion, which he brought with him from Alexandria. Schuerer writes: "Meanwhile the entire upper city was occupied by Romans. The military standards were set up and the hymn of victory sung. The soldiers ranged through the city, murdering,

burning and looting." Emil Schuerer, *The History of the Jewish People in the Age of Jesus Christ,* vol. 1, new edition, rev. and ed. Geza Vermes and Fergus Millar (Edinburgh: T&T Clark, 1973), 508. These were the circumstances the writer of our apocalypse looked back on. It is easy to understand how the early Christians interpreted this destruction of Jerusalem as punishment for the murder of Jesus, Son of Man.

17. This is another example of the *pesher* exegesis of Qumran (cf. "He is [encoded] wisdom: let him who has understanding reckon the number of the beast, for it is the number of a human being, and is number six hundred and sixty-six" [Rev. 13:18]).

18. Margaret Barker, *The Great High Priest: The Temple Roots of Christian Liturgy,* (London: T&T Clark, 2003); Rachel Elior, *The Three Temples: On the Emergence of Jewish Mysticism,* trans. David Louvish (Oxford: Littman Library of Jewish Civilization, 2004).

19. Lawlessness in the Greek is *anomia,* the source of Durkheim's *anomie* and a description in Girardian terms of the sacrificial crisis. The *katechon* holds back the advent of the sacrificial crisis.

20. The best account of this history, giving exhaustive citations to the primary sources in Flavius Josephus and Philo Alexandrinus, is in Schuerer, *History of the Jewish People,* 394–98.

21. René Girard, *Deceit, Desire, and the Novel: Self and Other in Literary Structure,* trans. Yvonne Freccero (Baltimore: The Johns Hopkins University Press, 1965), 256–314.

22. Fyodor Dostoevsky, *Demons, A Novel in Three Parts,* trans. Richard Pevear and Larissa Volokhonsky (New York: Vintage Books, 1995). See Vavara Petrovna to Stepan Trofimovich on his deathbed: "Do you remember, you empty, empty, inglorious, fainthearted, eternally, eternally empty man!" (659); "Let it be known to you then, Sofya Matveevna, that he is the paltriest, the emptiest little man" (661).

23. Dostoevsky, *Demons,* 7.

24. "Vavra Petrovna, who in twenty years had grown unaccustomed even to thinking that anything serious and decisive could proceed from Stepan Trofimovich personally, was deeply shaken." Dostoevsky, *Demons,* 662.

25. Dostoevsky, *Demons,* 654

26. Doetoevsky, *Demons,* 664; cf. "My friend, I have been lying all my life. Even when I was telling the truth. I never spoke for the truth but only for myself, I knew that before but only now do I see it. . . . perhaps I am lying now; certainly I am also lying now. The worst of it is that I believe myself when I lie. The most difficult thing in life is to live and not lie . . . and . . . and not believe one's own lie." Dostoevsky, *Demons,* 652.

27. Dostoevsky, *Demons,* 663.

28. Milan Kundera, "What Is a Novelist? How Great Writers Are Made," *New Yorker* (9 October 2006) 40–45. Kundera makes Flaubert his case in point, and writes of his *Madame Bovary* that it was a penance for the Romantic excesses of the *Temptation of St Anthony.* "It is the story of a conversion. Flaubert is thirty years old, the appropriate age for tearing away his lyrical chrysalis. Complaining afterwards that his characters are mediocre is the tribute he is paying to what has become his passion: the art of the novel and the territory it explores, the prose of life" (41). Kundera, however, lacks any theoretical content for his image of conversion, and for him it is conversion from a youthful lyricism to grown-up prose, a superficial disenchantment rather than a metaphysical transformation. Cf. Milan Kundera, *The Curtain: An Essay in Seven Parts,* trans. Linda Asher (New York: HarperCollins, 2006), 89–90.

29. Kundera, *The Curtain*, 655.

30. René Girard, *Violence and the Sacred,* trans. Patrick Gregory (Baltimore: The Johns Hopkins University Press, 1977).

31. René Girard et al., *Things Hidden since the Foundation of the World,* trans. Stephen Bann and Michael Metteer (Stanford, CA: Stanford University Press, 1987).

32. Lawrence's paper is an excellent comparative account of our major figures, together with an acute appreciation and critique of Girard.

33. Compare the following from Mark Halperin and John F. Harris, *The Way to Win: Taking the White House in 2008* (New York: Random House, 2006; as reported in the *New York Times,* 3 November 2006, B35). Bush views himself as a "national clarifier." His theory of leadership is as follows: "A successful leader will stand forthrightly on one side of a grand argument. Then he or she will win that argument by sharpening the differences and rallying his most intense supporters to his side." This is politics not as the art of compromise but as the separation of friend and foe.

34. Rossbach, *Gnostic Wars.*

35. Girard, *Deceit, Desire, and the Novel,* 257–314.

The Evangelical Subversion of Myth

René Girard
Académie française and Stanford University (emeritus)

In *Totem and Taboo,* Freud writes that long before he himself penetrated the secret of human origins, the Christian gospels had done so. "In the Christian doctrine," he says, "men were acknowledging in the most undisguised manner the guilty primeval deed."[1]

Here as elsewhere, the apparently unbelievable assertion of *Totem and Taboo* contains a gigantic insight. What Freud says here is literally true, except of course for his psychoanalytical interpretation of the primordial murder. In order to show this truth, one must go, not surprisingly, to those texts in the gospels that have the most unpleasant connotations to our ears, those most strongly repressed, even by the Christians, who avoid them more and more. Even they do not look closely at these texts because if they did, they might have to agree, they fear, with those who see a spirit of hatred at work in the gospels, a vindictive streak even in many words attributed to Jesus himself. Of all these texts, the so-called "Curses against the Pharisees," in Matthew 23 and Luke 11, have perhaps the worst reputation. They seem to confirm the opinion that the mind behind Matthew 23:35–36 still believes in the primitive blood curse (Gen. 4:10–12):

> On you will fall the guilt of all the innocent blood spilt on the ground, from innocent Abel to Zechariah, son of Berachiah, whom you murdered

> between the sanctuary and the altar. Believe me, this generation will bear the guilt of it all. (Matt. 23:35–36)

Abel is not a Jew. How could these lines be read in the context of the primitive blood curse of the Jews? To the ancient Jews, the Bible was more than a religious code and a history of national origins. It was the history of the entire human race, the sum total of all knowledge. The religious murders are limited neither to a single blood lineage nor even to a single religious tradition. After the well-known figure of Abel, who is the first murder victim in the Bible, a rather obscure figure is mentioned. Why? He is the last murder victim in the second book of Chronicles, which happens to be the last book of the Jewish Bible (2 Chron. 24:20–21).[2] Thus, the first and last victims in the Bible are mentioned. These two names obviously stand in lieu of a complete enumeration, which is impossible. There would simply be too many names. All the victims between the first and the last one are tacitly included.

This cannot fail to evoke the type of victimage I have been talking about, and the text of Luke gives us one more reason to believe in it.

If the word *beginning* (*arche*), which suggests the foundation of culture and is present in John (1:1), is absent from Matthew, it is present again or rather an even more significant word is present in the text of Luke, which runs almost parallel to the one of Matthew (Luke 11:49–51):

> This generation will have to answer for the blood of all the prophets shed since the foundation/beginning of the world, from the blood of Abel to the blood of Zechariah. (Luke 11:50)

The word that is translated by some as "beginning" and by others, better still, "as foundation," is *katabole*. The Greek says *apo kataboles tou kosmou*. *Apo* suggests a generative relationship rather than a merely temporal one. *Katabole* means the ordering or reordering that terminates some kind of disruption, the climactic resolution of a crisis. There is a medical use of it analogous to the purgative *katharsis*, or paroxysmal fit (Plato, *Gorgias*, 519a). *Kosmos* means order. The Latin Vulgate translates *apo kataboles tou kosmou* by *a constitutione mundi*—"from [or since] the constitution of the world," but still does not render the connotation of a paroxysmal process. In conjunction with murder, especially the type of murder we have at the beginning of the Bible, like the murder of Abel, the Greek expression *apo kataboles tou kosmou* cannot fail to evoke the dynamics of our myth and ritual. The tracing back of religious murders to Abel, the association of the first murder with the *kataboles tou kosmou*, cannot suggest a merely chronological coincidence between the first murder and the foundation of the world. There is collusion between human culture and murder that goes back to the beginning of humanity and that, according to Jesus, continues down to his own time, and is still operative among the Pharisees.

Mathew 23:35–36 and Luke 11:49–51 are a revelation of the original murder.

Now let us read another curse that evokes the mechanism we have uncovered in the previous readings:

> Woe unto you, lawyers and Pharisees. Hypocrites! You build up the tombs of the prophets and embellish the monuments of the saints, and you say, "If we had been alive in our fathers' time, we should never have taken part with them in the murder of the prophets." So you acknowledge that you are the sons of the men who killed the prophets. Go on then, finish off what your fathers began! (Matt. 23:29–32)

The Pharisees do not deny that the murders took place. Far from approving or ignoring the murders, they condemn them severely. They want to disassociate themselves from their murderous ancestors and religious forerunners. In the eyes of Jesus, however, they do not succeed; the religious behavior of the Pharisees paradoxically perpetuates the solidarity it denies, the solidarity with the murder of the prophets.

The murder of the prophets was a collective action and the arrogant denial of participation is also a collective action. "If we had been alive in our fathers' time, we should never have taken part with them in the murder of the prophets" (Matt. 23:30). In other words, we should never have surrendered to the mimetic contagion of the collective victimage. The Pharisees reassure themselves that they are incapable of such a deed.

In order to demonstrate their noninvolvement in violence, their own intrinsic innocence, the sons condemn their fathers; the original murders had been committed with a similar intent. The murderers murdered their victims, we found, in order not to perceive their own violence; this is the real significance of the scapegoat effect, which projects the violence of the community onto the victim. The sons, therefore, do exactly the same things as their fathers; they condemn them as murderers in order to achieve the same purpose as the murderers themselves, in order to obfuscate their own violence. The condemnation constitutes an act of violence that repeats and reproduces every feature of the original murder, except for the physical death of a victim. The sons have only shifted from one type of scapegoat to another. They are the spiritual murderers of their own murderous fathers and, as such, well worthy of these fathers from whom they think themselves separated by an abyss.

The continuity from generation to generation is insured, each time, by an effort to break with the past that always takes the form of an actual or symbolical murder of that past, of physical or spiritual victimage. Our hypothesis alone can make this "filiation" intelligible, because the original murder is already a means for the community to break with its own past violence, to forget the reality of that violence by thrusting its entire weight upon the collective victim. All later culture repeats the violent flight from violence; people repeat the violent burial of the truth that already characterizes even the most primitive forms of cultural foundation and elaboration. All human culture begins and continues with a violent burial of the truth.

In the case of the Pharisees, and Oedipus and his oracle, the victims seem to be vindicated, the murderers are condemned, the break with the violent seems complete; but this appearance is deceiving.

Past murders are denounced as the exclusive responsibility of the actual murderers, as something that is of no real concern to those who come after, to the pious Pharisees, except, of course, as a cause for self-congratulation. The old structure is reversed; the original murderers now occupy the place of the original victims and vice versa; the reversed structure serves the same purpose as the original one; it justifies the contemporaries by disengaging them falsely, because violently, from the violence of the past. The repudiation of the past is analogous to and continuous with the violence of the past.

Now I go to another text that has always appeared even more obscure, vindictive, and sinister perhaps than the ones already quoted, but it really means absolutely the same thing. It is John 8:43–44. The interlocutors inside the text are not designated as scribes or Pharisees but simply, this time, as the Jews.

It is true that this text is a historical source of Christian anti-Semitism, but one can show that it is only because the text is completely misunderstood by the Christians.

> Your father is the devil and you choose to carry out your father's desires. He was a murderer from the beginning, and is not rooted in the truth; there is no truth in him. When he tells a lie he is speaking his own language, for he is a liar and the father of lies [or of liars]. But I speak the truth and therefore you do not believe me. (John 8:44)

At least five themes in this enigmatic text are closely interrelated. Satan is described as an inexhaustible source of lies; the Jews are still imprisoned in these lies, because they share in Satan's desires. The Jews actively collaborate in a satanic delusion, which exists from the beginning and which is essentially connected with murder. Satan was a murderer from the beginning.

What kind of murderer can this be?

The designation of Satan as a murderer is usually interpreted as a veiled reference to the story of Cain and Abel. Most commentators rightly believe, in other words, that John 8:44 is not unrelated to the text: "On you will fall the guilt of all the innocent blood spilt on the ground, from innocent Abel to Zechariah," and so forth (Matt. 23:35).

This is true, up to a point. The murder of Abel comes first in the Bible chronologically, of course, but perhaps also in another and more fundamental sense.

We found that the murder of Abel is the primordial murder in the sense that it is the foundation of the Cainite culture, which is presented as the first human culture. Satan is the mimetic cycle itself, the mechanism of human culture. That is why his reign is really at an end, even though his triumph seems more complete than ever. We can understand very well why he would be a murderer from the beginning, and the father of all liars (meaning all the hearers of Jesus), the father of an entire culture that is not rooted in the truth. We can well understand why Jesus would speak of two languages, his own language, which reveals the original murder and is therefore the language of truth, and the language of his listeners, which is a lie because it is still rooted in the original murder. The one truth that these listeners resist the most is the truth being uttered at that very moment, in that very text, the truth of the original murder.

It is not wrong to relate this text of John to the story of Abel. The two are related; but the people who connect the one to the other do not understand the relationship; they do not perceive the genetic mechanism of culture behind the murder of Abel. From the phrase "Satan was a murderer from the beginning," they think that something is missing. The missing information would be the identity of the victim and of the murderer. We are told that the victim is Abel. In the text of the gospels we see a garbled murder mystery from which the names of the actors have been removed by mistake. We feel we add something to the text by supplying these names. This attitude is supremely significant. All interpreters always think they have a perspective, a methodology, another text that goes further than the gospel text. They do not realize that as long as they look for the individual or generic names of the victims and culprits, in specific episodes of murder, they remain imprisoned in mythology; they have not yet uncovered the truth. In order fully to uncover the truth, you must eliminate all proper names, all fictional elements. You must replace all the fabulous stories of origins by the semiotic matrix, by the genetic mechanism of all myths and rituals. This is exactly what the gospel text is doing when it says: at the beginning of human culture was murder and all human beings without exception are the sons and daughters of that murder. Down to the present day, they remain imprisoned in its lie because they have not yet really uncovered its operation.

If I am right, all modern attitudes are regressive and repressive in comparison with the text of the gospel.

With vertiginous speed but with complete clarity, a mechanism is formulated in John, the best formulation because it is purely abstract and universal, the most likely to be misunderstood. Now we understand that it is the same thing to be a son of Satan and to be a son of the men who killed the prophets. The surest means to perpetuate the lies that are rooted in the original murder and to generate more liars is to say, "If we had been alive in our fathers' time, we should never have taken part with them in the murder of the prophets."

The original murder is an inexhaustible source of falsified cultural meanings and values in which not the Pharisees alone, not the Jews alone, but all of humanity is still imprisoned.

The connection in John between Satan, murder, untruth, and the *arche*, the beginning, means exactly the same thing as the connection between murder, the denial of murder, and the foundation of the world in the Synoptic Gospels. The foundation and principle of this world, the devil and Satan are one and the same thing and they are none other than the spontaneous scapegoat mechanism as the source of all previous religion and all human culture, the mechanism of symbolicity itself.

Far from saying entirely different things and being rooted in a different spirit, the Synoptic Gospels and the Gospel of John say exactly the same thing. The vast effort of modern criticism to dismember the New Testament as well as the Old, and to compel each text to diverge from every other, resembles the attitude of many classicists toward the tragedic corpus of our Greek and European heritage; we must suspect that this immense enterprise of dissociation is not innocent; it must be part of our effort to elude the significance that is common to all these texts, to flee from a message that we go on treating more or less in the same fashion as those whose place is designated in the gospels as the first recipients of that message.

The traditional interpretation of the text tends to narrow down the scope of the text to the interlocutors inside the text who are, of course,

Jewish religious groups. Its traditional title, "Curses against the Pharisees," already constitutes an interpretation. This reading is obviously wrong. We can assert its essential deficiency even if already in the letter of the text that has come down to us certain details tend, if not to support the traditional reading, to suggest that the people who transcribed it had an imperfect understanding of that text. The reading we provide is too powerful, too faithful to the letter of the text not to sweep aside what still may appear to us as minor textual blemishes. These are not sufficient to discredit the present reading, which is both too coherent and effective in its relative complexity (*lectio difficilior*) to be refuted by such minor blemishes. These can be caused either by temporary lapses of the gospel writers, literally overwhelmed by the enormity of the message they had to record, and they can also be deficiencies on our own part, signs of our continued inability to grasp that same message in its entirety.

Whatever the case may be, the reading I give totally implicates the reader and suggests there cannot be any innocent misreading of such a text.

The gospels constantly claim that they bring into the world something that has never been heard before. The commentators take it for granted that this revelation is exclusively related to supernatural matters. The supernatural dimension in the gospels is essential but it cannot be assessed properly—it will always be confused with some kind of religious idealism—if the human aspect of the revelation is not perceived. There is a hidden dimension to human behavior (violence) that is an essential part of the revelation:

> There is nothing covered up that will not be uncovered, nothing hidden that will not be made known. You may take it, then, that everything you have said in the dark will be heard in broad daylight, and what you have whispered behind closed doors will be shouted from the housetops. (Matt. 10:26–27/Luke 12:2–3)

The Lukan instance of this saying comes immediately after the crucial passage in the "Curses," on the hidden collusion between murder and religious culture (Luke 11:49–51).

Another text that suggests that the revelation of human cultural origin is an integral part of Jesus's revelation is the borrowing by Matthew of Psalm 78:2, which is placed in the mouth of Jesus:

> I will open my mouth in parables; I will utter things that have been kept secret *since the foundation of the world*. (Matt. 13:35, quoting Ps. 78:2)

We have already noted the last words of the "Curses against the Pharisees," *à propos* of the original murder: "*all the innocent blood* shed since the foundation of the world" (Luke 11:50). Here, we have "things kept secret": *Kekroumena apo kataboles tou kosmou*. The only words that differ in the two sentences are "all the innocent blood" in one and the *kekroumena* in the other. The reference to "things kept hidden" is interchangeable with "all the blood that has been shed," because the one and the other refer to the same mechanism of collective violence that must remain hidden in order to remain the mainstay of human religion and culture, in order to go on functioning as it still functions with the contemporaries of Jesus.

No one today, not even most Christians, takes seriously the claim of the gospels that the words of Jesus, and his death, constitute the fulfillment of the Old Testament. To us it sounds like a particularly mischievous piece of mystical nonsense that can be maintained only by the most benighted religious provincialism in a particularly nefarious alliance with ethnocentric arrogance.

And it is true, indeed, that this assertion, in the past, has never amounted to much more than that. For the medieval Christian, the belief that the New Testament is the fulfillment of the Old and can account for everything in it is accepted as a principle of faith and it becomes the basis for the so-called allegorical or figural interpretation of the Bible, supposedly informed by a purely Christian understanding.

If you look at the allegorical interpretations of the Middle Ages, you will find that, in spite of certain early insights, to a large extent, the belief in the interpretive power of the New Testament remains a dead letter; it does not result in anthropological knowledge any more than it translates into a new religious formulation. Just as in the case of the modern exegetes who do nothing but refer John 8:44–45 back to Cain, for lack of anything else to say, the medieval allegorists, already, prefer to dwell with Old Testament stories, or, in the gospels, with purely parabolic discourse, rather than with statements as direct and pregnant as those we are now reading, which must remain a dead letter or worse until their real object is perceived, the original murder and its consequences.

Once this real object is perceived, we realize that the claims of the gospels in regard to the Old Testament must be taken seriously. We have found that a tendency to deconstruct the myths of collective violence is already at work in the Old Testament, but only in the gospel does this tendency become aware of its own significance because only there does it reach and understand its true goal, which is the reduction of all human religion and culture to its generative mechanism.

I wish I had space to examine with you other passages of the gospels that have found no explanation so far and that make a great deal of sense when they are read in the light of the reading I propose, in the light of the original murder as revealed in the gospels. When they confront such phrases as "let the dead bury the dead" or "where the corpse is, there the vultures will gather," the exegetes have nothing much to say; they surmise that these phrases must be proverbial, but they leave the significance of these proverbs undetermined.

I will also mention in passing the parable of the unfaithful vine growers (Matt. 21:33–46/Mark 12:1–12/Luke 20:9–19) who always unite against the messengers sent by the lord of the vineyard, who expel all of them and finally kill the son himself. After this parable Jesus ironically asks his listeners to interpret for him another Old Testament quotation: "The stone that has been rejected by the builders has become the keystone" (Ps. 118: 22–23/Matt. 21:42/Mark 12:10–11/Luke 20:17).

I also draw your attention to the possible relationship of what I am talking about with such sentences as the one uttered by Caiaphas in the gospel of John: "It is better for one man to die so that the whole people will be saved" (John 11:49–50).

One interpretation of the "Curses against the Pharisees" remains that still enables those who have adopted the gospels as their Holy Scripture and call themselves Christians to elude the full burden of the message. This interpretation is the traditional one, the one that sees in that text only that and no more, curses that would be exclusively directed against a Jewish sect, or perhaps Judaism as a whole and that would concern no one else.

This reading does once again what Jesus reproaches the Pharisees for doing. It suppresses the revelation of the semiotic matrix. It redirects the painful impact of the revelation toward someone else. Since the readers see themselves as followers of Jesus, they cannot choose him as their scapegoat; they have to turn against the only other people present in the picture, who are, of course, his direct interlocutors, the Pharisees. They are the last available victims. This time it is the Christian's turn to say: "If we had been alive in the time of our Jewish spiritual fathers, we should never have taken part with them in the murder of Jesus." If the Pharisees are said by Jesus to exceed the measure of their fathers, the traditional Christian reading of the "Curses" certainly exceeds the measure of the Pharisees. It does the same thing once more, but this time the victimizers never cease to read the text that condemns their own victimage as they go on with their victimage. They invoke as their justification the text that in reality condemns them in the most explicit fashion.

If we look back upon the traditional reading of texts like the "Curses against the Pharisees," we can see that the emphasis is not on the things that are said but on those to whom they are said, the immediate listeners of Jesus, the people he is personally confronting. The focus of the text is narrowed, its scope is diminished; a revelation that concerns all people equally, all religious and cultural systems, is turned into a denunciation of some people only, those belonging to one particular religion.

It is not insignificant, of course, that the Pharisees are the direct targets; but the significance is quite different from the one usually imagined. If there were, anywhere on earth, one religious cultural form—past, present, or future—that did not deserve the accusations proffered against the Pharisees, the gospels would not have the universal scope that the Christians themselves have always claimed, but that they perpetually deny in practice by restricting to Judaism those consequences of the Christian revelation they want to divert from themselves. If Pharisaism were not the highest mode of religious life yet attained by man, it could not stand for every other form; the words uttered by the gospel would not reach all cultural forms at the same time. This role of Judaism as representative of humanity as a whole is one with the idea frequently repeated in the New Testament itself that the election of Israel never has and never will be canceled, that they play a privileged role in the revelation of the entire truth.

Today we have reached a new stage in the history of our relationship to the Judaeo-Christian scriptures. Christian anti-Semitism is constantly repudiated and denounced. This repudiation, however, has not resulted in a greater understanding of the gospel text. Far from it: we find that the text has become a stumbling block even to the Christians themselves who see it as the cause of their own past violence. Thus, instead of seeking the source of that violence in themselves, they are still trying to project it onto some kind of sacralized scapegoat, and since all possible human victims have been exhausted, they must dispense with a human scapegoat and go directly to the text of the gospels, the text par excellence, the text that denounces victimage in all its forms and is itself denounced as the single greatest source of violence and hatred in our world. Even those who do not go that far think it advisable to turn away from the text; it is prudent not to acknowledge the doubts they may have in regard to its perversity.

For close to three centuries, in all institutions of higher learning, it has not been intellectually respectable to deal with the text except as an object of demystification, and every time we mention it we must take the ritual precaution of insulting it and reviling it in order to demonstrate that our attitude is the proper one, that we truly belong to the mimetic consensus of the modern intelligentsia. We must still reenact, vis-à-vis that text, gestures of ritual defilement that would be criticized as ethnocentric and regressive if they were directed at any non-Judaeo-Christian culture or religion.

We have reached the point where we can understand the enormous role played by the tomb in the texts we are reading. The Pharisees, we are told, like to erect funeral monuments to the long dead prophets; these tombs, by definition, are empty, but the Pharisees themselves and their culture are compared to real tombs, in other words, to tombs that still contain the remains of human beings:

> Woe unto you, scribes and Pharisees, hypocrites! For you are like unto whited sepulchers; they look well from the outside, but inside they are full of dead men's bones and all kinds of filth. (Matt. 23:27)

A tomb has two purposes. It is destined to honor a person who has passed away and also to dispose of a corpse, to hide it from the survivors, to make the ugly and dangerous reality of corruption and death invisible and inaccessible. Those two purposes are at odds with each other; they are never mentioned in the same breath. A tomb makes it possible to achieve both simultaneously. The tomb hides the material reality of corruption and asserts the spiritual continuity of human culture, the recollection and glorification of the past.

The rotting corpse inside and the beautiful structure around it resemble the entire process of human culture in its relationship to the original victim. The inside and the outside of the tomb recall and reproduce the dual nature of the primitive *sacra,* the conjunction in them of violence and peace, of death and life, of disorder and order. This structural homology must not be fortuitous. With the exception of tools, the most ancient traces of human culture are tombs, and tombs may well be the original monuments of humanity.[3]

Why did our still half-human or incompletely human forefathers invent such an institution as the burial of dead bodies? It is difficult to think that one fine day the idea simply occurred to them; they must have been under intense pressure to act in such a novel way. I personally believe that the pressure came from the mimetic crisis and victimage that we have encountered so many times and that, unlike the scheme invented by Freud in *Totem and Taboo,* is perfectly conceivable at the prehuman level as a mechanism of hominization. The inventors of burial were not dealing merely with a dead body in the naturalistic sense but with a collective victim against whom they had united and been reconciled. This collective victim they already regarded with a prereligious mixture of terror and veneration, and that is why they could not simply abandon him on the spot as their own animal forefathers had done, and burial was invented. The idea of the tomb does not come from the sacred; it may well be the first and essential manifestation of the sacred. The practice of religious burial suggests there never was such a thing as natural death for early humans; all people who died were automatically assimilated to the sacralized victim. That is why burial rites, all over the world, like all other rites, invariably amount to a reenactment of the mimetic crisis and scapegoat reconciliation. They include death and disintegration, therefore, but they end up with renewal; through the corruption of death they are trying to reach to the supreme power of life.

The idea that humans less intelligent and courageous than ourselves invented religion in order not to face death in the naturalistic sense, death as the end of everything, *period,* is nonsense. Death as a purely natural event is obviously a very recent invention; early humanity never had to elude that kind of death because it never learned about it. Death first appeared as sacred power through the misunderstood scapegoat mechanism, which is the universal mechanism of human culture. Far from being a mask for our naturalistic concept of death, the awareness of which would have come first and be falsified only later by ad hoc religious myth, religion comes first, and it turns early man into a builder of tombs because religion is the mythological face of the misunderstood scapegoat mechanism.

Thus we cannot say that the gospel text, the text of the so-called "Curses against the Pharisees," turns the tomb into a metaphor of human culture. It is human culture as a whole that is a metaphor of the tomb, and the tomb itself is the original metaphoric and pragmatic displacement of the misunderstood scapegoat reconciliation, the first and fundamental transformation of that mechanism into the first symbolic monument of human culture. However complex culture may become later, it remains an extension of funeral rites, an edifice erected around a sacrificial victim. If the tomb is really the original nucleus, and if all subsequent developments retain the tomb-like quality that is obviously present in the mechanism of self-deception associated by the gospels with the higher stages of religion, we should say not that our text is metaphorical but that it reveals the tomb as the first symbolic metamorphosis of victimage.

If all sacrificial culture is a tomb, so is every individual member of it, shaped and structured by the same protective misapprehension, by the same absence of radical crisis or critique that constitutes the whole.

> Woe unto you, scribes and Pharisees, hypocrites! For you are like unto whited sepulchers; they look well from the outside, but inside they are full of dead men's bones and all kinds of filth. (Matt. 23:27)

This passage cannot fail to recall the modern idea of an individual or collective unconscious, of human consciousness and behavior being governed by something that is part of us, that is most intimately ours and yet cannot be reached and does not want to be reached. We can easily verify, indeed, in everything I have said so far, that the victim inside the individual or collective tomb, the excluded scapegoat, operates as the unknown source of all cultural significance and behavior, individual and collective. This does not mean, however, that the gospel text should be interpreted as an anticipation or approximation of the psychoanalytical idea, that it is a still imperfect vision of something that Freud later perfected. In spite of its extreme brevity and concentration, the gospel text brings together in the most effective manner many ideas that are not really engaged by Freud because they were incompletely grasped; primarily, of course, the idea that the individual unconscious, even in modern man, is still rooted in some kind of primordial murder and that it is associated with the mourning of the dead.

Even though or perhaps because its metaphoric resources are always simple and easy to visualize, the gospel text outlines a scheme of self-deception more intellectually powerful and more rigorous than that of Freud.

We have found, for instance, that men can deplore the violence of their forefathers and yet retain the stamp of that violence, so that finally even our own repudiation of murder can really amount to a displaced reenactment of the murder mechanism. Thus, as culture, in appearance, moves farther and farther away from its origins and erases all traces of the collective violence that really came first, in reality, the entire process remains structurally homologous to the crudest manifestations of the misunderstood victimage phenomena. If sacrificial culture is a grave that presents itself almost explicitly as such, because again and again, victims are killed on a sacrificial altar, a later culture, in which blood sacrifice has lost much of its importance, or disappeared entirely, as it has in ours, is still a grave, but a grave that does not signal or even denies its own nature as a grave.

In order to represent the process visually, the gospel shifts from the tomb of the sarcophagus type, the visible monument that is erected above the ground, to the tomb that is underground and unmarked, invisible even as a tomb. The unmarked tomb makes not only its content invisible but itself as well. If any tomb is a means to disguise and to hide, the underground tomb is an improved and redoubled tomb, a tomb at the second power so to speak.

> Woe unto you, Scribes and Pharisees, hypocrites! For you are like graves that appear not, over which men may walk without knowing it. (Luke 11:44)

I certainly have neither the time nor the capacity to develop all the implications of a reading that does not arbitrarily narrow down the scope of the gospel text to one cultural world only. But one fundamental implication becomes clear. In these texts, something is completely revealed, more completely still than in the Old Testament and a fortiori in any work of literature. This something is the semiotic matrix of all mythology and ritual.

If we try to locate the gospels as a whole, we quickly realize that the whole text presents itself as a process that begins with a warning and an invitation by Jesus to the Jews first, then to humanity as a whole. The time has come for men to become reconciled to each other without sacrifices and other sacrificial means, because sacrifices are at an end.

The reaction of the listeners shows that they do not understand what is at stake any more than we do. The modern historical school, and now the structuralist school, is no more able to understand what the urgency of the message is about than the medieval and Christian commentators who believed in the apocalyptic threat but interpreted it in a supernatural and therefore a sacrificial way, as if the violence in the gospels still came from a violent god. The whole idea of a sacrificial pact between the Father and the Son, the sacrificial interpretation of the passion, which is completely absent from the gospels, is the central element, of course, in that sacrificial reading of the gospels. It is really the same old scapegoat misunderstanding, since it projects human violence onto a divine figure once again. The sacrificial reading is unable to conceive of a god that would be absolutely free of violence, which is what the gospel text is really about. My reading of the gospels is not a humanistic reading at all. It is almost impossible for human beings, and also terribly perilous, to conceive a divinity that would be absolutely free of violence.

As soon as this conception becomes intelligible, humans must realize that the violence is all theirs. All sacrificial protection is at an end and people can see their own violent truth for the first time. This is what is meant by the idea that the blood of all victims will fall upon the generations of those who hear the gospel, that all this blood will be required of this generation, that the post-gospel humanity will bear the guilt of it all. This has nothing to do with a primitive blood curse. It simply means that, even if they must be misinterpreted at first, and distorted in a sacrificial sense, the gospels have not been written in vain and the revelation will finally reach the consciousness of all men, making traditional culture impossible and compelling humanity to live in the full glare of its own truth, unprotected by sacrificial ritual and mythology.

The process described in the gospels is very carefully worked out. As people react more and more negatively to the offer of reconciliation, this offer becomes more pressing and the consequences of a refusal are more and more clearly spelled out. The texts we have read represent a crucial moment in that revelation, and they make it possible for us to understand what the central text of the four gospels, the Passion, is really about from an anthropological standpoint.

If human beings refuse the nonsacrificial reconciliation that must be substituted for the now exhausted sacrifices, they will inevitably attempt to suppress the knowledge that is provided to them by the gospels; they will try once more to close human culture upon itself and erect more violent barriers against their own violence. It is unavoidable, therefore, that an attempt to consolidate once more the culture of misunderstood scapegoat phenomena will include a new victimage, and the victim, this time, will not be arbitrary, in the sense that this time, he must be the One who threatens or seems to threaten the entire system through his untimely revelations of what human culture is really about. Unanimous victimage, in other words, will be reenacted, but this time it will be reenacted against the one who has revealed the very existence and function of that unanimous murder.

The truth once more will be buried, and, up to a point, it will be buried very deep, since everything is going to be interpreted once more in a sacrificial way. At the same time, however, the text of the gospels, however imperfect it may be in some of its details, remains intact, and, at any time, any interpreter who chooses to repudiate sacrificial distortions can see for himself or herself that, in that text, the truth of the original murder, after being revealed theoretically, so to speak, is also reenacted, and that murder must be reenacted because its truth is intolerable and humans refuse to hear it. In the Passion, humanity resorts once more to the original murder in order to go on deceiving itself about this same original murder.

The idea that the truth of the original murder cannot be uttered without triggering once more the original murder is very clear in the gospel.

> Then you acknowledge that you are the sons of the men who killed the prophets. Go on then, finish off what your fathers began. (Matt. 23:32)

In all gospel texts, the revelation in words always precedes the actual reenactment of the truth revealed, because the mechanism that must remain buried to be effective will inevitably be triggered once more by the fact that it is unburied, that it is re-surrected, so to speak.

It would take a long analysis to show that this is what happens in the case of the Passion. I have no time for this, of course, but I will go for one minute to a much briefer text, which belongs not to the gospels properly speaking but to the Acts of the Apostles and as such still retains gospel-like characteristics. This text is Stephen's martyrdom, which comes at the end and as a result of a speech that he makes before the Sanhedrin. All we need to quote are the last words of that speech, but they are crucial since they are nothing more nor less than a repetition of the "Curses against the Pharisees" and they are interrupted by the violent action of the crowd. It is undoubtedly these words, here, that reveal the role of collective murder in human culture, that trigger a violent and unanimous attempt to suppress this revelation, and this attempt inevitably reproduces the deed that mankind tries to deny and to suppress. Here is the text:

> Stiff-necked and uncircumcised in heart and ear, you always oppose the Holy Spirit, as your fathers did, so you do also. Which of the prophets have not your fathers persecuted? And they killed those who foretold the coming of the Just One, of whom you have now been betrayers and murderers. . . .
>
> Now, as they heard these things, they were cut to the heart and gnashed their teeth at him. But he, being full of the Holy Spirit, looked up to heaven and saw the glory of God, and Jesus standing at the right hand of God; and he said, "Behold, I see the heavens opened, and the Son of Man standing at the right hand of God." But they cried out with a loud voice and stopped their ears and rushed upon him all together. And they cast him out of the city and stoned him. (Acts 7:51–58)

Even before Stephen's vision of Christ in glory, his listeners are moving toward unanimous violence because of the words that link them up once more, and their whole culture, to the religious murders of the past. In the Anchor Bible edition of the Acts, Johannes Munck compares the last words of Stephen to "a spark that starts an explosion,"[4] a spontaneous and irresistible discharge of collective fury. There is no condemnation of Stephen by the Sanhedrin. It is true, on the other hand, that the murderers of Stephen manage to restrain their rage long enough to drag their victim outside of the city limits. This is another ritual precaution common to many societies. The pollution of violence and death must not be permitted inside the community. We seem to have an inextricable mixture of legal and illegal features, of ritual and of spontaneous elements. Here are the comments of Johannes Munck:

> Was this an examination before the Sanhedrin and the following stoning a real trial and a legally performed execution? We do not know. The improvised and passionate character of the events as related might suggest that it was illegal, a lynching.[5]

We are told that ritualism and spontaneity are poles apart; in our text, they are so much the same thing that they cannot be distinguished. From the standpoint of the ritual and cultural origin postulated here, this ambiguity has great significance. The scholars' hesitation between the most spontaneous and the most ritualized form suggests that the second may well be the scrupulous copy and mimicry of the first. The ritual form can always provide a satisfactory channel for a spontaneous outburst; it can become de-ritualized, so to speak, without important changes, because it is nothing but the ritualization of a first such outburst that has proved so successful in reestablishing the peace that its forms are carefully remembered and reproduced. That worldly wisdom we found in ritual stoning does not result from a statesmanlike calculation that would operate without a model and plan everything ex nihilo; it is patterned after a scapegoat phenomenon so effective that it remains unrecognized and it is read, in consequence, as an intervention of the divinity.

The unanimity of the participants is a quasi-technical indication here, which is more explicit in the Greek original *homothumadon*, and in its literal Latin translation in the Vulgate, *unanimiter*, than in most modern translations. The unanimity is required by the scapegoat ritual and it is the spontaneous result of the intolerable words uttered by Stephen, of the enormous scandal they provoke.

The lynching of Stephen has all the structural characteristics of the original murder I have been talking about. The lynching immediately follows the most decisive words of Stephen, those that repeat the "Curses against the Pharisees," the revelation by Jesus himself of the original murder. We can verify the paradoxical relationship between this murder and its motivation. The original murder reappears to keep the original murder covered up. Stephen is lynched in order to keep the truth of lynching hidden; but the truth of lynching is already out. It has just been expressed by Stephen when he repeats the words of Jesus. The proof that it is too late is that the lynchers *stop their ears* as they rush unanimously, *unanimiter*, against Stephen.

The Passion of Jesus is preceded by the revelation of the original murder in the "Curses against the Pharisees" and other texts. The Passion stands in the same relationship to these texts as the martyrdom of Stephen to the last lines of his speech. In both instances, the revelation is by both word and deed. First there is the word, then comes the deed, which confirms and corroborates the word, not because those who commit the deed want the word to be authenticated and confirmed but just the opposite. Those who commit the deed want to silence, suppress, and expel the word, but they unwittingly confirm it because the Word talks about its own suppression and expulsion.

But all these precautions are of no avail. Every word of the victim, every gesture of his victimizers is implacably recorded in the text of the Acts; this means, of course, that the collective violence against the truth, the attempt to bury that truth once more in a unanimous violence, is turned into a more complete revelation: everything covered up will be uncovered. First we have the words, which tell us about the violent repression of the truth, every time this truth is about to be uttered, and then we have the violent repression itself. Thus, the words of the revelation come first and they are immediately confirmed and verified by the action; this is as it should be if the revelation is true, since what the revelation reveals is the violent repression of its own violent truth by human culture.

We can understand why the Greek word for witness, *martyros,* has come to mean in our modern languages a victim in the sense of Stephen. To be a witness means not only to repeat the words of Jesus but also to pay for these words with one's life, not in some kind of meaningless and irrational sacrifice, but as a testimony to the truth of these words, as an immediate verification, so to speak. It is obvious from the preceding that Christianity claims no monopoly on innocent victims; it does not even claim a monopoly on those victims who die with the truth of their death in their mouths; from now on, all victims will die on the right side of truth, so to speak. They say that violence belongs not to God, as men have always believed, or to the specifically religious element in religion, as they now try to believe, but to the human cultural community as such and the human community immediately confirms this revelation by putting the witness to death. They will add to our knowledge rather than subtract from it.

As we understand this significance of the martyr, which cannot be reserved, of course, to the specifically Christian martyrs, we also understand the meaning of one more important passage in the "Curses against the Pharisees," a passage that is present both in Matthew and Luke (Matt. 23:34/Luke 11:49):

> The wisdom of God has said, "I will send them prophets and apostles; and some of them they will put to death and persecute so that the blood of all the prophets that has been shed from the foundation of the world may be required of this generation." (Luke 11:49)

Why the wisdom of God? The more men multiply victims, the more they reveal the truth they want to deny, the truth of human culture. It is not God's fault, of course, if this truth becomes accessible to men through more and more victims. It is the fault of humanity, which desperately tries to repress and exclude the knowledge that has been available to it.

> Woe unto you, lawyers! You have taken away the key of knowledge; you did not go in yourselves and those who were on their way in, you stopped. (Luke 11:52/Matt. 23:13)

"Those who were on their way in, you stopped." Who can these be? They can only be the Jewish people, insofar as they are exposed to the Old Testament, to that prophetic inspiration that keeps uncovering the truth of human culture, as we have said, but never entirely succeeds. If the Pharisees had wanted, they could have made further progress along the same route, just as Jesus himself has done and is doing, but instead, they have killed that inspiration and immobilized the Jewish religion in ritualistic complacency. All genuine inspiration has dried up or floundered in scholarly minutiae, in petty legalism.

Once the truth is out, once it has been inscribed in a text, it cannot be repressed any more. Beneath all the languages that keep repressing the truth, the language of mythology and ritual, the language of philosophy, or the language of modern ideology, another language is at work, another Logos that has nothing to do with the Logos of human culture.

Today, all efforts of modern criticism could be said to focus upon the notion of Logos, which signifies human culture itself insofar as it is one with language. Contemporary criticism effectively reveals that Logos as a whole is coming unstuck and falling apart. This criticism can show more and more how meaning has been assembled and put together, the logical and structural flaws in even the most beautiful constructions of human culture.

I fully agree with this criticism. I simply believe that it can be carried much further and that it is going to be carried to its logical end as the role of human violence in all cultural creation becomes more and more obvious.

One thing only is wrong with that criticism; it is distorted and spurred by one enormous illusion, and this is the strangest and most durable illusion of all Western thought. It is the illusion that the Greek Logos of Heraclitus and the Judaeo-Christian Logos are one and the same thing. This illusion is already present in medieval thought, which sees the Heraclitean Logos as a forerunner of John's Logos. It is present in the modern historical schools, which see John's Logos as a copy and usurpation of the Greek Logos. It is still present in Heidegger, the first one who tried to separate the Greek Logos from the Judaeo-Christian but who does not succeed because he sees the same violence in both. This assimilation of the Greek and the Judaeo-Christian is more than a mistake, of course, it is a fact of our history; it is, indeed, the major intellectual fact of our history.

In order to understand that the two cannot be the same, it takes very little; all that is needed, really, is to read the definition of the Christian Logos in the prologue of John. It seems that some invincible distraction has prevented us so far from reading these very simple lines. This is not surprising. These lines tell us that the Judaeo-Christian Logos, Christ as Logos, is really the truth that is not here, the truth that is always expelled, denied, and rejected. No wonder we could not read these lines; they constitute the most direct formulation of everything that is now at stake in our cultural crisis, in the disintegration of the Greek and cultural Logos. This Greek Logos is the logos built on violence and the misunderstanding of human violence; it is the Logos of expulsion whereas the Judaeo-Christian Logos is the expelled truth, or rather Truth itself, still expelled and rejected.

And the light shines in darkness,
and the darkness does not comprehend it. . . .
He came unto his own, and his own received him not. (John 1:5, 11)

NOTES

1. Sigmund Freud, *Totem and Taboo,* trans. James Strachey (New York: W. W. Norton and Company, 1950), 154.
2. The New Testament tradition has confused this Zechariah, who was, according to this

text in Chronicles, the son of Jehoiada, with Zechariah the canonical prophet, who was the son of Berechiah (Zech. 1:1). One might assume that Jesus used current idiom for an oft-used trope, "from Abel to Zechariah," to refer to the constant historical phenomenon of the murder of the messengers of God.

3. Cf. Robert Pogue Harrison, *The Dominion of the Dead* (Chicago: University of Chicago Press, 2003). This profound meditation by one of his younger colleagues and admirers is much in the spirit of Girard (Editor).

4. *The Acts of the Apostles,* trans., with introduction and notes, Johannes Munck; rev. William F. Albright and C. S. Mann (Garden City, NY: Doubleday, 1967), 70.

5. *Acts of the Apostles,* trans., with introduction and notes, Munck; rev. Albright and Mann, 68.

"Denial of the Apocalypse" versus "Fascination with the Final Days"

Current Theological Discussion of Apocalyptic Thinking in the Perspective of Mimetic Theory

Józef Niewiadomski

Institute of Systematic Theology, University of Innsbruck, Austria

A comprehensive assessment of the contemporary theological discussion of the apocalyptic problem will probably resemble René Girard's assessment of the discourse on the question of sacrifice; rather than answering the question itself, the discussion describes "a problem that remains."[1] In support of this view I quote Jürgen Moltmann:

> And yet it remains a theological puzzle why the early Christian congregations should have expected still further final apocalyptic struggles between God and the godless powers, between the archangel Michael and the Dragon, and between Christ and the Antichrist, even though they believed in Christ's eschatological victory in his cross and his resurrection, and in their doxologies extolled the lordship of Christ over the cosmos. Why does the scenario, battle, defeat, resurrection and victory, continually recur in the apocalyptic pictures of history? . . . How can the christological "once and for all" be reconciled with the apocalyptic expectation of new final struggles "again and again"?[2]

Because contemporary theological discussion obscures the drama of the New Testament, because it fails to heed the problem of the battle between good and evil becoming increasingly more intense as a result of the revelation that has taken place, it must content itself with acknowledging the mystery, with washing its hands in innocence and pointing to the unenlightened fundamentalists ridden by apocalyptic fever, smirking at them or, as of late, warning of their danger. The fundamental theological problem, that is, whether there is an apocalyptic dimension in God's acting in history that possesses present-day relevance, is thus downgraded to a cultural-historical question, and the God Who acts is replaced by the theologian who explains. The sects ridden by apocalyptic fever, on the other hand, are hardly aware of the drama. Since they are certain to join the side of the good in the end time struggle, and have long since safely identified the agents of the "dragon," they cannot be surprised by God's apocalyptic actions. Since the frontlines of the debate have hardly changed for decades, instead of a discussion of the apocalyptic dimension of God's acting in history, we find embittered trench warfare. The cannons are regularly fired in the direction of the opponent, and from time to time one's own equipment is modernized. Undermining the frontlines seems unimaginable. In what follows I would like to begin by describing the two frontlines and then proceed to discuss the attempt at undermining the frontlines that was developed in a congenial way in the dialogue between Girard and Raymund Schwager as well as other theologians from Innsbruck, and that in German-speaking countries is commonly known as "Dramatic Theology."[3]

A Longing for the Apocalypse

The fascination caused by the Apocalypse to this day finds its primary articulation in two correlated, yet separate, motifs. Those are the motifs of the imminent end of the world and of the Millennial Reign of Christ on earth, respectively. Within primitive Christianity we already find currents that expect the imminent return of Christ and the imminent end of the world. Even though the expectation of an imminent end of the world was disappointed and the official teaching of the Church interpreted the words concerning the imminent end in terms of individual death, the collective interpretation has never died out. Similar things can be observed with regard to the expectation of the Millennial Reign. Irenaeus and many second-century theologians took the biblical statements quite literally. According to the Book of Revelation (20:1–3), the Millennial Reign begins with the binding of Satan and his banishment into the abyss. This spectacular event starts an earthly reign of justice and peace. Eusebius of Caesarea linked this event with Roman

Emperor Constantine. Thereby he equated the Church, the Roman Empire, and the Reign of God. Yet Origen even earlier, and especially Augustine afterward, understood the Millennial Reign in terms of the Church only, and it was therefore seen as referring to a spiritual dimension. This description removed the Church from the field of mimetic rivalry with the state and conflict with an earthly reign. In this view, the "binding of Satan" does not represent a spectacular event in world history, which would bring with it a better reign; rather, it takes place in the conversion of each individual person and also in baptism. Since, however, it is impossible to separate the wheat from the chaff right in the midst of history, the Church itself is characterized by the ambivalence of sin and holiness, and it will have to live in the midst of this world with a certain serenity. As paradoxical as it may sound, for the bishop of Hippo the apocalyptic dimension of God's action is at one and the same time God's tolerance for sinners and God's wrath. This is why Augustine was not tempted into apocalyptic fever, either by the sack of Rome or by the clear foreshadowing of the sack of his own See of Hippo.

Despite this Augustinian hermeneutics, the hope of a "literal" Reign of Christ lived on in the Church. This expectation, as well as the hope for an early end of the world, has always motivated fringe groups, especially in troubled times. The increase in wars and social upheavals in the Middle Ages pushed both those hopes to center stage. In this context, then, the importance of the Cistercian abbot Joachim of Fiore can hardly be exaggerated. For in regard to the ensuing course of occidental history, it is true that Joachim is more alive than Augustine.[4] His exegesis of Scripture was different from the then dominant scholastic theology. In the context of this presentation, the following assumption of Joachim's is of primary importance. There is an immediate concordance between the history of Israel and the history of the Church. From a methodological standpoint this means that concordia had now taken the place long held by allegoria.[5] Isolated historical events could now be seen as paralleling other such events, and history as a whole was divided into various ages. Following the Age of the Father, which lasted until the coming of Christ, and the Age of the Son, which was marked by an imperfect (hierarchical) Church, now—through a great crisis—the Age of the Holy Spirit begins. Joachim's hope was not primarily focused on the Kingdom of God in the Afterlife but on the Church—changed by the Holy Spirit. The Church, which he continued to understand in a spiritual sense, stood at the center of his theology, but in a way that differed from Augustine's perspective. The concrete institution of the Church was now drawn into mimetic rivalry and conflict with the vision of the Millennial Reign. On the one hand Joachim drew a clear picture of who the foe was by pointing to the imperfect hierarchical condition; on the other hand his belief in the imminent dawning of a new age tempted him to look for a spiritual-political leader, the incarnation of Christ returning to the earth. Via the Franciscan Spirituals, Thomas Münzer, and other enthusiastic groups, his thoughts made their way into philosophy, were separated from the immediate ecclesiastical dream, and had a lasting impact on political developments in the modern era ranging as far as the trauma of the millennial Reich of the German nation.

Next, it is Luther's end time expectation that is important in the context of this presentation. Certainly, he perceived the papacy to represent the Antichrist, against whom the final struggle had to be fought. Because of this final struggle, he too expected the imminent end of the world. For radical groups and streams within the Reformation movement this end time expectation took on even greater importance. The greatest political impact of these groups came with the Puritan Revolution in England and, after its defeat there, in the United States. The hopes were transferred to the "New World," to the founding of a "city on a hill" in order to lead decadent Europe into a glorious new age. For centuries, the United States' national ideals were inspired by visions like these. And in this context, too, we can observe that the two motifs (the end and the millennial reign) are not neatly separated, as witnessed in the two expressions of hope that coexist in tension one with another: premillennialism and postmillennialism.[6]

Finally, it must not be forgotten that the rise of the natural sciences was accompanied by apocalyptic impulses and in part was inspired by them too. For Newton is not only the founder of modern physics, but also the interpreter of the book of Daniel and the Revelation of John. The natural sciences, however, in turn were the major driving force behind the transformation of the future-looking messianic faith into a purely secular belief in progress. This belief successfully rid cultural consciousness of the apocalyptic fever. Only unenlightened hicks could afford the luxury of a seemingly literal interpretation of the apocalyptic writings.

In the time of an enlightened consciousness, such a reading could only be found in classic American fundamentalist circles or—and we should not allow denominational opposition to fool us into not recognizing the deeper analogies—among Catholics. Among the latter it was mainly found in the context of the piety that points to all kinds of revelations and visions and that one could call "Marian apocalyptics." The reconstruction of the basic building blocks of this apocalyptic hermeneutic in the prevalent handbooks not only points to the fact that the abundance of religious images and statements is, in the final analysis, built on a small number of basic ideas, but also underlines the strong parallels between these statements and the worldview of the noncanonical apocalypses, for example, the Henoch Apocalypse, which were written at a time between the writing of the Old and New Testaments.

First, we find the conviction that we live in the last times on earth and that the final destruction is at hand. The founding of the state of Israel in 1948 and the Six-Day War have played an important role in intensifying this belief among evangelicals especially.[7] As God's acts go all but unnoticed in the present world, humankind is finally presented with the demonstration of His Divinity by means of His destructive actions on behalf of His people, Israel. In this view, God will surprise men with His destructive power and provide proof of His Divinity. This proof, however, will come at a heavy cost to His enemies: they will be identified as enemies of God, they will be humiliated, yes, even destroyed; the faithful—with whom the interpreters usually identify themselves—will be saved. Since the destruction of the godless world has already been decided by God it is impossible to delay it, let alone stop it from happening. This world has, because of its wickedness, been irreversibly given over to defeat. What counts is saving oneself, and as many "righteous and true Christians" as possible, to enter the new world. The concrete political situations of the present are integrated into this basic formal structure. Thus, perceived dangers and current political motifs of conflict are by way of concordia constantly pointed to as validating the veracity of the biblical teachings or the contents of (Marian) revelations. In this view, the biblical apocalyptic writings or the later visions unveil the real causes for the world crisis that is (at the particular moment) leading to the destruction of the world; they also describe the most recently developed and recently used weapons, they uncover political and Church-political developments and, most importantly, they identify political enemies as agents of Satan. The unclear relationship of apocalypticism with politically motivated ethics can lead to political passivity but from time to time can also reverse itself in the direction of activity. Someone fascinated by the end can try to speed it up or contribute to bringing it about. Yet does this not mean that even those who are marked by an eager desire for the apocalypse finally remain blind to the present relevance of the apocalyptic dimension of God's acting in history?

As long as this belief was found only in readily identifiable groups and circles, it did not cause much concern to enlightened theology or to the political sciences. On the contrary, the simple mention of the unenlightened fundamentalists was enough to cause self-righteous ignoring of the aporias of the present. A superficial analysis would suggest that the situation has fundamentally changed in the past few years. The crisis of belief in purely secular progress, a new awareness of catastrophes, and the worldwide surge in violence motivated by religion especially have led to a renewed interest in apocalyptic literature. In addition, the renewal of the fundamentalist debate in the last quarter of the past century has moved the locus in which apocalyptic fears and hopes are debated and lived more and more in the direction of a public realm that is structured by media. Apocalyptic fever could now even be turned into a media event. Messages sent by individuals or small groups, or even long-standing religious traditions, and the belief in the end of time are—by means of countless books, films, video clips, home pages, and even commercials—mixed together to form an apocalyptic stew and then brought to bear on the interpretation of world politics. It might sound paradoxical, but the renewed interest in apocalypses and the transposition of the discussion onto a global stage only emphasize the already established places of disagreement and by no means undermine them. Those ridden by apocalyptic fever still perceive God as the source of violence; "enlightened" realists ascribe this perception to the apocalyptically fevered fundamentalists themselves. The very fact that the topic is heavily marketed in the media distracts attention from the fundamental question, "What do we mean when we say that God acts in history?" Instead of facing the problem of the apocalyptic dimension of God's acting in history in all earnestness, we stare at the "evil" fundamentalists, who allegedly are responsible for our apocalyptic problem. In spite of the apocalyptic fever, our culture displays a certain apocalyptic blindness.

Apocalyptic Blindness in Academia

With its fixation on the questions posed by the natural and historical sciences in the nineteenth century, academic theological discussion itself contributes to establishing the traditional frontlines and to the widespread apocalyptic blindness. The attempt to keep up with the scientific standards of the age at first led to a relinquishing of biblical traditions. It was Ernst Troeltsch who delivered the decisive blow. Modern scientific cosmology does away with apocalyptic fears and hopes in one sweep: "The universe that now stands before us is immeasurably greater than the seven days' work of the Bible. . . . Science tells us that we appeared at a certain moment in time, and that at another moment, we will disappear—but it tells us nothing more. Just as the earth began without us, so too will it end without us. To put it in religious terms, this means that the end will not be an apocalypse."[8] Johannes Weiss and Albert Schweitzer did nothing but add fuel to the flames with their theses.[9] Their assumption that Jesus's message of the Kingdom of God and even His entire existence only make sense if they are understood against the backdrop of the imminent end of the world presents theology with a few seemingly clear-cut alternatives. As Jesus expected, even tried to bring about, the end of the world, the fact that it has not happened is clear proof that Jesus was wrong on that point. If therefore one wants to salvage Christianity, one consequently has to discard apocalyptic thinking. Some went about this salvaging by intensifying a liberal theology that perceives Jesus to be nothing more than a moral authority; others distinguished sharply between eschatology and apocalypse. But as the latter was given up in favor of a reinterpretation of the former, the specifically biblical aspect of eschatology was lost, namely, the idea that the battle between good and evil was intensified by the very fact that the revelation had taken place. The argument of the so-called eschatological reservation was designed to achieve an understanding of the temporal difference between the rule of God that was already present and that which did not yet exist and should be completed in the end of time. Eschatology became the twentieth century's favorite black box'; biblical criticism became criticism of the apocalypse itself. As everyone knows, Rudolf Bultmann led the charge. Even though he lived in the midst of war, he showed no consciousness of catastrophe. On the contrary, he passes a clear verdict against the biblical apocalyptic tradition: "Mythical eschatology is finished basically by the simple fact that Christ's parousia did not take place immediately as the New Testament expected it to, but that world history continues and—as every competent judge is convinced—will continue."[10] Bultmann's "Kerygma and Myth" radically excludes the experience of violence and continues the program of the "de-worldification" of theology. His existentialist theology also replaces political theology and political philosophy with the vast realm of the individual's internal experience. From that moment until now, a critical stance on apocalyptic topics became the identification card of academic theologians. Until further notice it was what set them apart from the theologians of the cults and sects. The question of whether there indeed is an apocalyptic dimension to the actions of God in history, and especially what it might consist of, could no longer even be asked by this kind of theology. In his provocative work, Ratlos vor der Apokalyptik (Clueless on the Apocalyptic), Old Testament scholar Klaus Koch in 1970 indeed provided a reminder of the unsolved question. He pointed to Ernst Käsemann and saw his theology as a new start, even a landmark in New Testament theology:

> Apocalypticism has been brought out of the closet of a peculiar area of specialization in religious history and brought to the attention of a wide theological public, at least in Germany and Switzerland. In this approach, apocalypticism is seen as a legitimate continuation of Old Testament ideas and thus as a medium to connect the Old and the New Testaments. While Käsemann's thesis had precursors and while other exegetes besides him advocated similar thoughts, only Käsemann's writings were met with excitement, even creating a sensation. For one, Käsemann had presented the problem in a more pointed way than anyone before him; in addition, however, a student of the famous New Testament scholar Bultmann was least expected to present such a view. Fellow students of Bultmann's and conservative exegetes alike were equally shocked. In the field of biblical studies apocalypticism had up to that time been a fringe subject in Old and New Testament studies, closely bordering on heresy. Käsemann all of a sudden declared the tributary to be the main stream which supposedly "feeds everything else at the end of the Old and the beginning of the New Testament."[11]

It was Johann Baptist Metz who in 1977 introduced the idea that apocalypse is the mother of all Christian theology into the widespread political discussion. But, turning against modern evolutionary thought, Metz wanted only to salvage the motif of near expectation. In the end, apocalypticism to him is at its core a teaching of the catastrophic nature of all ages:

> The Jewish-Christian apocalyptical vision has correctly been described by Ernst Käsemann as the "mother of Christian theology." It came to be regarded not as a mythical expulsion of time into a rigid world pattern, but rather as a process by which time could be restored to the world. In that case, we can see man's consciousness of catastrophe as expressed in the apocalyptical vision basically as a consciousness of time, not a consciousness of the time of catastrophe, but a consciousness of the catastrophic nature of time itself, of the character of discontinuity and the end of time.[12]

Is this attempt at salvaging apocalypticism convincing, especially in light of the decades of trench warfare between the fundamentalist sects rejecting academic theology and of academic theology simply smirking at the faith of the sects or deeming their faith dangerous? If one takes seriously the position of the believers who are fascinated by the end times, one would have to credit them more than anyone else with a consciousness of the catastrophic nature of time. But a concession of this kind still does not provide a critical instrument by which to distinguish between positions that may rightly be criticized and others that are to be accepted. The teaching of the "catastrophic nature of time" does not allow for a differentiated understanding of the apocalyptic dimension of God's acting in history. And in the framework of this hermeneutics it is altogether impossible to assess the noncanonical apocalypses. Should the small band of the righteous that feels itself entirely on God's side and sharply sets itself apart from the teeming masses of blasphemers, because those belong to the kingdom of Satan, also receive the benediction of Christian theology's nurturing motherhood? Such kinds of assessments are very much in vogue with a media-dominated public. This is precisely due to the fact that the public finds it easy to lump those "righteous ones," who remain entirely driven by a spirit of resentment and of vengeance, into a comprehensive apocalyptic stew together with the "Christian martyrs" and Islamic suicide bombers, and thus feeds its own prejudice that the apocalyptic problem stems solely from people with a perverse religious fantasy.

Congenial Solution by Girard and Schwager

With his description of the apocalyptic situation in *Things Hidden since the Foundation of the World*, Girard does not simply allow for an undermining of encrusted frontlines. To him, it is the uncovering of the violent sources of social trends by the Jewish-Christian revelation that really creates the apocalyptic situation. As humans are left without any sacrificial means to turn away the violence, they incur a degree of responsibility previously all but unknown to humanity. Thus it becomes clear that conversion is the only true alternative to scapegoats for the reaching of a social consensus, and thus conversion has become essential. Yet, because the hidden mechanism of the old consensus can no longer be covered up—and therefore sustained—and the radically renewed behavior does not materialize, the possibility of humanity's self-destruction follows logically. In accordance with this logic, the biblical apocalypses depict the destruction of the structures of human order.[13] However, they do not spring from a perverse religious fantasy; neither are they mere artifacts of a preenlightened culture; they merely take human conduct to its logical conclusion: self-destruction is the end of a humanity robbed of the (sacrificial) means of covering up and controlling violence yet unwilling to behave in a radically new way (because it is unwilling or unable to do so). The logic of this self-destruction is not bound to certain dates; rather it remains a permanent possibility. It shows the full urgency of the question of the apocalyptic dimension of God's actions in history. Inspired by Girard, Schwager has systematically organized many unclear and contradictory motifs of the theological discussion and has also shown clearly defined contours of the Christian faith in the apocalyptic age.[14] Thus the analogies and differences between legitimate Christian apocalyptic expectations and the undifferentiated fascination with apocalyptic scenarios become clearly apparent.

Even though Jesus associated himself with the apocalyptic tradition when he preached the imminence of the Kingdom of God, he clearly rejected the apocalyptic expectations of his environment. Thus he rejected all knowledge of dates and also any calculation of dates.[15] In doing so, he infused the common parlance of imminence with a new meaning. As the Kingdom of God first takes place in the experience of a personal closeness of God, it can come any- and everywhere. In this sense Augustine remains thoroughly faithful to Jesus's logic in his interpretation. In the first place, however, the Kingdom of God erupted in a singular way in Jesus's message and also in his own fate. The presence of the Father caused time to compress for Jesus. This allowed him to see the basic conflicts of mankind condensed in his own fate. This is also why the acceptance or the rejection of Jesus and of his message must be understood as the primary apocalyptic problem. The decisive theological difficulty does not lie in the temporal tension between a kingdom that meaninglessly has "already" come in Jesus but exists "not yet"; it lies, rather, in the question of the "opposing will" of humans who do not receive the message of Jesus. To this rejection Jesus reacts with his judgment discourse. And in these very texts Girard sees a privileged access to apocalyptic literature. What do these texts tell us about God's actions in history? By his teaching and his fate, Jesus transformed not only the understanding of the coming of the Kingdom of God but also the apocalyptic discourse of God's judgment. Jesus's words of judgment stem from a logic that stands in direct contrast to the apocalyptic (predominantly noncanonical) tradition and its undifferentiated black-and-white approach; in contrast to the idea of a violent God Who separates people one from another, Who Himself destroys the wicked or punishes them; and also in contrast to the self-righteousness of the apocalyptic seers who always know in advance who the agents of Satan are. Jesus's words are targeted not only at foes and enemies but at everybody. Thus they undercut any self-righteousness. In addition, they are structured by faith in a nonviolent God of love, even for His enemies, and therefore also for one's own enemies. This God therefore cannot possibly reveal His divinity through destructive works. His judgment must be seen as a judgment that humanity inflicts on itself by shutting itself up to the coming of the Kingdom of God.[16] Wherever this happens, the catastrophes announced in the judgment discourses are taking place. That is where fathers are pitched against sons, sons are pitched against fathers, and peoples destroy one another in series of wars. Why is it, then, that the Scripture describes this judgment as God's judgment? One reason is that God is the author of the whole created order. Another one is, however, that Christ's revelatory words unmask the connections of evil, lies, and violence. The immediate agents of judgment, however, are still humans themselves.

The apocalyptic traditions are not corrected merely in the teaching and practice of Jesus. His fate, particularly, condenses apocalyptic events and transforms them. From his fate it can be seen anew and in an even deeper way how the apocalyptic aspect of God's actions in history must be understood. When evil and violence were targeted directly at him, Jesus did not defend himself violently. Neither did he ask his Father to violently destroy his enemies. On the contrary, he prayed for them. He had even reinterpreted his own fate beforehand and thus had also broken down the spiral of violence and counterviolence that makes for apocalyptic resentment, that is, even the specifically apocalyptic hatred between victims and perpetrators. His Father did not step in violently in order to help His son. Nonetheless, God has unequivocally identified Himself with him and delivered him from death.

This understanding of the apocalyptic dimension of God's acting in history is of fundamental importance for systematic theology. Naturally it primarily states, "God judges!" However, He judges by permitting evil in the created order to have its wicked way between men. Even His own son had to experience this. This son was burdened with all the evil that humankind did not want to see within itself.[17] Today therefore Jesus's violent death must neither be seen as an accidental event nor as something that sprang forth from the will of an angry God. The idea of an angry God, indeed, is the last possible sacrificial reserve, which protects us in an untruthful way from beholding the "objective apocalyptic situation." By bringing Jesus's death into a positive connection with the will of God, by exposing the son in the sinner's place to the Father's wrath, tradition maneuvered itself into the impasse that closed its eyes to the real drama of the world, the situation that results from Christ's death. Because of that self-inflicted blindness, the fact that the Book of the Revelation (of John) not only incorporates a battle between good and evil but even intensifies it had to remain an enigma.

Moreover, a dramatic understanding of the apocalyptic dimension of God's acting also says, "God judges by raising man from the dead!"[18] Faith in the resurrection indeed is a fundamental part of apocalyptic perspectives.

Normally this belief is embedded in the climate of apocalyptic resentment or even in the framework of the victims' vengeance on their killers. The legitimate aspect (which features time and again in the theological debate) of justice and the hope that the murderer will not triumph over his victim are distorted beyond recognition in many apocryphal apocalyptic writings. In this world of lies and deception the "resurrection unto eternal shame" is mostly turned into a projection of one's own self-righteousness and an aggression against one's enemies that is stronger than death. The resurrection of Jesus does take up this apocalyptic motif, but also radically transforms it. For the one who is resurrected is the same one who embodied the God of love for one's enemy. This simple fact represents a radical challenge to the ostensibly very intense hatred directed at the godless. What is more, the faithful are presented with a clear criterion of verification when it comes to deciding between love or hatred, violence or nonviolence. And why is that? According to the apocalyptic logic of the Old Testament and the noncanonical literature, the resurrection of the dead remains inseparably linked to the end of the world, to the final judgment of God and also to the new heaven and the new earth. This logic says that it will be only in these complex future events that apocalyptic humanity will find proof of the veracity of its resentments. While this might at first sight seem like a temptingly convincing solution, a more critical reflection shows it to be a mere projection: nebulous figures of apocalyptic hope cannot be corrected by anything, anything at all. In contrast, the fate of Jesus provides a highly differentiated view of end time events, thus also transforming the apocalyptic expectation by resisting random projections. Because this resurrection takes place right in the midst of history, love and nonviolence are proved to be attributes of God; hate and violence on the other hand are disproved. In addition, Christians will always have to distinguish the end of the world in the temporal sense of the term from the end in the sense of finality. Even though Christ was raised, the history of the world continues. Therefore understanding the apocalypse only in terms of discontinuity is not an option for Christian thought.

The differentiations established in the preceding paragraphs are of enormous importance for discerning the ambivalent religious fears and hopes of those who are fascinated by the apocalypse. A destruction of political cultures, but also a possible destruction of humanity, even a destruction of our earth, may ultimately be the result of the self-judgment of humanity.

God's judgment could in this context only be seen in the form of His permitting that to happen. However, the destruction is in no way identical with the revelation of God's majesty and even less so with the coming of the new heaven and the new earth. Quite the contrary.

If Troeltsch and other theologians pitch natural scientific images of the possible end of humanity against the apocalypse, they overlook the fact that the fate of Jesus has already transformed the apocalypse into a real-symbolic drama.

Finally, the resurrection shows that the cross itself may be understood as an act of judgment. It is, however, a judgment that yet again undermines the hopes of the apocalyptic judgment. Even the perspective, suggested in the Gospel of Matthew 25:31–46, of two different camps, the goats and the sheep before the judging Son of Man, is corrected in the passion that follows. There, the judge himself is judged. He is turned into the victim. As a victim, he can forgive the perpetrators, because in the final analysis he sees in them primarily victims of sin. In this way he, the victim, can identify with them and undermine the apocalyptic separation into two groups of people. This separation does not happen in the way suggested by the noncanonical literature, that is, between the small band of the righteous and the teeming masses of the followers of Satan. Rather, it is a separation within man himself. As perpetrators of sin, humans stand allied against the "judged" judge; as victims, they remain within the sway of his saving power.

This is the reason why dramatic conflict does not relent after Easter. On the contrary, it is intensified.[19] Paul already writes about Christians who live worse than pagans in 1 Corinthians 5:1–5. The time after Christ's coming obviously is the time of the Church. Her history is just as dramatic as the fate of Jesus Christ. In her life the things that have fundamentally been accomplished in Jesus's life are now time and time again won anew on various levels. Since God will not make His Kingdom come against the opposition of human freedom, He allows history to continue. He will not forcefully bring the history of this world to an end. But he will definitely permit evil to have its way. In His saving work, however, He always starts at the very place where a person is at that moment. Even if the person is engaged in practicing evil. In the time following Easter, the drama of judgment is still present. If humans themselves are transformed by the power of identification with Christ, the victim, they no longer act as accusers but as forgivers; then they too transform, together with Christ, the immense potential of tears, curses, pain, and death. True, this is by no means realpolitik—not in the state, nor in society, nor in small groups, and not always in the Church. Despite the revealing power of the gospels, these social bodies remain structured by the mechanisms of accusation and scapegoating. This, however, is no argument against the belief that the undifferentiated apocalyptic logic has been exploded in Christ. Neither is it an argument against the hope that this salvation is available to everyone. If the end emphasizes conscious reconciliation over an apocalyptic separation into two, this hope has to create images that in turn motivate us towards a forgiving love and strengthen faith in the redefinition of judgment through the event of the cross. The ancient apocalyptic image of the final judgment now is to be purified in light of the thoughts above.[20] In the end, reflection gives way to narration. In pedagogical terms, the greatest educational effect is still achieved by way of a narration that creates meaning.

"The Last Judgment"

The Church believes in the resurrection of the dead. What does this mean concretely? Resurrection of the dead at first is the dream of the fulfillment of human desires as well as resentments. What does that mean? It is the chance, so important to all of us and often referred to on epitaphs, to encounter those who have been good to us, to meet with father and mother and all our loved ones. Resurrection of the dead is also the chance to encounter all of those who have done us harm, those we have cursed and on whom we wish vengeance. This, however, is where those human desires supported by the apocalyptic logic stop. But is resurrection of the dead not also a chance to encounter all those whom I have harmed? All those whom I have accused and all those whose space of life I have destroyed will also be confronted with me. Whenever the classic image of the Last Judgment spoke about a clear understanding of good and evil deeds, this clarity will in the first place relate to the relationship of victim and perpetrator within each individual human being. Let me put it in stark terms: when Hitler and his killers will be confronted with the victims of Auschwitz, and Stalin with those of the Gulag Archipelago, and the victims of Hiroshima with all the politicians and scientists who have caused their deaths; when we, the inhabitants of the developed world, will look the millions of children of the world's poorest countries straight in the eyes; and when, finally, the unborn or those cheated out of their right to live will demand their right, this encounter becomes all the more unbearable, if the extent to which the perpetrators themselves were nothing but victims is also laid bare. What gigantesque scenario of excuses and new accusations is there being realized?

There are two sides to this image. All those who have infringed my rights, who have done me wrong, whose victim I have become, stand before me as perpetrators. As their victim I will be able to adjudicate their righteousness. It is up to me. What will I demand? I will probably insist on my rights and demand retribution and vengeance.

At the same time, however, I will be confronted with all the victims of my conduct, my lies, my accusations. They will be entitled to the same judgment in my regard. They too will likely insist on their rights and demand retribution and vengeance. Yet I will profess my innocence by accusing others and passing the retribution and vengeance intended for me on to them. This could indeed become one true *dies irae*, a day of wrath in the "best" of biblical traditions, if everything depended solely on us on that day and if this judgment was to be nothing more than our self-judgment. Without God's interference, humans would mutually condemn one another to the hell of accusation, denial, and lies. Everyone would insist on victim status, demand retribution, and pass the retribution facing him or her on to others.

But there will be yet another confrontation on that day of wrath that is of decisive importance, namely, the confrontation with the unfathomable goodness of God and His readiness to forgive. This goodness, revealed in the history of the Bible and culminating in the fate of Jesus Christ, will be decisive—this, at least, is what Christians hope for. The scenario of the Last Judgment includes facing the apocalyptic judge of the world. In order to gain a systematic perspective on that, we will have to view the image of two camps from Matthew 25 together with the image of the lamb who was slaughtered from the Book of the Revelation of John.[21] In this context we have to carefully account for Christ's divine and human dimensions. In him, God's unconditional forgiveness and integration were embodied in a human life and death; in the Last Judgment Jesus will have to say something important also in his humanity. And it would be very surprising if he himself now did anything else but what he asked the Father to do, when he hung on the cross: forgive them.

By his example on the cross, Christ provided the basis for innumerable men and women throughout the history of Christianity to break out of the vicious cycle of accusation time and again by preemptive forgiveness and kindness, and even to partly transform that cycle ("breakthroughs of grace" in the discipleship unto Christ). Following Christ's example, many men and women have not passed on their potential of guilt, let alone increased it, but rather have declared it to be forgiven in advance by their prayers and by their deeds on behalf of the dead. And finally, when we realize that the man who prayed for his enemies on the cross and forgives all of us now in the final judgment is not just any man but the Son of God, who talks to us in perfect unity with God, so that in him we are confronted face to face with a God Who could have condemned us and left us in the self-inflicted hell of our own choosing, yet has accompanied us all the way into this hell of victimization, and then has once more opened us an exit out of the vicious cycle of claiming to be right and demanding retribution, we experience his radical grace of forgiveness face-to-face. For this reason hardly anyone will be able to inhibit this forgiveness and to insist on their rights and on retribution.

The fact that this confrontation will be "painful"—"as through fire"—is obvious in light of our experience. This, however, in no way changes our hope that the day of wrath will be transformed into a day of forgiveness, of grace, and of mercy.

NOTES

1. René Girard, *Violence and the Sacred*, trans. Patrick Gregory (Baltimore: The Johns Hopkins University Press, 1977), 1.
2. Jürgen Moltmann, *The Coming of God: Christian Eschatology*, trans. Margaret Kohl (Minneapolis: Fortress Press, 1996), 232.
3. Initiated by the Catholic Dogmatic theologian Raymund Schwager, S.J. (1935–2004), who also was the first president of the Colloquium on Violence and Religion (COV&R), this approach brings several theologians at the Institute for Systematic Theology in Innsbruck into close cooperation. The central characteristics of this approach are (1) a theological interpretation of mimetic theory; and (2) a view of revelation understanding it as a process of interdependent actions and reactions by different agents, including God. For more information, see *http://theol.uibk.ac.at/rgkw/xtext/research-0.html*.
4. Henri de Lubac, *La postériorité spirituelle de Joachim de Fiore*. 2 vols. (Paris: Lethielleux, 1979 and 1981).
5. In the allegorical method, biblical passages are interpreted in a way that transcends their immediate historical sense toward a deeper, hidden, meaning. Thus St. Paul, in Galatians 4:21–31, took the two wives of Abraham, Hagar and Sarah, to refer to the Old and New Testaments respectively. Concordia limits the range of possible allegorical interpretations because it demands a direct parallel between specific characters and events in the Old Testament and such specifics in the New Testament or Church history.
6. Premillennialism believes that the Second Coming of Christ will be before the Millennial Reign; postmillennialism regards the 1,000-year period as a precondition for the Second Coming.
7. Raymund Schwager and Jozef Niewiadomski, eds., *Religion erzeugt Gewalt—Einspruch!* (Münster, Germany: LIT, 2003), 17–19; 240–241.
8. Ernst Troeltsch, *The Christian Faith: Based on Lectures Delivered at the University of Heidelberg in 1912 and 1913*, foreword by Marta Troeltsch, ed. Gertrud von le Fort, trans. Garrett Paul (Minneapolis: Fortress Press, 1991), 58.
9. Johannes Weiss published his *Die Predigt Jesu vom Reiche Gottes in 1892;* Albert Schweitzer's *Geschichte der Leben-Jesu-Forschung* came out in 1906.
10. Rudolf Bultmann, "New Testament and Mythology," in *New Testament and Mythology and*

Other Basic Writings, selected, ed., and trans. by Schubert M. Ogden (Philadelphia: Fortress Press, 1984), 5. The German original of this text was published in 1941, and in 1948 it was integrated into the later famous "Kerygma and Myth."

11. Klaus Koch, *Ratlos vor der Apokalyptik: Eine Streitschrift über ein vernachlässigtes Gebiet der Bibelwissenschaft und die schädlichen Auswirkungen auf Theologie und Philosophie* (Gütersloh, Germany: Mohn, 1970), 11–12.
12. Johann B. Metz, *Faith in History and Society: Toward a Practical Fundamental Theology,* trans. David Smith (New York: Seabury Press, 1980), 175–76.
13. See the discussion in René Girard, *Things Hidden since the Foundation of the World,* trans. Stephen Bann and Michael Metteer (Stanford, CA: Stanford University Press, 1987), 196–205 and 253–62.
14. Raymund Schwager, *Jesus in the Drama of Salvation: Toward a Biblical Doctrine of Redemption*, trans. James G. Williams and Paul Haddon (New York: Crossroad, 1999); Raymund Schwager, *Banished from Eden: Original Sin and Evolutionary Theory in the Drama of Salvation*, trans. James G. Williams (Leominster, UK: Gracewing, 2006).
15. See Mark 13:22.
16. See Schwager, *Jesus in the Drama of Salvation*, 53–81.
17. See Schwager, *Jesus in the Drama of Salvation*, 116–18.
18. See Schwager, *Jesus in the Drama of Salvation*, 119–41.
19. See Nikolaus Wandinger, *Die Sündenlehre als Schlüssel zum Menschen: Impulse K. Rahners und R. Schwagers zu einer theologischen Anthropologie* (Münster, Germany: LIT, 2003), 238–239.
20. See Jozef Niewiadomski, Herbergsuche. *Auf dem Weg zu einer christlichen Identität in der modernen Kultur* (Münster, Germany: LIT, 1999), 167–86.
21. See Wandinger, *Die Sündenlehre*, 375–77.

Carl Schmitt's "Apocalyptic" Resistance against Global Civil War

Wolfgang Palaver
Institute of Systematic Theology, University of Innsbruck, Austria

To Paul Piccone (1940–2004)[1]

The deep political crisis our world faces today is most openly visible in the spread of global terror and the quite futile attempt to fight a war against it. Connected to this crisis is a growing gulf between Europe and its hope for a Kantian solution to this crisis—the constitutionalization of international law through the United Nations and the International Criminal Court—and the United States with a more Hobbesian understanding of its role as the world-police in charge of a *pax americana*. The international debate about these problems has also led to a growing discussion of the work of the German law scholar Carl Schmitt, especially of his writings on international law.[2] There are several reasons for this new interest in Schmitt. One is linked to a widespread conspiracy theory, according to which the foreign policy of the current Bush administration is nothing but the continuation of Schmitt's emphasis on the friend-enemy distinction, a position apparently connected to Schmitt's support of the Nazis. According to this conspiracy theory, Leo Strauss, who was in contact with Schmitt before he was forced to leave Germany, spread Schmitt's message during his time as an influential professor of political philosophy at the University of Chicago. Many of these superficial accusations are not worth talking about at all, but relating Schmitt's work to Bush's current war against terror might show us that it could be of some help in criticizing this current policy.[3] From Schmitt's perspective, however,

Bush's policy seems to be a perfect example of the dangers of a moralizing universalism. Of course, Schmitt would even more harshly and justly criticize those globalized terrorists who represent a violent universalism with its need of absolute enmity. Most of today's terrorists should not be confused with partisans who remain connected to their local homeland, fighting against a real enemy.[4]

The present article, however, will not enter into this quite superficial and often only accusatory debate about U.S. foreign policy. It will focus instead on some broader implications connected to Schmitt's work on international relations, leading us to the question of the apocalyptic situation of our contemporary world. In a first step I shall introduce Schmitt's major thesis on the danger of a global civil war following the breakdown of European international law after World War I. This part of the article will show how strongly Schmitt's work aims for the prevention of civil war. In a second step I shall analyze Schmitt's thesis with the help of René Girard's mimetic theory to conclude that the danger of a global civil war is linked to a world in which mimetic rivalry is no longer kept inside local or regional boundaries. Our globalizing world confronts us with a planetary mimetic crisis because of the erasure of cultural difference. The third section of the article deals with the political theology that characterizes Schmitt's thinking. Against widely held claims that Schmitt represents a fundamentalist believer in the Biblical revelation, I will show, in contrast to these superficial beliefs, how strongly he longed for a pagan version of Christianity to protect the political offspring of the old sacred from its complete dissolution. This rather futile attempt is linked to his endorsement of the *katechon*, a biblical concept that he interprets as a restrainer against the death of cultures by keeping political friend-enemy patterns alive. Dying closed societies should be replaced by new forms of political structures that still allow the channeling of internal rivalries to the outside. This last section helps us to understand how strongly Schmitt's work is linked to the apocalyptic crisis of our world that stems from the long-term impact of the biblical revelation. Focusing on his anti-apocalyptic endorsement of the *katechon* enables us to understand his work against the background of an apocalyptic world that is today justly addressed by more and more thinkers. The Jewish philosopher Jacob Taubes, who was in contact with Schmitt, saw himself, for instance, as an apocalyptic alternative to the German law professor: "Carl Schmitt thinks apocalyptically, but top-down, from the powers that be . . . ; I think from below."[5] Even the famous media theoretician Marshall McLuhan, who is usually known as a Panglossian prophet of the "global village," was well aware of the apocalyptic dangers that go along with electronic globalization. He called himself an apocalyptic thinker, underlining the importance of distinguishing Christ from Antichrist, something that has become more and more difficult to do.[6] Talking so openly about Antichrist one risks looking like an apocalyptic fundamentalist; but if it is true that we are today in the midst of an apocalyptic crisis, we cannot avoid these themes and questions. Ivan Illich's recently published interviews may serve as an exemplary model of how we have to overcome our hesitations in this regard. After overcoming the trepidations that accompanied him for 30 years, Illich clearly stated that our age is apocalyptic and not post-Christian, an age in which the corruption of the best leads to the worst.[7] My mimetic reading of Carl Schmitt's understanding of the *katechon* hopefully contributes to this most demanding task that we have to undertake today.

Global Civil War versus Clash of Civilizations

In order to understand the current state of our world we can draw more or less on two quite opposite paradigms. The first paradigm is Samuel P. Huntington's clash of civilizations, which was introduced after the Cold War ended and has attracted significant attention since the terrorist attacks of 9/11. According to Huntington, cultural differences play an important role in recent conflicts. "Culture and cultural identities, which at the broadest level are civilization identities, are shaping the patterns of cohesion, disintegration, and conflict in the post–Cold War world."[8] The former rivalry of the two superpowers "is replaced by the clash of civilizations."[9] Besides language, religion is in Huntington's view the most important element that distinguishes different civilizations.[10] Religion is the "principal defining characteristic of civilizations."[11] If we summarize this paradigm it rests on the assumption that differences, especially cultural and religious differences, are the most important source of human conflicts. But does this first paradigm really help us to explain our current situation?

Mimetic theory offers us an alternative paradigm. It assumes that human conflicts are more likely to arise if differences disappear and equality starts to characterize human relationships. Brothers not strangers are more likely to become enemies. According to mimetic theory, it is the disappearance of differences in our globalizing world that is most threatening. The more human beings become alike and the more everybody is able to compare himself or herself with everybody else, the closer we get to a world that is increasingly threatened by a global civil war. What Simone Weil remarked about the modern world in 1943 is even more true today: "There are far more conflicts than there are differences. The most violent struggles often divide people who think exactly, or almost exactly, the same thing. Our age is very fertile in paradoxes of this kind."[12]

Fundamentalist terrorism is not primarily rooted in cultural differences or in poverty and economic underdevelopment but, to the contrary, in a world in which people paradoxically become more resentful as they move closer to those who are better off.[13] The universality of modern media enhances resentment by enabling more and more people to compare themselves with others and by making any inequalities painfully obvious.[14] Contemporary terrorism is deeply rooted in a global disappearance of differences between cultures and nations, transforming our world into a global arena where enhanced competition increases envy and resentment at the same time. René Girard is right when he refers to the planetary mimetic rivalry that contributed to the terrorist attacks of September 11.[15]

Against the background of these two different paradigms, it is interesting to realize that Carl Schmitt's political theory has close affinities to both of them. Schmitt's most famous book, which appeared for the first time as an article in 1927, is *The Concept of the Political.* In this book he puts the deeper roots of enmity down to differences and strangeness, in a way close to what decades later became known as Huntington's paradigm of a clash of civilizations. According to Schmitt, the "political enemy" is the "other, the stranger; and it is sufficient for his nature that he is, in a specially intense way, existentially something different and alien, so that in the extreme case conflicts with him are possible."[16] One can find several parallels between Huntington's thesis and Schmitt's position in *The Concept of the Political.* Schmitt refers, for instance, to the long ongoing enmity between Christianity and Islam to prove that the biblical injunction to love our enemies does not interfere at all with his insistence on the necessity to have political enemies: "Never in the thousand-year struggle between Christians and Moslems did it occur to a Christian to surrender rather than defend Europe out of love toward the Saracens or Turks. The enemy in the political sense need not be hated personally, and in the private sphere only does it make sense to love one's enemy, i.e., one's adversary."[17] Similarly, Huntington refers to the different rules that the "nations of Christendom" used for dealing with each other and for "dealing with the Turks and other 'heathens'" to prove that "identity at any level—personal, tribal, racial, civilizational—can only be defined in relation to an 'other,' a different person, tribe, race, or civilization."[18] Like Schmitt,

Huntington sees no contradiction between an understanding of politics that is predicated on friend-enemy distinctions and the biblical message. According to him, all religions—regardless of their universalistic claims—differentiate between believers and unbelievers, between a superior in-group and an inferior out-group.[19]

During World War II and later, however, Schmitt's position moved closer toward a paradigm like mimetic theory. In his apologetic postwar journal, *Ex Captivitate Salus,* the enemy is no longer the stranger but the brother:

> Whom can I recognize as my enemy at all? Obviously only the one who can put me into question. And who can really put me into question? Only I myself. Or my brother. That's it. The other is my brother. The other turns out to be my brother, and the brother turns out to be my enemy. Adam and Eve had two sons, Cain and Abel. Thus begins the history of mankind. Thus looks the father of all things. That is the dialectical tension which keeps world history moving and world history has not yet come to an end. . . . The enemy is our own question embodied.[20]

To understand that the brother and not the stranger is more likely to become an enemy means systematically to prioritize civil wars over interstate wars. It is exactly the latent danger of civil wars inside a society that makes us long for the political distinction between friends and enemies.

Leo Strauss was one of the first readers of Schmitt's friend-enemy distinction who understood that the latent internal conflicts of a society necessitate a political enemy outside of it.[21] In a letter to Schmitt written on 4 September 1932, Strauss wrote about an apparently human need to create unity by joining together against a third party: "The ultimate foundation of the Right is the principle of the natural evil of man; because man is by nature evil, he therefore needs *dominion*. But dominion can be established, that is, men can be unified, only in a unity *against*—against other men. Every association of men is *necessarily* a separation from other men. The *tendency* to separate (and therewith the grouping of humanity into friends and enemies) is given with human nature; it is in this sense destiny, period."[22]

Often Schmitt's concept of the political is interpreted as a belligerent demand for war. The main reason for this claim is Schmitt's emphasis on the relationship between the political and the intensity of the distinction between friend and enemy, clearly including the possibility of combat and war.[23] The more intense the distinction between friend and enemy becomes, the more there exists the political: "The distinction of friend and enemy denotes the utmost degree of intensity of a union or separation, of an association or dissociation. . . . The political is the most intense and extreme antagonism, and every concrete antagonism becomes that much more political the closer it approaches the most extreme point, that of the friend-enemy grouping."[24] It is in keeping with this line that Schmitt calls the moments of a most intensive enmity the "high points of politics."[25] As an example he refers to the religiously underpinned enmity between Oliver Cromwell and "papist" Spain in the seventeenth century.

Schmitt's understanding of the political as relying on the intensity of enmity, however, is not rooted in a warmongering philosophy. Schmitt's main aim is the repression of civil war. In an article written in 1930, it becomes clearly evident how his emphasis on intensity is related to the overcoming of civil war:

> The political, correctly understood, is only the degree of intensity of a unity. Political unity can contain and comprehend different contents. But it always designates the most intensive degree of a unity, from which, consequently, the most intensive distinction—the grouping of friend and enemy—is determined. Political unity is the highest unity—not because it is an omnipotent dictator, or because it levels out all other unities, but because it decides, and has the potential to prevent all other opposing groups from dissociating into a state of extreme enmity—that is, into civil war.[26]

Schmitt's book on Hobbes from 1938 underlines this interpretation of *The Concept of the Political*. According to Schmitt, Hobbes's state is defined by its overcoming of civil war. The state "with great might perpetually prevented civil war," overcoming the "revolutionary, anarchistic force of the state of nature. . . . One of the monsters, the leviathan 'state,' continuously holds down the other monster, the behemoth 'revolution.'"[27] In order to overcome the state of nature, this chaotic and warlike condition has to be transferred from the inside of the state to its outside, to its relationship with other states. The more intensely the state is able to prevent the outbreak of civil war, the more intense its enmity to the outside becomes:

> Security exists only in the state. *Extra civitatem nulla securitas*. The state absorbs all rationality and all legality. Everything outside of the state is therefore a "state of nature." The thoroughly rationalized mechanisms of state command confront one another "irrationally." The more complete the internal organization of a state is, the less feasible it is for it to engage in

> mutual relations on an equal basis. The more and the more *intensely* each state is developed, the less it is able to maintain its state character in interstate relations. There is no state between states, and for that reason there can be no legal war and no legal peace but only the pre- and extralegal state of nature in which tensions among leviathans are governed by insecure covenants.[28]

Leo Strauss was right to claim that Schmitt's distinction between friend and enemy had a moral basis.[29] Schmitt affirms the state of nature between the states in order to prevent the state of nature—civil war—inside the state. War is for him an instrument to contain a more primordial form of violence between human beings. Therefore he views the interstate wars embedded in traditional European international law as the "opposite of disorder."[30] These wars are "the highest form of order within the scope of human power."

Due to Schmitt's view of interstate wars as a means to overcome civil war, he was alarmed by the breakdown of European international law after World War I. He criticized especially Great Britain and the United States for having fostered a universalism that has undermined traditional international law. Universalism and the return of the concept of a just war have led to a world that more and more turns into a global civil war. It was in 1938 that Schmitt started to criticize the emerging discriminatory concept of war—a concept that again distinguished between just and unjust wars—because it "transforms the war of states into an international civil war."[31] Later he coined the term "global civil war" (*Weltbürgerkrieg*).[32] He first used this term in an article published in 1942, in which he criticized the United States for being torn between isolationism and interventionism, a fact that would turn the world into a "global civil war" if the United States became the cornerstone of a new world order.

In a diary note from October 1947, in which he harshly criticized Jacques Maritain's integral humanism for its support of the concept of a just war, we can find a short summary of his thesis on global civil war: "Just war, i.e., the deprivation of the rights of the opponent, and the self-empowerment of the just side; that means: the transformation of state war (that is, of war in international law) into a war that is simultaneously a colonial and a civil war; that is, logically and irresistibly: . . . global civil war; and ceases to be interstate war."[33]

Later—especially in his book *The Theory of the Partisan* (1963)—Schmitt more and more emphasized the fact that the spreading global civil war leads to an intensification of enmity, to an absolute or total enemy that has to be annihilated. The final lines of this book document quite well Schmitt's position in this regard and help us to understand why so many scholars eagerly discuss his work today:

> The denial of real enmity paves the way for the destructive work of absolute enmity. In 1914, the nations and governments of Europe stumbled into WWI without any real enmity. Real enmity arose only out of the war, which began as a conventional war among states on the basis of European international law, and ended as a global civil war of revolutionary class enmity. Who will be able to prevent the rise of unexpected new types of enmity in an analogous but much greater extent, whose fulfillment will produce unexpected new forms of a new partisan? The theoretician can do no more than retain the concepts and call things by their names. The theory of the partisan flows into the concept of the political, into the question who is the real enemy and in a new *nomos* of the earth.[34]

In order to prevent a global civil war, Schmitt recommended a new world order—a new *nomos* of the earth—predicated on a division of the world into several independent great spaces. He favored a pluralism of *Großräume*, a pluralism of large blocs. According to Schmitt, since the beginning of the twentieth century the Western world has faced "an enormous alternative between a plurality of *Großräume* and a global claim to world power, pluralism and monism, polipoly and monopoly."[35] The Western world has either to "make a transition to a *Großraum* and to find its place in a world of other recognized *Großräume*, or to transform the concept of war contained in traditional international law into a global civil war."

Schmitt's diagnosis that our modern world has slowly moved toward a global civil war explains more convincingly our current situation than Huntington's clash of civilizations. Huntington's paradigm might even be interpreted as a futile attempt to recreate a politically divided world that prevents the outbreak of a global civil war. It is close to Schmitt's new *nomos* of the earth without, however, showing us the deeper—that means internal and anthropological—roots that seem to necessitate this political solution to the problem of human violence.

The Global Civil War Is a Planetary Mimetic Crisis

Mimetic theory enables us to understand Schmitt's political theory from an anthropological point of view. His concept of the political can be interpreted as an offspring of rituals rooted in the scapegoat mechanism overcoming a mimetic crisis. It is at least as old as Aeschylus's tragedy *Eumenides*. In this tragedy Aeschylus describes the overcoming of civil war by the establishment of a political order. The revengeful and violent Erinyes are transformed into the gentle and fruitful Eumenides. It seems that violence has fully disappeared from the city. This, however, is only superficially true. Open violence, in the sense of revenge, has been transformed into a form of structural violence that helps to create peace inside the city but can be used against foreign enemies and internal troublemakers at any time. The pacified Eumenides promise that common love *and* unanimous hatred will overcome civil war: "I pray that discord, greedy for evil, may never clamor in this city, and may the dust not drink the black blood of its people and through passion cause ruinous murder for vengeance to the destruction of the state. But may they return joy for joy in a spirit of common love, and may they hate with one mind; for this is the cure of many an evil in the world."[36] Civil war has to be overcome by enmity to the outside world. Wars against foreign enemies should help to create peace inside the city. Athena recommends political friend-enemy relations as an antidote to internal bloodshed. According to Girard, Aeschylus's tragedy *Eumenides* represents the political as an offspring of the scapegoat mechanism.[37] What was originally laid upon the scapegoat is now channeled outside the city. In rituals we can find the necessary link between the political and the scapegoat mechanism. The political builds upon the ritual channeling of internal violence toward the external world, whereas in the scapegoat mechanism a member of the group itself is killed. Rituals already tended to sacrifice foreigners. The political prolongs the ritual focus on the foreigner and takes a friend-enemy relationship between two different groups as an always already given starting point. Aeschylus's political is not the result of human reasoning but is rooted in pagan religion and represents an archaic type of political theology.

Mimetic theory not only enables us to understand the ritual origin of traditional forms of politics but it also helps us to understand the situation of our current world. What Schmitt calls a global civil war comes close to Girard's interpretation of our modern world as a planetary mimetic crisis brought forward by the biblical undermining of sacrificial cultures. Historical Christianity is partly a continuation of pagan culture, already including in itself, however, those elements that will lead to its own death in the long run. It has contained from the very beginning "the germs of the planetary society" that have resulted in the unprecedented "death of all cultures" typical of our modern world.[38] This universal crisis of our current world has an apocalyptic dimension, forcing us more and more to choose between the self-annihilation of humanity or the following of the rules of the Kingdom of God.

Enmity and Religion

By linking Schmitt's political theory to Aeschylus, we may recognize religion and political theology as dimensions of political concepts focusing on enmity. It is one of the predominant signs of our time to accuse religion in general of being responsible for an increase in violence, hatred, and enmity. Carl Schmitt is an oft-mentioned example in this respect. The German philosopher Heinrich Meier, who reconstructed the hidden dialogue between Carl Schmitt and Leo Strauss, claims that Schmitt is essentially a political theologian who believes in the truth of the Bible. It is belief in the truth of Genesis 3:15 that lays the foundation of Schmitt's political theology.[39] Schmitt is therefore a perfect example of a fundamentalist whose belief in the truth of the biblical revelation automatically makes him a political theologian prone to enmity and war.

Schmitt refers indirectly to Genesis 3:15 in his *Concept of the Political,* where he quotes a speech by Oliver Cromwell against Spain, which he sees as a perfect example of a form of enmity that is a "high point of politics": "'The Spaniard is your enemy,' his 'enmity is put into him by God.' He is 'the natural enemy, the providential enemy,' and he who considers him to be an 'accidental enemy' is 'not well acquainted with Scripture and the things of God,' who says: 'I will put enmity between your seed and her seed' (Gen. 3:15). With France one can make peace, not with Spain because it is a papist state, and the pope maintains peace only as long as he wishes."[40]

At first sight, this quotation seems to prove Meier's thesis. But is Meier's interpretation of this passage in Schmitt's *Concept of the Political* really appropriate? Is Schmitt's affirmation of the friend-enemy distinction really rooted in his belief in the biblical revelation? I think Meier's thesis is wrong or at least very superficial. A closer look at the above-quoted speech of Cromwell reveals conspicuous difficulties if it is interpreted in such a simple way. At first, Cromwell's speech seems to indicate that Schmitt's friend-enemy distinction ultimately favors a theologically motivated form of hereditary enmity; but how does this go together with Schmitt's claim in the same book that "the criterion of the friend-and-enemy distinction in no way implies that one particular nation must forever be the friend or enemy of another specific nation"?[41] And why should a Catholic thinker like Schmitt use the voice of the

Calvinist Cromwell—due to his "demonic rage" an outstanding example of an "anti-Roman temper"[42]—to express his central theological claim?

Meier's lasting contribution to the interpretation of Schmitt's work is his claim that Schmitt's thinking is based on a political theology. According to Martti Koskenniemi, Meier's thesis also applies to Schmitt's work on international law. It is true that Schmitt is a political theologian. But is it also true to claim like Koskenniemi—following Meier—that Schmitt's nomos "emerges from a political theology that is structurally homologous to Christian monotheism, historically continuous with religious teaching, and, above all, equipped by a supplement of faith that decides who is the enemy . . . in a concrete situation"?[43] Such a thesis is much too narrow to understand Schmitt's work and does not understand at all how religions and political theologies can substantially differ from each other. In this regard Meier and Koskenniemi are misleading.

I can prove my objection easily by showing how close Schmitt again and again came to a pagan type of political theology. To take an example we can look at his 1930 article, "Ethic of State and Pluralistic State," which we used to clarify his understanding of the relationship between the political and the intensity of enmity. This article is also important to understand how he tried to reconcile Christian monotheism with his emphasis on the necessity of a pluralism of political units. He tried to distance himself at this time from older political theologies that were closer to monotheism and monarchy, tending therefore to undermine pluralism in order to find a political theology more in concord with democracy. "In the system of 'Political theology,' the pluralism . . . corresponds with the era of contemporary democratic national states. . . . In accordance with the tendency of its ideas and logic, the monarchy is the more universalistic because it must derive from God when it does not justify itself democratically through the will of the people. In contrast, democracy leads to the recognition of each of the many peoples as a political unity."[44] Schmitt's pluralistic political theology supporting a pluralism of political unities was in need of a God who remains so high up in heaven that he no longer interferes in worldly affairs. "Universal monistic concepts like God, world, and humanity are the highest concepts, and are enthroned above—very high above—any plurality in concrete reality. They maintain their dignity as highest concepts only as long as they remain in their high position. They change their nature, and mistake their meaning and task, when they become mixed up in the scuffles of political life, and are recipients of a false power and a false proximity."[45] In Schmitt's *Constitutional Theory* (1928) we can see that this type of political theology leads politically to the divinization of the people.

The voice of the people becomes the voice of God because "in the area of the political, God can only appear as the God of a concrete people."[46] Schmitt turns out to be a prophet of the angels—or better demons—of the nations, typical of ancient paganism. Nothing related to the transcendent God should disturb the God of the people: "Rejection of every different and foreign authority which in the name of God wants to impose its will on the people, therefore rejection of all political influences and interferences that do not emerge from the substantial homogeneity of one's own people."[47]

It took Erik Peterson, an excellent theologian and former friend of Schmitt, to realize this shift toward paganism. Schmitt's emphasis that God should remain high up in heaven without any interference in worldly affairs, which in turn are completely given over to the divinized people, is a position that has affinities with modern deism and with ancient paganism at the same time. Deism applied the old French saying, "le roi règne, mais il ne gouverne pas" —the king reigns but does not govern—to God. It was Donoso Cortés—a reactionary Catholic thinker and Spanish statesman with whom Schmitt deeply identified in his *Political Theology* (1922)—who showed how deism ultimately leads to atheism.[48] In the late 1920s, Schmitt himself seems to have turned into someone who "excluded God from the world but held onto his existence."[49] By applying the French saying to ancient attempts to reconcile a universal God with many different local deities, Erik Peterson showed in his book *Monotheism as a Political Problem* (1935) how this kind of deism finds an analogy in paganism.[50] He especially refers to the political theology of Celsus, a second-century pagan who harshly criticized Christian monotheism for causing civil war (*stásis*) by trying to bring the whole world under the rule of one *nomos*.[51] According to Celsus, Christians should not destroy national and local cults, because these cults are all connected to particular demons or angels representing their people; they are cults whose power was assigned to them by the most high God.[52] Peterson clearly recognized that Celsus's claim that "the most high God reigns but the national deities govern" is nothing but a "political theology of the pagans."[53] His demand that people should rethink this connection "accurately" was a clear warning to people like Schmitt when in 1935 National Socialism was also trying to establish its own national cult. In Schmitt's last book, *Politische Theologie II* (1970), he recognizes Peterson's warning without, however, giving an answer to this problem.[54] Now Schmitt is content to show that Peterson's intensive use of the French formula *le roi règne, mais il ne gouverne pas* is an important proof of his own seemingly pure scholarly understanding of political theology, according to which "all significant concepts of the modern theory of the state are secularized theological concepts."[55]

Schmitt's political theology is much closer to the pagan theology of Aeschylus's *Eumenides* than to the core of the biblical revelation. A *concordia discors*—a disharmonious harmony—like that which characterizes Aeschylus's political theology is visible throughout Schmitt's work. In his early book, *Roman Catholicism and Political Form* (1923), where he indirectly refers to Léon Bloy's *Le Salut par les Juifs* (Salvation Is from the Jews) in this way endorsing Bloy's remark that there is an opposition within the Trinity itself, as well as in his very last book *Political Theology II* (1970), where he talks about *stásis*—enmity or civil war—he argues that in the Trinity we can discover an ambivalent image of God typical of the pagan sacred.[56] But it would also be an oversimplification to understand Schmitt as a purely pagan thinker. His political theology is rather a pagan or sacrificial version of Christianity.

In order to understand the deeper meaning of this characterization, we have to focus more closely on the complex relationship between religion and enmity. Pagan enmity is not just aiming at the destruction of the adversary but is already a form of moderation of human conflicts. Due to its origin in the scapegoat mechanism, it participates in the "double transference, the aggressive transference followed by the reconciliatory transference" that means the demonization followed by the divinization of the victim, who is blamed for causing the crisis and blessed for its overcoming.[57] In the pagan world the enemy is sacred like the original scapegoat. He is seen as an evil and as a person to be respected—a curse and a blessing—at the same time. Both Simone Weil and Hannah Arendt recognize, for instance, a moderate form of enmity in Homer's *Iliad*.[58] The pagan sacred protects human beings from their own violence. Taking revenge is often left to the gods and is not a purely human activity. René Girard clearly describes how enmity changed its character with the emergence of our modern world:

> The more socially "efficient" scapegoating is, the more capable it is of generating a positive transfiguration of the scapegoat, as well as the negative transfiguration of fear and hostility. The positive transfiguration is still present in the feudal and even the national traditions of military warfare. The enemy is respected as well as intensely disliked. This positive aspect weakens more and more in the modern world, as civil and ideological conflicts tend to predominate. The class enemy of the modern revolutionary never becomes ritualized as a good, even sacred enemy.[59]

It is this difference between the sacred enemy of the old world and the enemy in the modern world that is no longer protected by the pagan sacred and therefore faces annihilation that plays a central role in Schmitt's political theory.

The biblical undermining of sacrificial culture has deprived the enemy of the protection of the pagan sacred. He is now threatened by dangerous demonizations caused by heretical offspring of the biblical revelation. These heresies are a result of the biblical uncovering of the scapegoat mechanism on the one hand and their rejection of the biblical demand for love of the enemies on the other. Modern scapegoaters are aiming at the annihilation of the enemy because they are no longer able to divinize their victims. But despite its detachment from pagan religion, we can also discover a religious temptation in the modern world that increases human violence. Schmitt talks about an "age of masses with its pseudo-theological enemy-myths" and about the terror of the "pseudo-religion of absolute humanity."[60] Less and less protected by the theologically motivated pagan sacred, theologically motivated hatred becomes more aggressive than ever before. The religious wars at the dawn of our modern world are an early example of that temptation. Traditional international law has distanced itself from religion in order to overcome this religious threat. In his *Nomos of the Earth,* Schmitt calls this distancing from religion a "detheologization."[61] Schmitt himself is part of this differentiation. In his postwar journal he underlines his own detheologization, something systematically left aside by people like Heinrich Meier: "Theologians tend to define the enemy as someone who has to be annihilated. But I am a jurist not a theologian."[62] At the same time, however, he realizes that to give up all connections with traditional religion will lead to an even more dangerous world, deprived of all the protections provided by the pagan sacred.

It is due to this insight that he distinguishes holy wars from modern just wars because holy wars still "enshrine something from the primordial character of an ordeal," a way of longing for sacred arbitration, whereas just wars rely solely on human judgment.[63] Traditional international law remained, according to Schmitt, connected to the legacy of holy wars despite its distancing from theology. The authority of jurisprudence "has become secularized but not yet profanized."[64] In order to keep enmity moderate and tame, Schmitt tried to distinguish politics and religion without losing all sacred protection. A note in his diary illustrates his complex position:

> Humanization of war means above all a de-divinization, a reduction to a purely human relation renouncing all balances and reliefs, which result from transcendent forces and powers. . . . Based on pure humanity, on a pure *homo homini homo,* the humanization of war will not last for long. Man

> rather becomes the being of all beings; he becomes God and animal, and the enemy has to be treated simply like an animal because he cannot be divinized.[65]

Schmitt's critical reference to the formula *homo homini homo* is more than revealing. It refers to Francisco de Vitoria's repudiation of the Christian conquest and oppression of the Indians in Latin America. Schmitt accused de Vitoria of having dissolved all sacred differences between human beings, leading toward universalism and its humanistic unleashing of war. De Vitoria, however, was not a humanitarian warmonger but belonged to a Christian tradition of desacralizing war leading back to Augustine.[66] His position culminated in the statement that "difference of religion is not a cause of just war." He therefore opposed holy war, "the doctrine that right religion sanctions war against unbelievers and the confiscation of their property."[67] De Vitoria represents the biblical tradition that dissolved the archaic amalgamation of religion and war and was rightly criticizing his adversaries as leaning toward paganism. Schmitt's rejection of de Vitoria's position underlines once more that his political theology is not primarily representing biblical revelation but a pagan version of it. By clinging strongly to the old sacred protections of enmity, he tries to keep as much paganism alive as is possible in an age strongly influenced by Christianity.

Schmitt's Anti-Apocalyptic Endorsement of the *Katechon*

Although Schmitt thought of himself as a Catholic Christian,[68] he was at the same time forced to oppose the biblical revelation in its undermining of pagan culture. Schmitt's personal tragedy is linked to this odd position of which he was only partly aware. There are a few remarks in his diary that show us his insight into the biblical dissolution of sacrificial culture.[69] In August 1948, he wrote a note in which he argues against a positivistic reading of the Bible. Schmitt points out that the perfect parallel between Moses's escape from Egyptian child murder (Gen. 2:1–10) and Jesus's escape from the massacre of the innocents (Matt. 2:13–23) is a sign of truth not of forgery; but when he turns to the parallel between the Gerasenes demanding Jesus's departure (Matt. 8:34; Mark 5:17) and the grand inquisitor's plea to Jesus to go away and never come back, Schmitt is uncertain: "Is this sameness a sign of truth or of forgery?"[70] Though Schmitt sided with the grand inquisitor throughout his life, this little question shows how much he was aware of his model's affinity with paganism. In a most revealing diary note written about a year later, he sides with the grand inquisitor in a way that again makes the subversive force of the biblical revelation explicit:

> Thomas Hobbes' most important sentence remains: Jesus is the Christ. The power of such a sentence works even if it is pushed to the margins of the conceptual system, even if it is apparently pushed outside the conceptual body. This deportation is analogous to the domestication of Christ undertaken by the Grand Inquisitor of Dostoevski. Hobbes articulated and provided scientific reason for what the Grand Inquisitor did: to make the effect of Christ harmless in the social and political sphere; to deanarchize Christianity but to leave to it at the same time some kind of legitimating effect in the background and in any case not to do without it. A clever tactician gives up nothing, at least as long as it is not totally useless. Thus Christianity was not yet spent. Therefore we may ask ourselves: who is closer to Dostoevski's Grand Inquisitor: the Roman Church or Thomas Hobbes' sovereign? Reformation and Counter-Reformation point in the same direction. Tell me your enemy and I tell you who you are. Hobbes and the Roman Church: the enemy is our own question embodied.[71]

Like Leo Strauss and Eric Voegelin, Schmitt feared the anarchic and subversive force connected to Christianity.[72] It is this subversion that makes the apocalyptic threat of a global civil war possible.

Mimetic theory is able to explain this interrelation. It is the disclosure of the scapegoat mechanism that undermines sacrificial culture in the long run, indirectly enabling the possibility of a global civil war. According to Girard, the biblical revelation slowly turned all closed societies emerging from the scapegoat mechanism into our globalizing world of today: "The gradual loosening of various centers of cultural isolation began in the Middle Ages and has now led into what we call 'globalization,' which in my view is only secondarily an economic phenomenon. The true engine of progress is the slow decomposition of the closed worlds rooted in victim mechanisms. This is the force that destroyed archaic societies and henceforth dismantles the ones replacing them, the nations we call 'modern.'"[73] Globalization, however, is a dangerous state of affairs. Without the protection of the political divisions provided by the pagan sacred, human beings need to follow the rules of the Kingdom of God to prevent the unleashing of planetary violence. It is for this reason that Girard claims that "a radically Christian appropriation of history could only be apocalyptic."[74]

Schmitt, in contrast, is an anti-apocalyptic thinker.[75] This can be best illustrated by his understanding of Christian history. In his private notes on 19 December 1947, he wrote the following: "I believe in the *katechon;* he is the only possibility for me to understand history and find its meaning as a Christian."[76] A similar remark can be found in his *Nomos of the Earth* (1950): "I do not believe that any historical concept other than *katechon* would have been possible for the original Christian faith."[77] By using the term *katechon,* Schmitt is referring to 2 Thessalonians 2:6–7.[78] and a particular political interpretation of this passage that identifies the Roman Empire with the *katechon* who holds back the coming of the Antichrist. Schmitt's approval of this interpretation of the *katechon* shows his anti-apocalyptic attitude. His main concern is the restraining of the Antichrist, whom Schmitt identifies with chaos and anarchy.

It was especially his concern about a global civil war that led him to the concept of the *katechon.* He referred to it for the first time in the 1942 article in which he first used the term global civil war. Throughout his life, he saw a unified world as the reign of the Antichrist, a Kingdom of Satan, or the attempt to build the Tower of Babel.[79] The reign of the Antichrist would be a unified and centralized world without war, politics, states, or *Großräume.* It would create "peace and security" in the sense of 1 Thessalonians 5:3, which was, according to medieval Christianity, the sign of the reign of the Antichrist that ultimately results in destruction.[80] Following medieval Christianity, Schmitt hoped for a *katechon* to prevent a satanic unification of the world. This new *nomos* of the earth, a plurality of *Großräume,* becomes the *katechon* that holds back the unified world of the Antichrist. To some extent, a pluralistic world resembles anarchic chaos. In this specific sense, however, anarchy is not a threat but a remedy. It has to fulfill the role of the *katechon.* It is nihilism rather than anarchy that must be contained. "Anarchic chaos is better than nihilistic centralization. One can recognize the *katechon* by the fact that he does not strive for world-unity."[81]

Theologically, however, the *katechon* is an ambiguous concept. The *katechon* is both poison and antidote. As a restrainer, it is a means to prevent destruction. At the same time, however, it also uses anarchy or violence to prevent the total outbreak of anarchy or violence. Theologically speaking, it not only postpones the reign of the Antichrist but it also holds back the second coming of Christ. This ambiguity of the concept of the *katechon* is rooted in the pagan sacred.[82] The *katechon* contains violence in both senses of the word "contain." Again, Schmitt's particular use of this concept reveals how strongly his political theology is characterized by a pagan version of Christianity.

The concept of the *katechon* allows, however, a quite different use compared to the one we know from Schmitt. It may even help us to find appropriate political, ecclesiastical, and spiritual solutions in a world endangered by a global civil war. The German Protestant theologian Dietrich Bonhoeffer used the term *katechon* in his *Ethics* in order to explain the role of the state and other forces of order that—besides the Church—have to prevent the destruction of the world: "The 'restrainer' is the force which takes effect within history through God's governance of the world, and which sets due limits to evil. The 'restrainer' itself is not God; it is not without guilt; but God makes use of it in order to preserve the world from destruction."[83] How should the Church deal with the *katechon*? According to Bonhoeffer, first the Church should be aware that it has a completely different task. It should prove to the world that Christ is the living Lord. "The more central the message of the Church, the greater now will be her effectiveness. Her suffering presents an infinitely greater danger to the spirit of destruction than does any political power which may still remain."[84] But this difference between the Church and the forces of order does not prevent a close alliance between them in the face of imminent chaos. By preaching the risen Jesus Christ, the Church compels the "forces of order to listen and to turn back,"[85] without, however, rejecting them arrogantly by claiming a moral superiority. According to Bonhoeffer, the Church preserves the "essential distinction between herself and these forces, even though she unreservedly allies herself with them."

The apocalyptic state of our world is a moment of decision, returning to an important topic always close to the heart of the decisionist thinker Carl Schmitt.[86] Contrary to Schmitt, however, it is not important only to take a decision but also to choose the right side. Ultimately it means to side with Christ and follow him by taking the rules of the Kingdom of God seriously. This is not only a spiritual task but also a way of political importance. Pope John Paul II's reflections on the velvet revolutions of 1989 emphasize the importance of the example of Christ to those people who successfully changed the political landscape without violent means. By referring to the "narrow path" between cowardice and violence, he challenges both the European and the United States' perspective of today on the current crisis in international politics:

> The events of 1989 are an example of the success of willingness to negotiate and of the Gospel spirit in the face of an adversary determined not to be bound by moral principles. These events are a warning to those who, in the name of political realism, wish to banish law and morality from the political arena. Undoubtedly, the struggle which led to the changes of 1989

called for clarity, moderation, suffering and sacrifice. In a certain sense, it was a struggle born of prayer, and it would have been unthinkable without immense trust in God, the Lord of history, who carries the human heart in his hands. It is by uniting their own sufferings for the sake of truth and freedom to the sufferings of Christ on the cross that people are able to accomplish the miracle of peace and are in a position to discern the often narrow path between the cowardice which gives in to evil and the violence which, under the illusion of fighting evil, only makes it worse.[87]

NOTES

Scriptural quotations are from the New Revised Standard Version of the Bible (1989).

1. I dedicate this article to Paul Piccone, the founding editor of the journal *Telos*, who encouraged me more than a decade ago to publish several articles on Schmitt. He died in July 2004 in his hometown, New York; at the same time a little group of scholars gathered by Robert Hamerton-Kelly convened at Stanford to discuss the work of Carl Schmitt, Leo Strauss, and Eric Voegelin with René Girard. On Piccone, see Russell Berman, "Introduction" *Telos* 128 (2004): 3–7; and Gary Ulmen, "Paul Piccone and *Telos*," *Telos* 131 (2005): 4–12.
2. The English translation of Schmitt's major book on international law, *The* Nomos *of the Earth*—written during the final stages of World War II and originally published in Germany in 1950—appeared in 2003. In 2004, different English translations of Schmitt's 1963 book, *The Theory of the Partisan*, were published. Several journals recently issued special sections dealing with these two books or relating Schmitt's work to current political problems. See *Telos* 127 (Spring 2004); 132 (Fall 2005); *CR: The New Centennial Review* 4, no. 3 (2004); *Constellations* 11, no. 4 (2004); *South Atlantic Quarterly* 104, no. 2 (Spring 2005); and *Leiden Journal of International Law* 19, no. 1 (2006).
3. See Chantal Mouffe, "Schmitt's Vision of a Multipolar World Order," *South Atlantic Quarterly* 104, no. 2 (2005): 245–51; and Mouffe, *On the Political* (London: Routledge, 2005), 76–83.
4. Carl Schmitt, *The Theory of the Partisan: A Commentary/Remark on the Concept of the Political*, trans. A. C. Goodson (East Lansing: Michigan State University Press, 2004), 76. This text is also accessible at *http://msupress.msu.edu/journals/cr/schmitt.pdf*.
5. See Jacob Taubes, *Ad Carl Schmitt: Gegenstrebige Fügung* (Berlin: Merve Verlag, 1987). The English translation is quoted from Joshua Robert Gold, "Jacob Taubes: 'Apocalypse from Below,'" *Telos* 134 (Spring 2006): 141. See also Robert G. Hamerton-Kelly, "Die paulinische Theologie als politische Theologie: Ethnizität, Ideologie und der Messias," in *Vom Fluch und Segen der Sündenböcke: Raymund Schwager zum 60. Geburtstag*, ed. Jozef Niewiadomski and Wolfgang Palaver (Münster, Germany: LIT, 1997), 41–160.
6. See Marshall McLuhan, *The Medium and the Light: Reflections on Religion*, ed. Erick McLuhan and Jacek Szlarek (Toronto: Stoddard, 1999), especially 57–65. Also see Erik Davis, *TechGnosis: Myth, Magic and Mysticism in the Age of Information* (London: Serpent's Tail, 2004), 299–304.

7. Ivan Illich, *The Rivers North of the Future: The Testament of Ivan Illich as Told by David Cayley*, with foreword by Charles Taylor (Toronto: Anansi, 2005), 59–63, 169–170, 177–180.

8. Samuel P. Huntington, *The Clash of Civilizations and the Remaking of World Order* (New York: Simon and Schuster, 1996), 20.

9. Huntington, *Clash of Civilizations*, 28.

10. See Huntington, *Clash of Civilizations*, 47, 59, 66.

11. Huntington, *Clash of Civilizations*, 253.

12. Simone Weil, *Oppression and Liberty*, trans. Arthur Wills and John Petrie (London: Routledge, 2002), 171.

13. See Alan B. Krueger and Jitka Malečková, "Does Poverty Cause Terrorism? The Economics and the Education of Suicide Bombers," *New Republic*, 24 June 2002, 27–33; and Jean Bethke Elshtain, *Just War against Terror: The Burden of American Power in a Violent World* (New York: Basic Books, 2003), 118–20.

14. See Bernard Lewis, *The Crisis of Islam: Holy War and Unholy Terror* (London: Phoenix, 2004), 50, 62, 101–2, 111–13, 125, 132.

15. See René Girard, *Celui par qui le scandale arrive* (Paris: Desclée de Brouwer, 2001), 8, 22–25; and Girard, "Ce qui se joue aujourd'hui est une rivalité mimétique à l'échelle planétaire: Propos recueillis par Henri Tincq," *Le Monde*, 6 November 2001. Also see Jean-Pierre Dupuy, *Avions-nous oublié le mal? Penser la politique après le 11 septembre* (Paris: Bayard, 2002), 43–67.

16. Carl Schmitt, *The Concept of the Political*, trans., with introduction and notes, by George D. Schwab, with Leo Strauss's Notes on Schmitt's Essay, trans. H. Lomax, and foreword by T. B. (Chicago: University of Chicago Press, 1996), 27.

17. Schmitt, *Concept of the Political*, 29.

18. Huntington, *Clash of Civilizations*, 129.

19. Huntington, *Clash of Civilizations*, 97.

20. Carl Schmitt, *Ex Captivitate Salus: Erfahrungen der Zeit 1945/47* (Cologne: Greven Verlag, 1950), 89–90. Quoted in Jan-Werner Müller, *A Dangerous Mind: Carl Schmitt in Post-War European Thought* (New Haven, CT: Yale University Press, 2003), 55.

21. In Strauss's later work, *Natural Right and History* (1953), he again emphasizes the friend-enemy distinction as an essential element of civil society in his description of classical natural right. Drawing on Bergson's distinction between the closed society and the open society, he states that "if the society in which man can reach the perfection of his nature is necessarily a closed society, the distinction of the human race into a number of independent groups is according to nature" (Leo Strauss, *Natural Right and History* [Chicago: University of Chicago Press, 1971], 132). Natural law, however, which acts as "dynamite for civil society" (*Natural Right*, 153), reveals the "inevitable self-contradiction" of the "citizen-morality" (*Natural Right*, 149): "Civil society as closed society necessarily implies that there is more than one civil society, and therewith that war is possible. Civil society must therefore foster warlike habits. But these habits are at variance with the requirements of justice. . . . Civil society is . . . forced to make a distinction: the just man is he who does not harm, but loves, his friends or neighbors, i.e., his fellow-citizens, but who does harm or who hates his enemies of his city." This self-contradiction can only be solved by transforming the city into the "world-state." But

this solution obviously "transcends the limits of political life" (*Natural Right,* 151), because "no human being and no group of human beings can rule the whole human race justly. Therefore, what is divined in speaking of the 'world-state' as an all-comprehensive human society subject to one human government is in truth the cosmos ruled by God, which is then the only true city, or the city that is simply according to nature because it is the only city which is simply just" (*Natural Right,* 159–60).

22. Strauss is quoted in Heinrich Meier, *Carl Schmitt and Leo Strauss: The Hidden Dialogue,* including Strauss's notes on Schmitt's *Concept of the Political* and three letters from Strauss to Schmitt, trans. J. Harvey Lomax, foreword by Joseph Cropsey (Chicago: University of Chicago Press, 1995), 125.

23. See Schmitt, *Concept of the Political,* 32–33.

24. Schmitt, *Concept of the Political,* 26, 29.

25. Schmitt, *Concept of the Political,* 67.

26. Carl Schmitt, "Ethic of State and Pluralistic State," trans. D. Dyzenhaus, in *The Challenge of Carl Schmitt,* ed. C. Mouffe (London: Verso, 1999), 195–208, 203.

27. Carl Schmitt, *The Leviathan in the State Theory of Thomas Hobbes: Meaning and Failure of a Political Symbol,* foreword and introduction by George Schwab, trans. George Schwab and Erna Hilfstein (Westport, CT: Greenwood Press, 1996), 21. I have made some slight corrections to the translation.

28. Schmitt, *Leviathan,* 48–49. Again, I have made slight corrections to the translation; the emphasis is mine.

29. See Leo Strauss, "Notes on Carl Schmitt, The Concept of the Political," in Schmitt, *Concept of the Political,* 81–107. See especially 101–4.

30. Carl Schmitt, *The* Nomos *of the Earth in the International Law of the* Jus Publicum Europaeum, trans. and annotated G. L. Ulmen (New York: Telos Press, 2003), 187. See also 150–51.

31. Schmitt, *Leviathan,* 48. See also Carl Schmitt, *Die Wendung zum diskriminierenden Kriegsbegriff* (Berlin: Duncker and Humblot, 1938), 1–2.

32. Carl Schmitt, *Staat, Großraum, Nomos: Arbeiten aus den Jahren 1916 bis 1969,* ed. Günter Maschke (Berlin: Duncker and Humblot, 1995), 435.

33. Carl Schmitt, *Glossarium: Aufzeichnungen der Jahre 1947–1951,* ed. E. Freiherr von Medem (Berlin: Dunkler and Humblot, 1991), 2: quoted in Gary Ulmen, "Carl Schmitt and Donoso Cortés," *Telos* 125 (2002): 76 n. 29. See also Jacques Maritain, *Integral Humanism: Freedom in the Modern World; And a Letter on Independence,* vol. 11, *The Collected Works of Jacques Maritain,* ed. Otto Bird, trans. Otto Bird, Joseph Evans, and Richard O'Sullivan (Notre Dame, IN: University of Notre Dame Press, 1996), 307:

> With regard to the *morality of the means,* it is clear that force and, generally speaking, what I have called the carnal means of war are not intrinsically bad, because they can be just. Theologians and moralists explain to us on what conditions these are just, and thereby they perform a work of mercy, enabling us to live on this earth. They do not take the lead, it is not their business to open new doors to violence; but once these doors are open, they justify what can be done, and give us light in order to advance into the dark defiles of history. Force implies also violence and terror and the use of all the means of

> destruction. These things also can be just in certain defined conditions. . . . The worst anguish for the Christian is precisely to know that there can be justice in employing horrible means.

During World War II, Maritain criticized Schmitt's understanding of the political as the revelation of the "essence of *pagan* politics and of the foundations of the Pagan Empire." See Jacques Maritain, *The Twilight of Civilization,* 2nd ed., trans. L. Landry (New York: Sheed and Ward, 1945), 37.

34. Carl Schmitt, "Theory of the Partisan: Intermediate Commentary on the Concept of the Political," *Telos* 127 (2004): 78. See also Teodoro Klitsche de la Grange, "The Theory of the Partisan Today," *Telos* 127 (2004): 169–75; Chantal Mouffe, *On the Political;* and William E. Scheuerman, "Carl Schmitt and the Road to Abu Ghraib," in *Constellations* 13, no. 1 (2006): 108–24.

35. Carl Schmitt, *The* Nomos, 296.

36. Aeschylus, *Aeschylus: Agamemnon, Libation-Bearers, Eumenides, Fragments,* with an English translation by H. Weir Smyth, ed. H. Lloyd-Jones (Cambridge, MA: Harvard University Press, 1983), line 977–87.

37. See René Girard, *Job: The Victim of His People,* trans. Yvonne Freccero (Stanford, CA: Stanford University Press, 1987), 146–53; see also Wolfgang Palaver, *Die mythischen Quellen des Politischen: Carl Schmitts Freund-Feind-Theorie* (Stuttgart: Verlag W. Kohlhammer, 1998), 38–45.

38. René Girard, *Things Hidden since the Foundation of the World,* trans. Stephen Bann and Michael Metteer (Stanford, CA: Stanford University Press, 1987), 249, 441.

39. Gen 3:15: "I will put enmity between you and the woman, and between your offspring and hers; he will strike your head, and you will strike his heel."

40. Quoted in Schmitt, *Concept of the Political,* 68.

41. Schmitt, *Concept of the Political,* 34.

42. Carl Schmitt, *Roman Catholicism and Political Form,* trans. and annotated by G. L. Ulmen (Westport, CT: Greenwood Press, 1996), 3.

43. Martti Koskenniemi, "International Law as Political Theology: How to Read *Nomos der Erde?*" *Constellations* 11 no. 4 (2004): 499.

44. Schmitt, "Ethic of State," 204.

45. Schmitt, "Ethic of State," 204–5.

46. Carl Schmitt, *Verfassungslehre,* reprint based on the 1928 first edition (Berlin: Duncker and Humblot, 1993), 238.

47. Schmitt, *Verfassungslehre,* 238.

48. See Juan Donoso Cortés, *Selected Works of Juan Donoso Cortés,* trans., ed., and introduced by Jeffrey P. Johnson (Westport, CT: Greenwood Press, 2000), 81–82, 110.

49. Carl Schmitt, *Political Theology: Four Chapters on the Concept of Sovereignty,* trans. George Schwab, 2nd ed. (Cambridge, MA: MIT Press, 1988), 59.

50. See Erik Peterson, "Der Monotheismus als politisches Problem: Ein Beitrag zur Geschichte der politischen Theologie im Imperium Romanum," in *Theologische Traktate.*

Mit einer Einleitung von B. Nichtweiß (Würzburg, Germany: Echter Verlag, 1994), 23–81. See 27, 39, 44, 58, 66, 72.

51. Peterson, "Der Monotheismus," 43; see also Origen, "Against Celsus," in *The Ante-Nicene Fathers: Translations of the Writings of the Fathers down to A.D. 325*, ed. Alexander Roberts, Vol. 4, reprint of 1885 ed. (Peabody, MA: Hendricks, 1995), 8.2. See also Carl Andresen, *Logos und Nomos: Die Polemik des Kelsos wider das Christentum* (Berlin: Walter de Gruyter and Co., 1955), 189–238.

52. See Origen, "Against Celsus," 7.69.

53. Peterson, "Der Monotheismus," 58, 72.

54. Carl Schmitt, *Politische Theologie II: Die Legende von der Erledigung jeder politischen Theologie* (Berlin: Duncker and Humblot, 1970), 55.

55. Schmitt, *Political Theology*, 36. See also Schmitt, *Politische Theologie II*, 51–56; Schmitt, *Verfassungslehre*, 290.

56. Schmitt, *Roman Catholicism*, 33. See also Schmitt, *Politische Theologie II*, 116–20; Leon Bloy, *Le Salut par les Juifs*, 2nd ed. (Paris: G. Cres, 1924), 88–90; Palaver, *Quellen*, 59–65; Jacques Derrida, *Politics of Friendship*, trans. George Collins (New York: Verso, 1997), 108–109; and Müller, *A Dangerous Mind*, 157–59.

57. Girard, *Things Hidden*, 37.

58. Simone Weil and Rachel Bespaloff, "The Iliad, or the Poem of Force," in *War and the Iliad*, with an essay by Hermann Broch, trans. M. McCarthy, with an introduction by C. Benfey (New York: New York Review Books, 2005), 37. See also Hannah Arendt, *Between Past and Future: Eight Exercises in Political Thought* (Harmondsworth, UK: Penguin Books, 1993), 262–63.

59. René Girard, "Generative Scapegoating," in *Violent Origins: Walter Burkert, René Girard, and Jonathan Z. Smith on Ritual Killing and Cultural Formation*, ed. Robert G. Hamerton-Kelly (Stanford, CA: Stanford University Press, 1987), 94.

60. Schmitt, *Ex Captivitate Salus*, 89; Carl Schmitt, "A Pan-European Interpretation of Donoso Cortés," *Telos* 125 (2002): 113.

61. See Schmitt, *The* Nomos, 128, 140–41, 159.

62. Schmitt, *Ex Captivitate*, 89.

63. Schmitt, *Ex Captivitate*, 58; See also Schmitt, *Die Wendung*, 2; Schmitt, *Glossarium*, 293–96; Schmitt, *The* Nomos, 58; and René Girard, *Violence and the Sacred*, trans. P. Gregory (Baltimore: The Johns Hopkins University Press, 1977), 299, 314–15. Surprisingly close to Schmitt, Dietrich Bonhoeffer also underlined the fact that as soon as wars are no longer seen as ordeals they become total wars, turning enemies into criminals: "War . . . always remained a kind of appeal to the arbitration of God, which both sides were willing to accept. It is only when Christian faith is lost that man must himself make use of all means, even criminal ones, in order to secure by force the victory of his cause. And thus, in the place of a chivalrous war between Christian peoples, directed towards the achievement of unity in accordance with God's judgment in history, there comes total war, war of destruction, in which everything, even crime, is justified if it serves to further our own cause, and in which the enemy, whether he be armed or defenseless, is treated as a criminal" (Dietrich Bonhoeffer, *Ethics*, ed. E. Bethge, trans. Neville Horton Smith [New York: Touchstone, 1995], 94.) One could question here, however, if Bonhoeffer's use of the term "Christian

faith" is completely appropriate. It seems rather that Bonhoeffer refers to the protective shelter of the pagan sacred.

64. Schmitt, *Ex Captivitate,* 72.

65. Schmitt, *Glossarium,* 270.

66. See Roger Ruston, "The War of Religions and the Religion of War," in *Studying War—No More? From Just War to Just Peace,* ed. Brian Wicker (Kampen, The Netherlands: Kok Pharos Publishing House, 1993), 129–41. See especially 134–37.

67. Ruston, "The War," 136.

68. See the following two entries in Schmitt's diary from 1948: "For me the Catholic faith is the religion of my fathers. I am Catholic not only by confession but also by historical origin, if I may say so, by race"; and "This is the secret keyword to my entire mental and authorial life: the struggle for the authentically Catholic sharpening" (Schmitt, *Glossarium,* 131 and 165). These entries are quoted in Michael Hollerich, "Carl Schmitt," in *The Blackwell Companion to Political Theology,* ed. Peter Scott and William T. Cavanaugh (Malden, MA: Blackwell Publishing, 2004), 110.

69. Another example would be Schmitt's specific type of anti-Semitism. He did not criticize Judaism in general, but distinguished clearly between pre-exilic and post-exilic Judaism. Only the latter has fostered the de-territorialization typical of our modern world. A closer look at this matter would show that ultimately Schmitt's critique is directed against the central thrust of the Biblical revelation itself (see 112–25 in Wolfgang Palaver, "Carl Schmitt on *Nomos* and Space" *Telos* 106 [1996]: 105–27).

70. Schmitt, *Glossarium,* 192.

71. Schmitt, *Glossarium,* 243.

72. According to Leo Strauss, the Bible made the global vision of humanity possible by slowly undermining those closed societies based on a friend-enemy distinction that he preferred, following Plato: "Classical political philosophy opposes to the universal and homogeneous state a substantive principle. It asserts that the society natural to man is the city, that is, a closed society" (Strauss, *Liberalism Ancient and Modern* [Chicago: University of Chicago Press, 1995], x); see also Strauss, *Natural Right,* 130–64; Strauss, *The City and Man* (Chicago: University of Chicago Press, 1978, 73); John Ranieri, "The Bible and Modernity: Reflections on Leo Strauss," *Contagion: Journal of Violence, Mimesis, and Culture* 11 [2004]: 55–87). In his private side notes to his comment on Schmitt's *Concept of the Political,* he refers to the "*religious* origin" of the idea of a political unity of all men. Following Celsus, he refers to Christianity as the origin of a global *nomos:* "Celsus: the Monotheism of the Christians is *stasis*" meaning sedition or civil war, using Schmitt's translation. Strauss, *Hobbes's politische Wissenschaft und zugehörige Schriften—Briefe* (Gesammelte Schriften 3), ed. H. and W. Meier (Stuttgart: Verlag J. B. Metzler, 2001), 239–41; Schmitt, *Concept of the Politicalt,* 29. Likewise, Eric Voegelin affirms in his *New Science of Politics* (1952) Celsus's insight into the revolutionary character of Christianity (see John Ranieri, "What Voegelin Missed in the Gospel," *Contagion: Journal of Violence, Mimesis, and Culture* 7 [2000]: 125–159): "The Christians were persecuted for a good reason; there was a revolutionary substance in Christianity that made it incompatible with paganism. . . . What made Christianity so dangerous was its uncompromising, radical de-divinization of the world" (Eric Voegelin, *The New Science of Politics: An Introduction,* with a new foreword by D. Germino [Chicago: University of Chicago Press, 1987], 100). According to Voegelin, Celsus did not believe in the possibility that different national cultures would ever "agree in one *nomos.*" Celsus "understood the

existential problem of polytheism; and he knew that the Christian de-divinization of the world spelled the end of the civilizational epoch and would radically transform the ethnic cultures of the age" (Voegelin, *New Science,* 101). Although Voegelin relates the Biblical revelation to Bergson's distinction between the closed society and the open society—the "idea of a universal God" has as its "logical correlate the idea of a universal community of mankind" (Voegelin, *New Science,* 156)—he remains highly critical of all those who think that the revelation would result in "the replacement of the closed society by an open society" (Voegelin, *New Science,* 158). He claims that a tension between these two types of truth "will be a permanent structure of civilization." In this respect he sides with Plato and criticizes Christian Fathers like Ambrose and Augustine because they "did not understand that Christianity could supersede polytheism but not abolish the need of a civil theology." Both Strauss and Voegelin follow Erik Peterson's interpretation of Celsus in his 1935 book, *Monotheism as a Political Problem,* which indirectly criticized his former friend Schmitt for his leanings toward paganism.

73. René Girard, *I See Satan Fall like Lightning,* trans., with a foreword, by James G. Williams (New York: Orbis Books, 2001), 165–66; see also Girard, *Things Hidden,* 194; and René Girard, *Oedipus Unbound: Selected Writings on Rivalry and Desire,* ed. and with an introduction by Mark R. Anspach (Stanford, CA: Stanford University Press, 2004), 89–90.

74. Girard, *Things Hidden,* 250.

75. See Jacob Taubes, *Ad Carl Schmitt: Gegenstrebige Fügung* (Berlin: Merve Verlag, 1987), 16, 21–22, 72–73.

76. Schmitt, *Glossarium,* 63. See also Gopal Balakrishnan, *The Enemy: An Intellectual Portrait of Carl Schmitt* (London: Verso, 2000), 224–25.

77. Schmitt, *The* Nomos, 60.

78. 2 Thess. 2:6–7: "And you know what is now restraining him [the lawless one], so that he may be revealed when his time comes. For the mystery of lawlessness is already at work, but only until the one who now restrains it is removed."

79. Palaver, "Carl Schmitt," 117–19.

80. 1 Thess. 5:3: "When they say, 'There is peace and security,' then sudden destruction will come upon them, as labor pains come upon a pregnant woman, and there will be no escape."

81. Schmitt, *Glossarium,* 165. See also Schmitt, *The* Nomos, 187.

82. See Wolfgang Palaver, "Hobbes and the *Katéchon:* The Secularization of Sacrificial Christianity," *Contagion: Journal of Violence, Mimesis, and Culture* 2 (1995): 57–74; and Girard, *I See Satan,* 185–86.

83. Bonhoeffer, *Ethics,* 108. With regard to Bonhoeffer's theological understanding of the *katechon,* we can find a somewhat similar concept in Paul's view of the Law as a "custodian" protecting us from our own violence in Gal. 3:19–24: "It makes perfect sense that the Law, as the instrument of sacred violence, was given only to contain trespasses for the time being . . . ; and not directly by God but through angels, because God is not a God of violence. Nevertheless, it served the negative purpose of holding bad violence in check by good violence, holding society together until the truth could be made known. As a product of the surrogate victim and the double transference, it was an advance on the primordial chaos of unconstrained mimetic rivalry" (Robert G. Hamerton-Kelly, *Sacred Violence: Paul's Hermeneutic of the Cross* [Minneapolis: Fortress Press, 1992], 76).

84. Bonhoeffer, *Ethics,* 109.

85. Bonhoeffer, *Ethics,* 110.

86. See Oliver O'Donovan, *The Desire of the Nations: Rediscovering the Roots of Political Theology* (Cambridge: Cambridge University Press, 1996), 156–57, 284. See also Schmitt, *Political Theology;* and Wolfgang Palaver, "A Girardian Reading of Schmitt's *Political Theology,*" *Telos* 93 (1992): 43–68.

87. John Paul II, *Centesimus annus: On the Hundredth Anniversary of Rerum novarum* (Washington, DC: United States Catholic Conference, 1991), #25.

Philosophy, History, and Apocalypse in Voegelin, Strauss, and Girard

Fred Lawrence
Boston College

Systematic Framework

For the sake of ordering the reflections that follow, I shall frame my interpretation of politics and apocalypse in Voegelin, Strauss, and Girard by transposing a fundamental idea in Catholic theology into the contemporary context of historical mindedness. This framework can be formulated in a proportion: nature is related to supernature as history is related to eschatology. At the core of the first part of the proportion is a methodically controlled idea regarding the basic structure of the universe, which is grounded in the isomorphism between the structure of human knowing and the structure of the universe of being.[1]

Nature and Supernature

We begin with knowing. Whenever we come to know something, the data presented by our senses and represented by our imagination spontaneously give rise to questions for understanding: What? Why? How? Once we inquire about data as presented or represented, then we may undergo an act of insight or understanding that grasps in the imaginative representations the intelligibility that is *possibly* relevant for a correct answer to our question; this understanding enables us to express what we have grasped in guesses or hypotheses. In order to ascertain whether the intelligibility grasped and formulated is *actually* relevant, a further kind of question arises, demanding that we check or verify the intelligibility grasped in relation to the data. By gathering and examining evidence, we may understand whether it is sufficient to warrant our judgment—Yes, No, Probably, Possibly—as the case may be. So let us speak of the threefold structure of human knowing in terms of experience, understanding, and judgment. Through these activities we come to know what is true about reality. What is global warming? Is it a proximate danger, or not? To answer these questions correctly or truly, we have to perform these operations repeatedly, until there are no further relevant questions.

What is known by experiencing, understanding, and judgment is a combination of data conditioned intrinsically or extrinsically by space and time (potency, matter), intelligibility (form), and actual occurrence or existence (act). Hence, the proportion:

experience/data	:	understanding/hypothesis	:	judgment/verification
potency	:	form	:	act

Thomas Aquinas made a point important to our discussion: the object proportionate to the human capacity to know adequately is always a "quiddity [intelligibility, form] existing [act] in matter [potency]." But human beings yearn to know what transcends their capacity to know adequately. For instance, Thomas Aquinas said that once people learn the primitive meaning of the word God, they have a natural desire to know *quid sit Deus?* This question stands for the fact that, in general, we desire to know more than we are able to understand and judge adequately—everything about everything. So, as Thomas stated repeatedly, we can know *that* God is, but in our present wayfarer's condition we can never know *what* God is essentially by means of our natural capacity to know. What we can know adequately is intrinsically or at least extrinsically conditioned by space and time, and because God is in no way conditioned by space and time, God is ever mysterious to us.

Hence, in our proportion—nature : supernature : history : eschatology—the term "nature" refers to the entire range of what human beings can properly or adequately understand and judge. "Supernature" refers to the range of what we can know in the light of absolutely supernatural grace, that is, to what we can know solely either by the light of grace or faith, or by the light of glory after we die. Once God graciously reveals his mystery to us, strictly supernatural revealed truth can be correctly understood and truly judged by human beings, not properly or adequately, but only analogically. Analogical understanding may be descriptive and expressed in metaphors, myths, and symbols; or it may be explanatory, and so expressed in terms of a scientifically controlled use of technical terms and relations.

This may be exemplified by the term "supernatural" itself. Prior to 1230, the term was used in ordinary and theological parlance as a kind of emphatic epithet. This usage continues today in such phrases as "Tales of the Supernatural." Aristotle's conception of nature *tout court* made it possible to give the term a precise theoretical meaning in the theological distinction between nature and supernature. Above, I have delineated nature and supernature in terms of the limits of adequate human knowledge. Now if what Bernard Lonergan has called the theorem of the supernatural was made possible by the entry of Aristotle's philosophy into the Latin West, its purpose was to do justice to the gift-character of God's gracious self-communication to finite and sinful human beings. In the Middle Ages, *fides quaerens intellectum* elaborated "the theory of two orders, entitatively disproportionate: not only was there the familiar series of grace, faith, charity, and merit, but also nature, reason and the natural love of God."[2]

History and Eschatology

Our guiding idea is that eschatology is to history as the supernatural is to nature. This is an extended analogy. The first part of the analogy between nature and supernature refers to the natural human capacity and desire for happiness vis-à-vis God's solution to the humanly intractable problem of evil together with God's gracious fulfillment of human capacity and desire in the gifts of the Incarnation, of God's unmerited favor (grace), and of the vision of the blessed. The second part of the analogy relating history to eschatology implies a shift from nature to history. Lonergan enjoyed quoting Robert O. Johann's claim that "[w]ith man's emergence from nature, the world becomes unstuck."[3] Early symbolic and descriptive awareness of history (in what Voegelin would call "cosmological" symbolisms) thought of it in light of natural cycles and regularities—the part of the world that does *not* come "unstuck." The emergence of history as a philosophical problem in the eighteenth century and of historical consciousness in the nineteenth calls for an explanatory grasp of history that takes into account the unique changes in the world's becoming due to the agency of human acts of apprehension and decision. With regard to historical events it is not enough to say, "Plus ca change, plus c'est le meme chose."

Let us understand history, then, as the general field of human process. Within the total field of emergent probability, it includes the whole range of historical *possibilities,* the whole field of historical *probabilities,* and the whole manifold of *actual* historical occurrences.[4] I am distinguishing history from nature in the same way that subhuman nature is distinguished from human nature. The entry of subatomic particles into the elements of the periodic table, the entry of chemical elements into compounds, of compounds into cells, and of cells into myriad combinations and configurations, and of these combinations and configurations into the constitution of the incredible variety of plant and animal life take place in time, but they are not strictly what we mean by historical.[5] So too the evolution of lower species into higher ones involves temporal processes, yet in and of themselves they are not historical. But individual and collective human development is historical.

So-called postmodern thought has brought into prominence the idea that history is a project of human self-construction. Following Rousseau and Nietzsche, postmodern thinkers extrapolated from the chancy character of human development to the cult of human originality, creativity, and uniqueness—in short, of self-realization.[6] In doing so, they mistakenly not only completely separated human self-construction in history from nature, but also set it in opposition to subhuman nature, conceived as just a heap of resources to be tamed, transformed, and exploited. In a more adequate account, first, the human being itself is a *synholon* (as Aristotle put it)—a synthesis of inanimate, vegetative, animal, and rational elements.[7] This means that human self-construction is a higher integration of the subhuman nature that it takes into itself.[8] Second, and more crucially, history is what we humans have done and what we are doing with our capacity to be intelligent, reasonable, and responsible within a natural ecology made up of many recurrent schemes such as the solar system and the nitrogen and hydrogen cycles. Moreover, far from being reducible to subhuman and unconscious elements and drives, as behaviorists and positivists believe, human intelligence, reasonableness, and responsibility arise spontaneously as spiritual and conscious demands within us. These conscious demands reveal to us that the human self-construction of history can be either natural or unnatural.[9] It is natural to the extent that we act intelligently, reasonably, and responsibly, respecting the integrity of our enabling natural environment; it is unnatural to the extent that we do not conduct ourselves in this way. On this account, then, history sublates nature, in the sense of presupposing it, elevating it, and carrying it forward. In the movement from the simple intelligibility of nature to the intelligent intelligibility of the human being, history perfects nature rather than dominating, suppressing, or eliminating it.

History, then, is a challenge to the exercise of our human intelligence and freedom. People not only have to make their history but they have to make sense of it as well. The commonsense way of making sense of history is through the great myths or stories and rituals.[10] And so, as Voegelin says, "Human society . . . is as a whole a little world, a cosmion, illuminated with meaning from within by the human beings who continually create and bear it as the mode and condition of their self-realization."[11]

If a catholic theology has to account for the total possibility both of history and of nonhuman nature, still its focus is the comprehensive drama of humanity in relation to God as creator and redeemer. This embraces the universal human story of creation, fall, and divine redemption, and so it involves not just history but eschatology, in the sense of the theological claim that, paradoxically, salvation is future yet present in relation to history. Moreover, as supernature transcends nature, so eschatological events such as the death and resurrection of Christ transcend history. Eschatology both erupts from the space/time continuum and interrupts the sinful gravity-force of human historicity.

Eschatology and Apocalyptic

There has been a tendency for theologians to lose their balance in relation to eschatology, either keeping history and rejecting eschatology (as perhaps Oscar Cullmann and Wolfhart Pannenberg have done) or keeping eschatology at the cost of history (in the manner of Albert Schweitzer and Rudolf Bultmann). Be that as it may, one of the chief ways religious tradition—and especially Judaism in the second temple period—expresses the distinctness and discontinuity of eschatology from history is the literary form and symbolism of apocalyptic, whose common meaning has to do with the expectation of the imminent end of the world. For more recent scholarship, the broader purpose of apocalyptic is to invest historical and political events with a theological—that is, eschatological—significance, and does not necessarily imply the univocal view that history will come to an end via a cosmic catastrophe that ushers in a new age.[12] So as a descriptive approximation, eschatology refers to T. S. Eliot's "intersection of the timeless with time." In New Testament terms, according to N. T Wright, "Jesus and some of his contemporaries expected the end of the present *world order,* i.e., the end of the period when the Gentiles were lording over the people of the true god, and the inauguration of the time when this god would take his power and reign and, in the process, restore the fortunes of his suffering people."[13] From a Catholic perspective, the future dimension of eschatology is roughly analogous to the traditional teaching that grace initiates our pilgrimage to glory; and the present dimension of eschatology is somewhat analogous to the teaching that Christ's death and resurrection, though past, still reach us in the present and occur to us in the sacraments of Baptism and Eucharist.

If, in the medieval context, the answer to the problems induced from without by the entry of Aristotle into the Latin West and from within by the need for an adequate conception of the relationship between divine grace and human freedom was achieved in the distinction (not separation) between supernature and nature, the modern concern with history and eschatology calls for an integration of the two in such a manner that neither dimension is eliminated or conflated with the other. On this issue, the work of Voegelin, Strauss, and Girard is both symptomatic of the problem and illuminative of the solution sought by contemporary theology.

Voegelin, Strauss, and Girard

What the Authors Chiefly Have in Common

Both Eric Voegelin and Leo Strauss are self-consciously philosophers, and both are concerned with theology, in the sense that each recognizes in his own way that political philosophy, as motivated by resistance to human corruption, begins with the question of the right way to live and so must engage what Spinoza called the theologico-political problem. As for René Girard, it is not clear to me that he ever claims for himself the mantle of philosopher rather than that of a scholar of literature, anthropology, and psychology. But if we define philosophy broadly as comprehensive reflection on the human condition, then he, too, must be considered a philosopher.

These three figures have worked as scholars in the modern sense of interpreting and assessing the meaning of historical data *sine ira et studio,* outside the sway of any authoritative traditions. Each bases his argument on its capacity to provide the most satisfactory account of the works with which he deals, be they primordial myths or composed texts such as the works of Plato and Aristotle or the so-called books of the Hebrew and Christian scriptures. Each is willing to seek guidance from ancient as well as modern texts. In a sense, all three have used historical interpretation of the ancient writings as their preferred mode of propaedeutic to teachings directly related to the question about the right way to live.

An initial distinction between Voegelin and Strauss on one side and Girard on the other is that Voegelin and Strauss are political philosophers, while Girard has to do with politics only indirectly, inasmuch as the political is implicit in his more directly social and cultural approach to comparative literature. Girard would argue that what is meant by the political order in the classic sense of the question of the regime is de facto generated by and imbued with the mimetic and scapegoating processes upon which he focuses, so that he grants a primacy to the religious and the cultural over the political. Voegelin and Strauss would argue instead that reflection upon the human being, in relation to other human beings within the environment of nature and as related to the ground of being, is architectonically handled in establishing a regime that for better or worse implements the society's or culture's normative meanings and values. Therefore they both seek to discern a human order that is, in Aristotle's phrase, "right by nature" (*phusei dikaion*);[14] and their efforts as philosophers have been in great measure to retrieve a notion of nature not as a dogmatic set of precepts but as a heuristic framework for asking and answering questions about human order.

Despite this crucial difference that separates Voegelin and Strauss from Girard, each of the three thinkers clearly intends to offer his readers a true account of the human condition that takes fully seriously both the historical access to the basic data on man and the historical character of human being itself. None of them would ignore relative differences that emerge in time, but none of them would agree that such differences prevent the thoughtful person's arriving at transcultural absolutes that are invariant over time and historical development. Each would have no patience with either relativism or historicism, let alone what Allan Bloom has termed the "easy-going" nihilism that dominates the academy in the West today, often under the guise of postmodernism.

In summary, each of these thinkers seeks a comprehensive perspective in quest of a true account of the ultimate determinates of human being that is fully open to the religious or theological dimension of the human being. Girard believes the cultural and religious sphere to be more primordial than the political, while Voegelin and Strauss contend that the determinative factor in human order is political, however conditioned by religion and culture it may be. And so while Girard has uncovered the most fundamental structures affecting human existence, Voegelin and Strauss have sought a theoretical viewpoint that permits the analysis of all the basic human formations and deformations and enables both diagnosis and remediation of the contemporary crisis.

On Voegelin's General Orientation

Eric Voegelin's project is perhaps the most sweeping and comprehensive of the three thinkers. For Voegelin, philosophy emerged when Socrates, Plato, and Aristotle resisted the disorder of fourth-century B.C.E. Greek society. Max Weber's example as an explorer of the structures of reality, in the period between the end of the nineteenth century and the beginning of a new age, by means of critical rational scholarship or science set the tone for Voegelin's approach to the philosophy of order.[15] Voegelin's philosophic response to the disorder of our age was aimed at theoretically regrounding the science of historical and social order. Inspired by a theoretic and methodological insight into the equivalences of experience and symbolization of meaning, he abandoned the writing of a (still extraordinary) history of political philosophy in the conventional genre of the history of political ideas in favor of a comprehensive reflection on the history of order traced through the history of the symbolizations of order.[16] To refound human sciences caught up in Marxist or positivist counterpositions, a standpoint for answering the basic questions about order and disorder, truth and untruth, in our time was needed.

In his attempt to lay bare an experiential self-knowledge of the human being and humanity's place in the cosmos, Voegelin shared the Aristotelian notion of a man as a *synholon* (mentioned above), whose physical, vegetative, animal and psychic dimensions are to be integrated by the rational spirit's capacity for *phronesis*. "Man, when he experiences himself as existent, discerns his specific humanity as that of the questioner for the wherefrom and the whereto, for the ground and the sense of his existence."[17] Beginning with society as a "cosmion of meaning," Voegelin sees that the human answers to these questions are initially a matter of sociocultural self-understandings expressed in the manifold of myths, religions, ideologies, art and literature, and philosophic and political reflection: "the principles must be regained by a work of thematization which starts from the concrete, historical situation of the age, taking into account the full amplitude of our empirical knowledge."[18]

According to Voegelin's hypothesis concerning the equivalences of experience and symbolization, less-differentiated consciousness can also symbolize the meaning and ground of humanity, in relation to God, human being, and world, and to society and history, if only in global and compact terms.[19] Voegelin tried to enucleate the common core manifest in the multiplicity of extant symbolisms through philosophical reflection upon the experiential complexes of people and their different social and historical orders. He focused on human consciousness as a sensorium that is the origin of every human experience of order, inasmuch as people open themselves to the formative power of a transcendent, non-object-like, pre-personal reality, which is the ground of being. This is the anthropological principle of his investigations. Here is a dramatic statement of how Voegelin conceives the philosophical purpose of his historical work:

> [It is] to penetrate to the spiritual-historical form of the other to its experience of transcendence, and in such penetration to train and clarify one's own formation of transcendent experience. Spiritual-historical understanding is a catharsis, a *purificatio* in the mystical sense, with the personal goal of *illuminatio* and *unio mystica:* in fact if it deals systematically with great chains of material, it can lead to the working out of sequences of order in the historical revelation of the spirit; and finally it can in this way produce in fact a philosophy of history.[20]

In *The New Science of Politics* (the first great work after his "turning") Voegelin speaks of the philosophers Plato and Aristotle as "mystic" philosophers, who achieved maximum differentiation of consciousness. *Order and History,* volume 3, *Plato and Aristotle* depicts philosophy largely in terms of a "leap in being," which enables the shift from cosmological to anthropological symbolizations of order.[21] The leap in being denotes the historical, experiential discovery of divine transcendence. Its Kierkegaardian overtones connote the two dimensions of (1) a conversion or attunement as something suffered rather than properly achieved on one's own; and (2) a differentiation that marks both the consciousness of those symbolizing and the symbolic complexes expressive of the differentiated conscious experiences. The elements of conversion, attunement, and differentiation remain to be elaborated in many helpful ways after the expression "leap in being" falls into disuse. Differentiation in contrast to more global and compact symbolizations becomes a key to all of Voegelin's investigations. For instance, in *The New Science,* more compact cosmological symbolizations give way to both anthropological and soteriological differentiations, which undergo the "Gnostic" derailments that Voegelin says are the basis of modern ideologies.

Any symbolism is correlative to the experience that generated it. From the perspective of experience, there is the spontaneous, existential[22] search for meaning or direction in the flow of experience—a meaning or direction that may be missed or lost by default. Hence, any symbolism, too, either may indicate existence in truth or may express derailment if expressive of debased experience. In either case, symbolisms are not completely under the control of symbol-makers, even though they do arise from powerful experiences of the human soul.[23] In *Anamnesis*, Voegelin retrieved Plotinus's account of the originating experience of the symbolizer that has to be reenacted by the interpreting philosopher:

> Recollecting is the activity of consciousness by which what has been forgotten, i.e., the knowledge latent within consciousness, is raised up out of unconsciousness into a specific presence of consciousness. In the *Enneads* (IV, 3, 30), Plotinus described this activity as the transition from non-articulated to articulate, self-perceiving thought. The non-articulated knowledge (*noema*) becomes conscious knowledge by an act of perceptive attending (*antilepsis*); and this antileptic knowledge is moreover fixed by language (*logos*). Recollecting, then, is the process in which non-articulated (*ameres*) knowledge is elevated into the realm of linguistic representability (*to phantastikon*) and through expression, in the pregnant sense of taking external shape (*eis to exo*), and attains linguistically articulated presence of consciousness.[24]

The correlation between experience and symbolization lies at the heart of Voegelin's interpretative method of meditative exegesis, which is an anamnetic movement on the part of the interpreter through the symbol or complex of symbols to the originating, generative experience. Without this reenactment, the symbols do not have their rightful meaning.

Yet such an interpretive movement is fraught with peril. It can be that a person's experience is either so derailed or the person is in such a state of deculturation (in the sense that his or her cultural formation amounts to a deformation or a closedness to differentiation) that the symbol does not necessarily provide access to the generative experience. The person may either lack the requisite conversion or not be open to the needed differentiation of consciousness.

In any case, for better or worse, any individual person is overwhelmingly conditioned by his or her environing culture. Using the Platonic parable of the cave as a paradigm, the possibility of conversion has to be taken into account as something that, as Aristotle phrases the emergence of consciousness in *The Generation of Animals*, "comes in from outdoors." Conversion is not under an individual person's control but has the gift-character of a "theophanic event" that draws the human being into an "epochal advance" in differentiation. Personal control becomes an issue only of responsive openness or closure.

Both Voegelin and Leo Strauss wanted to recover the classic experience of reason. In terms of Voegelin's theory of equivalences, this experience has to be conceived, more broadly than Strauss conceived it, as an act of *anamnesis*, remembrance, or recollection that unfolds the dialectic between symbol and engendering experience. Such philosophical recollection is an enactment of reason, in which Voegelin's understanding of reason contrasts sharply with Strauss's. Strauss accepts from the medieval Arabs and Jews—and from the Catholic tradition on reason vis-à-vis revelation[25]—the dogmatic distinction between faith and reason and between philosophy and theology. For Voegelin, philosophy as essentially meditative exegesis in an anamnetic mode cannot help but be a case of "fides quaerens intellectum" (faith seeking understanding), in Anselm of Canterbury's Augustinian phrase. For Voegelin, in contrast to Strauss, the philosophically reflective asking and answering of questions sooner or later reduces to the tension between divine appeal and human quest or response.[26] For all his unwillingness to merge faith and reason, Strauss might not be able to dispute Voegelin's interpretation of Aristotle's account of noetic experience, even though (to my knowledge) he remains silent about it:

> The unrest in a man's psyche may be luminous enough to understand itself as caused by ignorance concerning the ground and meaning of existence, so that the man will feel an active desire to escape from this state of ignorance (*pheugein ten agnoian, Metaphysics* 982b18). The analysis thus requires further language symbols: "ignorance"—*agnoia, agnoiein, amathia;* "flight from ignorance"—*pheugein ten agnoian;* "turning around"—*periagoge;* "knowledge"—*episteme, eidenai.*[27]

Strauss is perhaps unwilling to agree with Voegelin that Aristotle as *philomythos* was equally a lover of wisdom, whereas Voegelin insists that, as such, he was also participating in that "wondering" (*thaumazein*) by which "all humans naturally desire to know."[28] Strauss conceives of philosophy as the replacement of opinions about what is highest and best by true and certain knowledge, which means *episteme* in accord with the logical ideal of knowledge Aristotle set forth in the *Posterior Analytics*—a standard of rigor to which neither Aristotle nor Voegelin hold themselves when it is unsuitable to the demands of the subject matter of their philosophic inquiries.

Voegelin on History and Apocalypse

We can grasp what history means for Voegelin in his Schelling essay in "Last Orientation." Voegelin describes Schelling's distinction between two senses of history: "first, the actual course of natural and human events in the universe; and this course of events becomes history in the second meaning if it is understood by man as a meaningful unfolding of the universe." He goes on to explain that the second sense of history involves an "internalization of the course of events" or an "immersion of the external process into a movement of the soul," which "itself is part of the stream." Hence, "when the soul gives meaning to the stream, it discovers the stream and its meaning in itself. In this sense the soul is knowledge, and history is a science of the soul."[29] This distinction remains operative, I believe, throughout Voegelin's post-1952 work. *The New Science* and four of the five volumes of *Order and History* (from 1956 to 1974) intend to be a philosophical exploration of the order of humankind, of society and history, in relation to the divine ground of being, within limits set by empirical scholarship.

Voegelin deals mainly with history in the second sense in his examination of the self-interpretative world of human experience enclosed in the symbolic worlds throughout history. Hence, his interpretative categories have to do with distinguishing and analyzing the various symbolisms that have emerged so that human beings might make sense of their lives in history in the first sense.

In this analysis, the central issue is humanity's break with the order of cosmological experiences and compact, consubstantial mythological consciousness. No longer captivated by the divine cosmic order of the ancient high civilizations, Hellas and Israel respond to the crisis of cosmological societies by undergoing the supreme acts of differentiation of their experience and their symbolization. In Israel there is the rise of properly *historical existence* in virtue of an interpretation of the Word of a transcendent God experienced as the community-founding ground of all things, who calls them out to be representative of the truth for all humankind. Ancient Israel's development of a universal order of humanity under God gave rise to the human self-understanding in accord with which human beings are the subjects of history.[30] In parallel fashion, there emerges in the context of the Greek city-states (*poleis*) the discovery of the rightly ordered human soul as the "invisible measure" or standard of human order in both cosmos and polis. In Voegelin's words, "without the discovery of the Logos in the psyche and in the world, without the creation of philosophic existence, the problem of history would not have become a problem of philosophy."[31]

Order and History, volume 4, *The Ecumenic Age*[32] marked a second great turning point in Voegelin's intellectual career. His empirical research compelled Voegelin to give up the dominant vision in volumes 1–3, whose axis turned on the emergence in Greek philosophy and in Jewish and Christian experience of humankind's consciousness of itself as *the* subject of history. The Western symbolic form of universal history, which follows a linear evolution of social and symbolic forms of order, had to be relinquished. In an investigation ranging from 800 years before Christ until 800 years afterward, Voegelin described the constitutive elements that emerged during the Ecumenic Age and that are proper to the precisely universal consciousness of humanity. These include spiritual outbursts in experiences of differentiation, and (concomitantly with the forms shaping world empires) the uncovery of human historicity as articulated by the symbolic form of historiography. Parallel fields of development proper to a *global* humanity no longer fit into the vision of humankind as the subject of the history of a *single* civilization. Voegelin thus realized that the subject matter of his investigation was "an open historical field of major and minor divine-human encounters, widely distributed in time and space over the societies who together are humanity in its history."[33]

In *The Ecumenic Age*, Voegelin makes fully explicit what was mainly implied in earlier volumes of *Order and History*, namely, historiography. It is an anthropological differentiation that symbolizes a spiritual irruption that dissolves the primary experience proper to cosmological symbolizations by breaking through to encounter the ground of being beyond the intracosmic beings. This gives rise to the clear distinction between immanence and transcendence. Voegelin describes the significance of such a breakthrough in the anonymous Essene document, *The Apocalypse of Abraham:*

> When the soul opens . . . in an act of transcendence, the beyond of the world is not experienced as an object beyond the world. The text makes admirably clear the tension of the search—of God seeking man, and man seeking God—the mutuality of seeking and finding one another. Not a space beyond space but the search is the site of the meeting between man and the beyond of his heart; and God is present even in the confusion of the heart that precedes the search through the realms of being. The divine Beyond thus is at the same time a divine Within the world. Subtly, the unknown author traces the movement from the search of the unknown that is present in the search as it was in the confusion, and further on to the call from beyond—until what in the beginning was a disturbance in

> that part of being called the heart has dissociated into the "Here am I" and "I am He."[34]

This is an experience of transcendence typically disrupting the primary, compact experience of the cosmos. In Israel, Greece, and China the experience of transcendence expressed in historiographical symbolism is a response to the experience of empires, whose only rationale is the senseless expansion of sheer power. We recall that Voegelin specifies two meanings of history: the course of historical events accessible to empirical verification; and a given society's story of that history, by which it makes sense of the factual field. Historiography is a form of mythic-speculation that people under the pressure of empire employ to communicate in narrative form the meaning of life in the tensional presence of the transcendent ground. For Voegelin, the further form of mythic-speculative symbolism named historiogenesis melds the symbolisms of theogony, anthropogony, and cosmogony into historiography.[35] "In the production of historiogenesis, myth and speculation cooperate with the historiographic intention."[36] Such narrative is correlated with the rituals by which people reenact a healing and renewing cosmogony. As Voegelin, introducing the notion of apocalypse, explains:

> Eliade's diagnosis of the ritual as an attempt to "annul the irreversibility of time" recalls the "*statisation*" *du devenir* attempted by apocalyptic speculation. The apocalypses of Jewish antiquity metamorphose the correlative but separate symbolisms of historiogenesis and rhythmic renewal into the one process of history that will issue into the perfect realm. To the believer in a creator-god, the cosmos has dissociated into "this world" of imperfection and the perfect divine ground of being; hence, he does not believe either in the concord of his society with cosmic order nor in the possibility of repairing actual disorder by repetitions of the cosmogonic act. Nevertheless, even if the embracing cosmos is gone, the tension is still experienced, and if the waste of order can no longer be overcome by rituals, the tension can now be dissolved by a metastasis that will put an end to the imperfection of existence forever.[37]

In *The Ecumenic Age*, Voegelin sets apocalyptic symbolism in the context of contrast between two radically different exoduses within reality, exemplified historically by "the sequence of structurally equivalent symbolisms of the Deutero-Isaianic exodus of Israel from herself into an ecumenic mankind under Yahweh with Cyrus his Messiah, the Stoic exodus from the polis into the imperial ecumene of the cosmos, the Christian exodus into a metastatic ecumene providentially prepared by the imperial ecumene, the Hegelian ecumenic reconciliation and the Marxian ecumenic revolution." First, there is the exodus as concupiscential (that is, a function of disordered desire), which Voegelin relates to Herodotus in his comment on Jacob Burckhardt's statement on "ages, peoples, individuals, who destroy the old and make room for what is new without being capable of a happiness of their own": "Their renovative power has its source in a permanent discontent that is bored by every achievement and presses toward new forms."[38] This points to the insight that although "the most obvious strain in conquering expansion is the 'violence' and 'selfishness' which Burckhardt stresses, there is also in it the strain of 'boredom' and 'discontent' with every achievement and of imaginative enterprise that will assuage the unrest."[39] The concupiscential exodus is ultimately a flight from the *conditio humana.* Second, there is the spiritual exodus that transcends reality while remaining within reality as aetiologically and directionally structured.

Voegelin notes that apocalypticism emerges from understanding that the succession of empires in pragmatic history and the sequence of imperial dominations did not create "the field in which the true order of personal existence could expand into the order of society. . . . As the Jewish apocalyptics ever since Daniel had seen, the realization of the humanly true order under God in society would require the apocalyptic transfiguration of the 'historical' reality in which the truth of order had emerged as insight."[40] Apocalyptic, then, represents a deformation of spiritual exodus:

> In apocalyptic consciousness, the experience of the movement within reality beyond its own structure has split into the conviction that history is a field of disorder beyond repair by human action and into the metastatic faith in a divine intervention that will establish the perfect order of the realm to come. The tension between order and disorder in the one reality dissociates in the phantasy of two realities following each other in time.

In *Israel and Revelation,* Voegelin had already remarked on what he deems the inherently unauthentic character of "metastatic" faith in terms of its utter disregard for the exigencies of pragmatic history.[41] However, what the healing apocalyptic consciousness is aware of needing is clarified not in the "noetic differentiation" of consciousness exemplified by Plato and Aristotle, but in the "pneumatic differentiation," the prime analogate of which is Paul's "vision of the Resurrected."[42] The pneumatic differentiation involves both a heightened sense of the one drawing the human heart to itself and a sense of transfiguration, due to the pleromatic representation of the divine in the risen Christ. Thus, "meaning in history is constituted through man's response to the immortalizing movement of the divine pneuma in his soul." Those undergoing the pneumatic differentiation are typically incapable of giving an adequate analysis of it, and so the "effective history" (to use Gadamer's phrase)[43] of this differentiation becomes bedeviled by misinterpretation.[44]

Even though the noetic differentiation is the outcome of a "noetic theophany," for Voegelin it has definite limitations:

> [It] did indeed proceed from the personal order of the immortalizing response to the paradigm of immortalizing order in social existence, and ultimately to the historical symbolism of the Nous as the Third God; the three dimensions of order—personal, social, historical—were fully differentiated. But they conducted their analysis within the limits set by the fundamentally intracosmic character of the theophany to which they responded. . . . The classic analysis reached the divine *aition* as the source of order in reality; it differentiated the structure of existence in the Metaxy, but it did not extend to the structure of divine reality in the pneumatic depth of creation and salvation. Only through Paul's response to his vision did the philosopher's *athanatizein* expand into the pneumatic *aphtharsia;* the paradigmatic polis into the organization of man's spiritual as distinguished from his temporal order; and the Third Age of the Nous, into the eschatological structure of history under the one God of all ages.[45]

A correct understanding of pneumatic differentiation enables Voegelin to distinguish the *eschatological* meaning of transfiguration, correctly conceived, as a theophanic effect within history that continually impels persons beyond history as they continue the struggle within history "in fear and trembling": in the life of the wayfarer or pilgrim as a member of universal humanity. But apocalypticism incorrectly imagines transfiguration to be something that metamorphoses the person or the community beyond history in the sense of going outside history, of ending history. This is the result of an incomplete and so distorted reaction to the deeply felt reality of concupiscential exodus through conquest.

For Voegelin, the term eschatology is inseparable from universal humankind, which "is not a society existing in the world, but a symbol which indicates man's consciousness of participating, in his earthly existence, in the mystery of a reality that moves toward its transfiguration. Universal mankind is an eschatological index."[46] Voegelin goes on to describe the basic options of the Ecumenic Age:

> When the primary experience of man's existence in the cosmos has dissociated into the opacity of concupiscential expansion and the luminosity of spiritual consciousness, the bond that prevents the two pieces of reality from falling apart into the two realities of apocalyptic and Gnostic thinkers is found in history. On the level of the truth of existence, the transfiguring process takes place of the *okeanos* as the horizon of the universally divine mystery for a mankind that has become ecumenic through the concupiscential exodus. Hence, the triad of the ecumenic empire, spiritual outburst, and historiography expresses equivalently the structure in reality that had been compactly expressed by the *oikumene-okeanos* symbolism.[47]

Thus, apocalyptic symbolism is ambiguous. One of the texts most often quoted favorably by Voegelin as an example of divine-human encounter is the first-century B.C.E.. Essene document, *The Apocalypse of Abraham,* mentioned above. It was written in the context of the brutality of imperial conquest. It also bears the expression of the deformation of epochal consciousness in the "apocalyptic brutality" that is also present in the New Testament's "blood-dripping avenger-Christ of the Revelation of John" (19:11–16). Unfortunately, the problem is perennial:

> The apocalyptic deformation of epochal conscious observed by Paul has remained a constant in Western civilization. In the eighteenth century, Kant recognized it in the progressivist intellectuals who believed the meaning of history to be fulfilled in their own existence and degraded all humanity to the status of "contributors" to the glory of the present. In the twentieth century, we are still plagued with the same deformation in the sect of apocalyptic sociologists who have invented the dichotomy of "traditional" and "modern" societies, and still pursue Concorcet's policy of destroying "traditional" societies by "modernizing" them. And we find the apocalyptic deformation in Bultmann's thesis that the Old Testament is of no concern to the Christian theologian. The Pauline admonition, "Remember the root sustains you," cannot be repeated often enough.[48]

Before *The Ecumenic Age,* Voegelin's account of history reached its apex of meaning in the noetic and pneumatic differentiations of consciousness. At that time he had a balanced view of the complementarity of the two differentiations, especially when it came to dealing with ecumenic conquests, spiritual outbursts, and historiography. The symbol of universal humanity as the subject of an eschatological exodus by which the structure of reality moves beyond itself was a product of *both* the noetic and the pneumatic irruptions.

Finally, for Voegelin, apocalyptic has a negative valence, but the negativity is not moralistic, because in the originating sense of Jewish apocalyptic, the failure of apocalyptic imagination has more to do with its experiential context than with the overweening need for certainty that usually leads to an escape from history.

On Strauss: Politics, History, and Apocalypse

Leo Strauss, like Voegelin, emigrated in flight from Hitler's Nazism to the United States. Unlike Voegelin he was a Jew; but like Voegelin, he could say that his lifelong preoccupation was with two questions: God and politics. As a youth Voegelin flirted with Communism; Strauss wrote to Karl Löwith that as a young man he was fascinated by the writings of Nietzsche.[49] Voegelin's youth in Vienna exposed him to a wider range of cultural artifacts and history than was probably available during Strauss's education in Kirchhain, Marburg, Freiburg, and Hamburg. Strauss's lively inquisitiveness led him into early and deep contact with Zionism in its religious, cultural, and political forms; and thinking his way through these alternatives prepared him for engagement with political philosophy in relation to the issue of religious belief throughout his lifetime.[50]

The title of an important essay, "Progress or Return?" expresses the central issue of Strauss's work.[51] He tells us that the question came to the forefront for him because of his intellectual confrontations with two of the leading and most influential thinkers of post–World War I Germany: Carl Schmitt, Germany's leading professor of constitutional law, who collaborated in formulating the German constitution of the racist National Socialist regime; and Martin Heidegger, often acclaimed as the greatest philosopher of the twentieth century in spite of his involvement with Nazism.

Carl Schmitt's theory of friend/foe was unapologetically a secularized political theology.[52] Strauss saw that Schmitt's critique of liberalism stood itself within the framework of one of the great founders of liberalism, Thomas Hobbes. Indeed, Schmitt was only following Hobbes's principles in contending that the state alone could guarantee social justice, since it alone could protect its citizens from internal and external enemies; that the state alone could suffice to ensure law and order in the community, for it alone is guided by the principles of leadership and loyalty. As Strauss put it: "The critique of liberalism that Schmitt has initiated can therefore be completed only when we succeed in gaining a horizon beyond liberalism."[53]

Heidegger's importance to Strauss is evidenced by the way the philosopher of Messkirch helped him "gain a horizon beyond liberalism." Everyone interested in philosophy in the early 1920s heard rumors that Heidegger was the "hidden king of thought." He radicalized Husserl's break from the then neo-Kantian dominance of German academic philosophy. Prior to his encounter with Heidegger as a younger man, Strauss, like Voegelin, had the highest esteem for Max Weber as a scholar.[54] But, as Strauss told Franz Rosenzweig on the way home after first listening to Heidegger lecture in Freiburg, he made Weber seem "like an orphan child"[55] in comparison. Strauss observed that Heidegger understood the phenomenologist's motto—Back to the things themselves!—by interpreting the expression *Sachen* (here translated as things but also denoting subject matter, issue, affair, business) not in terms of Husserl's preferred object of pure sense perception but in terms of *pragmata,* or matters of practical concern (Aristotle, *Ethics*), and of *pathemata,* issues about which one is passionate (Aristotle, *Rhetoric*). Moreover, Heidegger's radicalization of phenomenology was grounded in a return to reading the great works of the ancients independently of their being "kept" by traditions such as scholasticism. Without the filter of an authoritative tradition, Heidegger read ancient authors with the conviction that they are capable of teaching us truths today. Such reading became a hallmark of Strauss's project of "return."[56]

It is also significant that the radical connotations of the Hebrew prophets' *return* (*teshuvah*) are as important for Strauss's enterprise as are the religious connotations of conversion and attunement for Voegelin's. Alerted to the weaknesses of Schmitt's philosophy, Strauss reread Baruch Spinoza's *Theologico-Political Treatise* carefully.[57] He came to the realization that Hermann Cohen, the leader both of Marburg neo-Kantianism and of modern German Jewish thought, had not quite understood that proto-modern Jewish philosopher because for all his fidelity to Judaism he was too caught up in the horizon of modernity to see that Spinoza was in the process of creating that horizon. This led Strauss to reexamine Spinoza's relationship to the greatest of premodern Jewish thinkers, Moses Maimonides. Here—not without the aid of that other great modern Jewish thinker, Gotthold Lessing—he rediscovered the art of esoteric writing[58] as well as the key to the Enlightenment critique of religious belief, which he realized was in its way perhaps shallower than the false belief itself.

Strauss became convinced that one could comprehend what either Spinoza or Maimonides was saying only if one took expressly into account the art of esoteric writing, which philosophers both ancient and modern resorted to in order to avoid the danger of persecution.[59] The modern escape from Plato's cave, he saw, involved the discovery of specifically premodern and pre-Enlightenment philosophic writing through the careful study of the ancient authors, Jewish, Arabic, and Greek. This enabled Strauss, whom Voegelin regularly defended as a painstaking scholar and philologist,[60] to explain that the fundamental option for philosophic thought today is whether to return to the study of the ancients or to remain committed implicitly or explicitly to the horizon of progress inaugurated by modernity.

The rediscovery of premodern thought, which Strauss and his followers came to call the Great Tradition, also demanded the reappropriation of the questions from which the works of that tradition originated: What is the right way to live? What do we look up to? What do we bow down to? What is the best regime? Voegelin reoriginated political philosophy through a meditative exegesis engaged by the dialectic between symbol and originating experience. Strauss reoriginated political philosophy by taking his bearings from Plato and Aristotle,[61] who started from the political and moral concern of the ordinary person at any time and place, and ascended to the asking and answering of the fundamental theoretical questions first clarified in a comprehensive and decisive manner by Socrates in terms of the great struggles between philosophy and the city, or philosophy and poetry.[62]

Philosophy's commitment to questioning threatens the city because it reveals the problematic character of people's basic beliefs as expressed by the poets, whose inspiration was purportedly the gods. As the public world of human affairs, the city is a permanent cave, ultimately incompatible with philosophic knowledge.[63] Philosophy's quest to replace opinion with true and certain knowledge of things by their universal and necessary causes remains *the* standard of true cognition for Strauss. He presupposed it in his formulation of the tension between Athens and Jerusalem, which he insisted is constitutive of the vitality of the Great Tradition, as well as in his formulation of *the most basic* of fundamental questions: Why philosophy?[64] As he wrote to Voegelin in 1951:

> I believe still today [that is, 15 years after writing *Philosophy and Law*] that the *theioi nomoi* is the common ground of the Bible and philosophy—humanly speaking. But I would specify that, in any event, it is the problem of the multitude of *theioi nomoi* that leads to the diametrically opposed solutions of the Bible on the one hand and of philosophy on the other.[65]

Jerusalem represents the world of belief—in the creation of the world, in the miracles, and in the need of divine revelation for the guidance of life. Robert Sokolowski correctly noted that as a Jew, Strauss always articulated a voluntarist conception of God based on the primacy of unfathomable will, in contrast to the intellectualist tradition of the Christian Thomas Aquinas, which grants primacy to the divine wisdom.[66] In the *scriptum*[67] that forms the centerpiece of Meier's rendition of the theologico-political problem, the version of Christian faith focused upon is also the voluntarist one of Luther and Calvin,[68] rooted in a notion of divine transcendence for which everything seems possible because it knows nothing as impossible.[69] Correlatively, Strauss portrayed orthodox belief as a decision to assent to the truths revealed by others. Without benefit of the supernatural light of faith, which Strauss rejects, belief becomes virtually arbitrary and is equated with blind obedience. In contrast, according to the Thomist analogy of light, the mysteries of faith are held to be intelligible, but with an intelligibility that is not immediately accessible to the light of human reason alone. Aquinas compared the human intellect's power in relation to the divine intelligibility to the eyesight of an owl in daylight, for which the sunlight is too bright—God is in no way associated with irrationality or arbitrariness. Similarly, as Ernest Fortin often pointed out, at the start of the *Summa theologiae* Thomas Aquinas could do something unheard of within either a Jewish or Islamic community or a post-Lutheran Protestant world, namely, to ask whether there is a need for any other wisdom besides philosophy, thus placing theological wisdom on the defensive.[70]

For Strauss, Athens represents premodern rationalism, which is most perfectly embodied in great Arab philosophers such as Alfarabi, Avicenna, and Averroës and great Jewish philosophers such as Halevi and Maimonides.[71] Premodern rationalism restricts truth to what can be established in accord with the demands of Aristotle's logical ideal of knowledge. It is distinguished from the modern rationalism of either (1) the unequivocal, even hyperbolic, adoption of the Aristotelian logical ideal in Descartes, Hobbes, and so forth, or (2) the relegation of the teachings based on belief in divine revelation to the realm of imagination in a pejorative sense, as in Hobbes's "vain imaginings" or Spinoza's assessment of the cognitive status of the authors of the biblical narratives.

In *Philosophy and Law,* Strauss showed that, pushed to its most radical consequences, the basic alternatives for modern rationalism are not orthodoxy or Enlightenment but orthodoxy or atheism.[72] Premodern rationalism, motivated by respectful awareness of the human need, on the part of the many who are incapable of the ascent to philosophy, for religious beliefs and dogmas for the sake of morality, arrived at a reconciliation with orthodox belief; premodern rationalism also understood the political dangers of widespread atheism. A premodern rationalist like Maimonides had no difficulty reconciling Jewish law with natural law as discernible by unaided reason alone on the basis of Deuteronomy 4:6: "Keep them and do them; for that will be your wisdom and understanding in the sight of the peoples, who, when they hear all these statutes, will say, 'Surely, this great nation is a wise and understanding people.'"[73] Conscious that religious beliefs cannot be rationally refuted by Aristotelian *apodeixis,* he sought to protect simple believers' fidelity to salutary verisimilitudes or "noble lies." In accord with premodern rationalism, Strauss was critical of the modern rationalists' unquestioned assumption that belief is no different from prejudice, in the pejorative sense of being based on passions or superstition that ought to be extirpated.

Strauss agreed with Rousseau's comment that the Enlightenment had a prejudice against prejudice. He underlined Spinoza's intellectually honest admission that just as the miracles justifying religious belief cannot be proven apodictically, so also they cannot be disproved; and he agreed with Lessing that the ultimate critique of a religion is mockery.[74] The young Strauss boldly argued: "The Jewish tradition has a more appropriate response to the question of the original ideal of the Enlightenment than does cultural philosophy."[75]

Rather than throwing in his lot with political as opposed to cultural and religious Zionism, Strauss dedicated himself to the renewal of political philosophy. He claimed that it "is not a historical discipline," although he was highly skilled in historical work. He, like Voegelin, knew that "political philosophy is fundamentally different from the history of political philosophy itself."[76] Strauss's unconventional reading of the history of modern philosophy contrasts sharply with that of typical histories of political philosophy, whose social-scientific or cultural-historical approaches level crucial differences by failing to appreciate the significance of the eighteenth-century "quarrel between the ancients and the moderns," not to mention the fact that, according to Strauss, the question *quid sit deus?* is coeval with philosophy.

Strauss explains this failure by a rather neat extension of the metaphor of the cave from Plato's *Republic.* The *doxai* pictured in Plato's cave did not possess the cognitive status of true knowledge (*episteme*) but that of natural beliefs without which the city could not function or exist. The cumulative errors of modernity have generated an artificial cave, distinct from that natural cave depicted by Plato. Hence, before beginning the ascent from the cave to the sun, the philosopher must first deal with people in this "second, 'unnatural' cave"[77] by, as it were, elevating them back to the more natural cave of premodern beliefs.

> To that end, and only to that end, is the "historicizing" of philosophy justified and necessary: only the history of philosophy makes possible the ascent from the second, "unnatural" cave, into which we have fallen less because of the tradition itself than because of the tradition of polemics against tradition, into that first, "natural" cave which Plato's image depicts, to emerge from which into the light is the original meaning of philosophizing.[78]

Besides the tension between Athens and Jerusalem, Strauss's attempt to revive classic political philosophy always includes the contrast between ancient and modern forms of rationalism. So the analysis of our contemporary situation in terms of the twofold contrast between Athens and Jerusalem and between ancient political theory as a higher viewpoint and modern political theory as a decisively lower viewpoint (even if it is not to be condemned outright for that reason) takes on a quite practical relevance. In fact, liberal democracy makes the world safe for philosophy, and if one can give ancient rather than modern arguments for supporting it, perhaps it can be salvaged from the ravages of the crisis of our time. Strauss's hermeneutic strategy is then clear:

> It is safer to try to understand the low in the light of the high than the high in the light of the low. In doing the latter one necessarily distorts the high, whereas in doing the former one does not deprive the low of the freedom to reveal itself fully as what it is.[79]

The contrast with the horizon analyzed by Strauss as the outcome of the "three waves of modernity"[80] is significant for our discussion, because it clarifies that what the standpoints of Athens and Jerusalem have in common is of far greater significance than what either of them shares with modernity. This is a startling finding, since, like Hegel, many take for granted that modernity's principles of equality and liberty simply implement what are essentially Christian principles through a strategy Hegel called "the lowering of heaven."

What about Strauss's hypothesis of the "three waves of modernity"? One can certainly read it as a detailed account of what Voegelin called a process of deculturation or the replacement of reality by "Second Realities."[81] That hypothesis also seems to be fully compatible with Voegelin's differing statement of these matters in his essay on liberalism.[82] In his relentless push back to the origins of modern political thought from within a horizon beyond modernity, Strauss revealed how both Hobbes and his chief modifier, Locke, turn out to be disciples of Machiavelli, the initiator of the first wave of modernity.[83] Strauss discovered that Machiavelli inaugurated the revolution against the medieval synthesis, beginning a succession of lower syntheses characteristic of the sociocultural decline described by Voegelin in terms of the eclipse of reality. In the 15th chapter of his odd little book, *The Prince,* Machiavelli wrote the fateful words:

> many have imagined republics and principalities which have never been seen or known to exist in reality; for how we live is so far removed from how we ought to live, that he who abandons what is done for what ought to be done will rather learn to bring about his own ruin than his preservation. A man who wishes to make a profession of goodness in everything must necessarily come to grief among so many who are not good. Therefore it is necessary for a prince who wishes to maintain himself to learn how not to be good, and to use this knowledge and not use it according to the necessity of the case.[84]

In Lonergan's phrase, Machiavelli opted to "develop 'realist' views in which theory is adjusted to practice and practice means whatever happens to be done."[85] This option becomes the matrix for three trajectories of political thought stretching in one wave from Machiavelli through Hobbes, Locke, Smith, and Montesquieu, a second wave from Rousseau through Kant, Hegel, and Marx, and a third wave from Nietzsche to the present.[86]

Conventional secular intellectual historians would generally agree with Herbert Butterfield[87] in ascribing the greatest importance by far to the scientific revolution in the sixteenth and seventeenth centuries vis-à-vis the Reformation and the Renaissance. For Strauss the unquestionably crucial factor in this revolution is a specifically Machiavellian offshoot of the "new" science's concern for utility. Thus, it demanded autonomy from theological or philosophic hegemony, and it excluded questions irresolvable by appealing to observation or experiment. Hence, the scientistic propaganda of Condorcet, Diderot, D'Alembert, and Comte lends plausibility to the Machiavellian argument that true answers to the question of how we ought to live are so far removed from how we do in fact live as to be practically or politically irrelevant. A political science governed by *verità effettuale* entails the separation of politics from morality and invites the tandem of scientific experts and managers to take control of our lives.

Strauss argued that the radically Machiavellian reorientation toward nature as *fortuna* inspired the scientistic or Cartesian (manipulative) derailment of modern science. Bacon admitted being "much beholden to Machiavel and others, that write what men do and not what they ought to do,"[88] and proclaimed that the sole purpose of science was "the relief of man's estate." The specific difference of scientific knowledge is power. So, too, the Baconian motto of *parendo vincere* lies at the heart of Descartes' *Discourse on Method*, especially in his own expression of intent in Part Six: "to make men the masters and possessors of nature"[89]—an aim to which the vaunted *Cogito* and hyperbolic doubt are subordinated.

Machiavelli's original dissociation of ethics and politics also prepared the way for the privatization of human ends and the breakdown of the common or public good as the *raison d'être* of political order. Henceforth, what Aristotle (*Politics*, III, v, 1280a25–1281a9) held to be but an apolitical precondition of politics is posited in Hobbes's *Leviathan* as the sole reasonable motive for politics:

> The passions that incline men to peace are fear of death; desire of such things as are necessary to commodious living; and a hope by their industry to obtain them. And reason suggesteth convenient articles of peace, upon which men may be drawn to agreement. These articles are they, which otherwise are called the laws of nature. (chap. 13)[90]

And while John Locke, the putative grandfather of liberal democracy in the United States, quoted "the judicious Hooker," Strauss demonstrated that he actually followed Hobbes's teaching that the purpose of polity is neither "eternal life" nor "the good life," but comfortable self-preservation. Locke's reduction of political concern to the protection and security of the private individual is precisely expressed in his *Letter Concerning Toleration*:

> The commonwealth seems to me to be a society of men constituted only for the procuring, preserving, and advancing their own civil interests.
>
> Civil interests I call life, liberty, health, and indolency of body; and the possession of outward things, such as money, lands, houses, furniture, and the like.

The bias toward considering human activity as essentially a matter of maximizing privately defined pleasure or minimizing privately defined pain is central to the liberal tradition, so that the concern for the common good of order and value is subverted to the interests of private advantage, whether of individuals or of groups. As Strauss wrote:

> Locke's teaching on property, and therewith, his whole political philosophy, are revolutionary. . . . Through the shift of emphasis from natural duties or obligations to natural rights, the individual, the ego, had become the center and origin of the moral world . . . man owes almost everything valuable to his own effort.[91]

For Strauss, Rousseau was the initiator of the second wave of modernity and the first to see bourgeois politics for what it is. The famous statement occurs in *The First Discourse on the Arts and Sciences:* "Ancient politicians incessantly talked about morals and virtue, those of our time talk only of business and money."[92] But there was a disequilibrium between his desire to restore the nonutilitarian virtue of the classical republics, on the one hand, and his typically modern question about the reconciliation of the needs and desires of the individual with the authority and constraints of society as a whole on the other: "Man is born free, and everywhere he is in chains. . . . How did this change happen? I do not know. What can make it legitimate? I think I can resolve that question."[93]

In a context where it is taken for granted that human beings in civil society have nothing in common but the joint pursuit of individually determined goals, Rousseau displaced the traditional question of politics posed in terms of the common good with the question of political legitimacy. Kant's avowal of the primacy of practical reason was based on Rousseau's general will as bolstered by civil religion. Nor does Kant's democracy of "good will" suppose for a moment that most men and women are capable of more than "a wide range of self-regarding responses to the carrot and the stick."[94] Like Rousseau, Kant pinned his hopes for a political solution to the problem of reconciling universal autonomy with the anarchy of self-interest on the creation of proper institutions and of laws "with teeth in them." Acknowledging this split between personal morality and efficient constitutional planning, Kant even envisioned a perfectly just civil society composed entirely of devils, on the basis of enlightened self-interest.[95]

After Hegel's abortive attempt to patch up the rift between political institutions and morality, Karl Marx went on to criticize liberal capitalist political economy in the name of a complete liberation from illegitimate bondage. But he never unequivocally suggests a motivation for revolution other than the maximization of satisfactions. Even the famous slogan, "from each according to his capacities and to each according to his needs,"[96] can be interpreted this way—and Alexandre Kojève famously did so.[97] The utopian communist society that "makes it possible for me to do one thing today and another tomorrow, to hunt in the morning, fish in the afternoon, breed cattle in the evening, criticize after dinner, just as I like"[98] decisively rejects the division of labor but not Locke's or Smith's primacy of economic man. In both liberal capitalist and communist political thought, the classical political orientation, which judged the desire for wealth, glory, and freedom to do what one pleased utterly subordinate to the requirements of the good life, is turned upside down. The political order is governed strictly in the light of the standards of security, comfort, and disoriented freedom. For what use is the good life if you are not alive? And what does it avail a man to live well if he is not well off?

Strauss credited Nietzsche, the devastating critic of "the last man" in the prologue to *Thus Spake Zarathustra,* with starting the third wave of modernity, in which we still live. It is a matter not just of the death of God but of the degeneration of the human being under either communism or liberal democracy, which he regarded as secularized versions of Christian pity based on *ressentiment.* Nietzsche's desire for a more integral human being was the apotheosis of historicism for Strauss, opening the way to its pair of catastrophic implications—relativism and nihilism. Strauss was willing to grant that Nietzsche's intimations of deprival were intended to overcome nihilism by confronting it without succumbing to *ressentiment,* but I do not think he was convinced that Nietzsche was fully capable of adequately elucidating or inviting people to "a genuine conversion from premoral if not immoral concern with worldly goods to the concern with the goodness of the soul" instead of merely pivoting on "the calculating transition from unenlightened to enlightened self-interest."[99]

Strauss develops this three-wave hypothesis at length in his perhaps best-known and most influential work, *Natural Right and History,* in terms of the transformation of the central category of nature. "Nature is older than any tradition; hence it is more venerable than any tradition. . . . By uprooting the authority of the ancestral, philosophy recognizes nature as an authority."[100] For Strauss, Greek philosophy's opposition between *physis* or nature and *nomos* or conventional belief is a transhistorical criterion. His understanding of what is "right by nature" (*physei dikaion*) is as nuanced and flexible as Voegelin's in the essay in *Anamnesis.*[101] Even so, in deploying this standard, Strauss wants to release the philosophic account of the difference between right and wrong from the relativities of space and time, of opinion and human agreement. For Strauss, this standard of morality and politics was articulated for virtuous gentlemen in Aristotle's *Ethics* and *Politics*. From this standard, each wave of modernity defaults with increasing radicality. Ancient political philosophy made virtue the great theme; modern politics replaced that theme with power. For ancient natural law emphasizes duty or obligation, while modern natural right stresses self-centered claims. This string of oppositions could be extended virtually indefinitely.

Nature is the key for Strauss. It marks the antithesis both to socially accepted deviations from nature and to historicism as either relativism or nihilism. From the perspective of premodern rationalism, this concept of nature excludes supernatural eschatology only to the extent that it is "irrational." Strauss's notion of nature is certainly not unintelligent, but, if he remains open to it, he regularly fails to take into account God's solution to the human crisis, and so remains within what Voegelin would call the noetic differentiation of consciousness. For him, "necesse est philosophari." This perhaps explains his anti-historicist penchant, which leads to a comparative unwillingness to deal with the details and scope of world history.

Voegelin would say that the philosophies of Plato and Aristotle are incapable of dealing adequately with the problem of apocalyptic, because it is conditioned by circumstances not given in their historical milieu. But Strauss would say that they alone provide access to what Allan Bloom called "a rich and concrete natural consciousness of the political phenomenon";[102] and they alone reflect on political things by putting them within the context of the whole or what is highest and best, not so much giving us answers but showing us what the fundamental political problems for all times are.

> Historicism sanctions the loss, or the oblivion, of the natural horizon of human thought by denying the permanence of fundamental problems. It is the existence of that natural horizon which makes possible "objectivity" and therefore in particular "historical objectivity."[103]

The political philosopher is one who demonstrates the ongoing political relevance of reflecting on the political situation at any time in light of these fundamental problems.

Nature, then, means the direct experience of political things together with the re-raising of the fundamental political problems through time.

> The recognition by philosophy [originally by Socrates] of the fact that the human race is worthy of some seriousness is the origin of political philosophy or political science. If this recognition is to be philosophic, however,

> this must mean that the political things, the merely human things, are of decisive importance for understanding nature as a whole.[104]

History is only relevant insofar as the reading of the ancient authors makes accessible that natural experience of politics and those fundamental questions.

> History, that is, concern with the past as thought of the past, takes on philosophical significance if there are good reasons for believing that we can learn something of utmost importance from the thought of the past, which we cannot learn from our contemporaries. History takes on philosophical significance for men living in an age of intellectual decline. Studying the thinkers of the past becomes essential for men living in an age of intellectual decline because it is the only practical way in which they can recover a proper understanding of fundamental problems. Given such conditions, history has the further task of explaining why the proper understanding of fundamental problems has become lost in such a manner that the loss presents itself at the outset as progress.[105]

Apocalyptic, as a function of divine revelation, is to be dealt with in the way those who conceive their religion as *law*—typically, Islam and Judaism in their nonmystical, *sharia/hallacha*-oriented versions—would do. Strauss was convinced by the medieval Arab opinion of Alfarabi that the fundamental treatment of the problem of revelation or prophecy is to be found in Plato's *Laws*. In Strauss's opinion, the *Laws* is the fundamental complement to *The Republic,* which constructed the best regime in speech alone. As one moves from "speech alone" toward implementation in practical reality, indispensable dogmas by which the many can live the lives of good citizens are needed. Common people are more likely to pay heed if those who fashion the *nomoi,* in Rousseau's phrase, "attribute their own wisdom to the gods."[106] Not only is there no room in Strauss's framework for apocalyptic in its usual meaning but he also explicitly rejects the eventuality that the basic problems of historical living can ever be decisively solved. The possibility of a solution—the institution of the best regime of Plato and Aristotle—is indeed never apodictically excluded; but Strauss believes that such a regime would unfortunately be impossible to sustain.

In conclusion, I take Strauss to be doing political philosophy in his expressed sense of "the political, or popular, treatment of philosophy, or the political introduction to philosophy—the attempt to lead the qualified citizens, or rather their qualified sons, from the political life to the philosophical life."[107] Whatever his own true orientation may be, I take him to be neither a crypto-Nietzschean nor a conservative elitist as this is vulgarly conceived. As Carnes Lord put it, he believed that "elites set the tone for the larger society, exemplifying a way of life and nurturing ideas and values—the deeper meaning of the notion of 'regime' that Strauss found in Plato and Aristotle."[108] I think his esteem for Churchill was not exoteric; that he genuinely took Churchill at his word about Aristotle's *Ethics* as the adequate expression of the morality by which he lived; and that he is far from being anti-democratic, as is evident from this statement from Strauss's "Eulogy for Churchill," cited by Harry V. Jaffa:

> The tyrant stood at the pinnacle of power. The contrast between the indomitable and magnanimous statesman and the insane tyrant—this spectacle in its clear simplicity was one of the greatest lessons one can learn at any time.[109]

Strauss agreed with Churchill that democracy, with its "low, but solid" basis, is the worst regime, except for all the others. Strauss's statement—"Democracy in a word, is meant to be an aristocracy which has broadened to a universal aristocracy"—adequately formulates the educational project to which any red-blooded university teacher today is dedicated; and Voegelin's remark that a critical mass of virtuous citizens is the condition of the possibility of democracy as opposed to tyrannies supported by plebiscitary majorities gives us a reasonable goal to shoot for.

Girard—The Unabashed Christian Solution: Unexpected Fulfillment of Apocalypse

Although I am less familiar with René Girard's work than with that of the others,[110] Girard is in many ways the most radical of the three thinkers, and the most sympathetic to a theologian. Prescinding from the details of Girard's mimetic theory and the massive role he assigns it in the archaic origins of culture, myth, and religion,[111] here I want to underline his unequivocal judgment that universal humanity confronts a problem that cannot be solved on a purely human basis, in accord with the Christian doctrine of moral impotence. He is altogether bold in stating that the solution is God's, that it is a supernatural solution, in accord with the Christian teaching that salvation comes to us by grace alone. He is altogether clear that the solution's decisive historical revelation and occurrence is the life, death, and resurrection of Jesus of Nazareth, specifically as emerging from the Jewish tradition that had already begun exposing the nonsacrificial nature of God's love for human beings.[112] This accords with the teaching that God's forgiveness and the sending of the Holy Spirit happen to all human beings *propter Christum*.

Relevantly for our discussion, Girard unhesitatingly uses the term apocalyptic in a conventionally biblical and Christian sense.[113] For Girard, apocalypse possesses the heightened eschatological twist that involves a build up of evil into a climactic crisis, a transformative event that constitutes a *metabasis eis allo genos,* expressed by Paul's phrase, "a new creation" (2 Cor. 5:23). The possibility of existence on a plane completely liberated from mimesis, violence, scapegoating, and sacrifice is both pointed toward and actualized in the life, death, and resurrection of Jesus.[114] For Girard, then, eschatology and apocalypse converge on and, in a sense, expand from the death and resurrection of Jesus, who in his words and deeds reveals God's way of dealing with violence in a manner that only a divine person who is fully human could do. This expresses in terms of historical causality the Chalcedonian doctrine that the one person of the Word is truly divine and truly human. What more could an orthodox Roman Catholic theologian ask for?

Now Girard is aware of the point of the story told by the Montreal émigré psychiatrist convert to Christianity, Karl Stern, about the Hassidic rabbi who looked out the window and said, "So what's changed?"[115] In *Things Hidden from the Foundation of the World,* Girard recognizes how the slow absorption of the Gospel in history is accompanied by a build up of the panorama of displacement, distortion, and evil, which seems to be mounting to a crux, a crisis. Girard describes this situation as apocalyptic. He insists that the apocalyptic expectations of Second Temple Judaism in first-century Palestine are fulfilled, but not in the catastrophic, mimetic fashion of finally settling the score by vengeance. Jesus's action of suffering the effects of human evil in history and offering unconditional forgiveness to the perpetrators goes completely against the grain of mimetic ways of confronting evil.

Girard's use of apocalyptic integrates the central scandals of the Christian faith—that grace is unmerited and that God becomes human in Jesus. He unabashedly asserts them after arriving at them chiefly by his own intellectual probity, following the line of questioning his research has opened for him—from mimesis through scapegoating and sacrifice to Christian redemption. Moreover, this voyage of discovery occurred to a scholar led by the exigencies of insight and a remarkable concern for truth and beauty.[116] In the process of acquiring a rare interdisciplinary scholarly expertise, Girard passed from being a generalist university teacher in the humanities at Indiana University into the fields of literature and literary criticism[117] at Johns Hopkins, and from there to comparative anthropology and psychology and biblical interpretation while at Stanford.[118] This is not unlike Voegelin, whose breadth of historical and world-cultural learning compelled him to an ever deepening and broadening apprehension of the requirements of the political scientist in our day. Nor is it altogether different from Strauss, whose thinking through cultural, religious, and beyond political Zionism led him from an engagement with the post- and pre-Enlightenment Jewish tradition to the study of the Western tradition of practical and political philosophy from Plato and Xenophon to Nietzsche, Weber, and Heidegger.

If I have a hesitation with regard to Girard's analysis, it is mimetic theory's apparent naturalization of sin. Not strictly a theologian by profession, Girard has been liable not to distinguish his theory from those radical modern analyses of the Christian doctrine of original sin.[119] However, the teaching of the Bible differs significantly from the teachings of Hobbes, Locke, and Rousseau, because in Genesis mimesis is a *deformation* of the human being rather than an expression of humanity's God-given nature.

What is at issue here? If Genesis is correct, then the state of nature accounts of Hobbes, Locke, and Rousseau are at best descriptions of human beings as fallen, not of human beings as either natural or elevated to mutual friendship with the persons of the Holy Trinity. Hobbes, Locke, and Rousseau fallaciously eliminated the light of faith and truncated the light of reason into a merely calculating faculty in order to establish the foundations of civil society on the "low but solid basis" of damage control: people can pursue mimetic desires without killing each other. The concomitant secularization of civil society and privatization of true Gospel values leads to what Strauss, speaking of Locke, called "the joyless quest for joy." It is a joyless quest for joy because physical and psychological violence in civil society—if not preventive attacks against threats from outside—is often disguised. Girard alone among the three sees the apocalyptic consequences of, in Pascal's formulation, making people think concupiscential desire is the same as charity.[120]

In brief, Girard could use the theoretic construct of nature to give a more adequate account both of human formation and of human deformation by mimesis to communicate more effectively the human transformation wrought by God in Christ Jesus. This would be the theoretic context for dealing adequately with apocalyptic and politics. And I believe this was well initiated by his disciple, Raymund Schwager.[121]

Jerusalem and Athens in Girard, Strauss, and Voegelin

The differences among the three become most clear when we examine their respective stances on Jerusalem and Athens. Strauss discovered that premodern rationalism held the two in tension, although many of his greatest followers let the tension go in favor of Athens. Perhaps as an atheist motivated by intellectual probity, Strauss favored Athens on the basis of a conscience rooted in Jerusalem. Therefore, the axis of his thought rotates around what may be attained by reason unaided by belief or revelation, although he studied the Bible with great care. Strauss noted that the Bible does not have a term for nature, and a philosophic grasp of nature was the focus of his enterprise.

Voegelin, doing something that Strauss could not do either as a philosopher or as a Jew, joins Paul in crediting Jesus as the pleromatic presence of divinity in history. Yet like Strauss, he perceives great dangers in the possible imbalance to which the pneumatic differentiation may be prey, due to its intense experience of the personalized and loving goal toward which the tension draws the converted. At the same time he appreciates the moral contributions to society of sincere Christian believers. Voegelin is indistinguishable from Strauss insofar as his *bête noire* is any kind of metastatic faith, of which apocalypticism is a chief species. While one wonders whether Voegelin was too greatly influenced by the Bruno-inspired Schelling, so that he leaned more toward Athens than Jerusalem, still, he asked that the Psalms be read at his deathbed, and requested a Christian burial, if that were possible.[122]

Girard's criterion for historical judgment comes straight from the Gospel of Matthew 25: the measure to which a person lives in accord with the Gospel and imitates Jesus who identifies with victims. For Girard, then, Jesus is the only person absolutely free of negative mimesis; he freely gives his life for all the rest of humanity, whose members are subject to mimesis, violence, scapegoating, and sacrifice in the pejorative sense. Thus, Girard stands firmly on the side of Jerusalem.

It is important that what is significant for Girard is not loyalty to one side or the other (since that would probably have a mimetic motivation), but truth. Thus, if Strauss as an atheist had a Jewish conscience, we might also say that Girard had the Catholic penchant to use reason to clarify what goes beyond reason,[123] whether it be the mimetic process on one side of the apocalyptic divide, or God's answer to mimesis in Christ Jesus on the other. What drives Girard is neither the possessive individualism of the first wave of modernity nor the expressive individualism of the second wave, but, in common with Nietzsche, the quest for a more integral kind of humanity than the first two waves could muster; and unlike Nietzsche, Girard's commitment is to Jesus alone, not to Dionysus, nor to "Caesar with the heart of Christ" (which Catholic theologian Hans Urs von Balthasar interpreted as biblical morality without Christianity).[124]

My sense is that Girard transcends Nietzsche's and Strauss's vantage of the third wave because he uncovered the mimetic root underlying Hobbes and Rousseau's state of nature analyses at the source of the first two waves. Hobbes and Rousseau's accounts of the state of nature are geared to their modern project of separating traditional religious opinion from political power. They had two purposes: first, to replace the biblical account of the Fall, and, second, to revise or overcome the premodern account of nature. Hobbes concentrated on the power of the weakest to kill the strongest in the scarcity-ridden, asocial state of nature, exacerbated to the extreme by the vanity of a few. In the *Second Discourse on the Origins of Inequality,* Rousseau transposed the Hobbesian problematic into the realm of social psychology. He focused on the dawning of the alienating realization that one's estimation of oneself is dependent on others' estimation of one's self. This leads to the displacement of the primal amiable beast's spontaneous self-love (*amour de soi*) and the atrophy of the original human compassion because of the vanity (*amour propre*) of the rational human being. This being's capacity to compare leads to envy and jealousy. Girard's mimetic theory lays bare the generative force that produces the effects of physical and psychological violence (which we associate with both archaic and so-called civilized human beings) in Hobbes and Rousseau.

Girard's analysis of mimesis, scapegoating, and sacrifice enables him to assert what Strauss seems to realize but never quite expresses, and what Voegelin tends to articulate quite generally in terms of the Augustinian opposition between the concupiscential (or pneumopathological) soul and the open soul. According to Girard, the human condition, dominated by mimetic desire, cannot be held in check by a calculating contract (Hobbes's *Leviathan*), or remedied either by the emotional faith of the Savoyard vicar or by the sublimation of eros by female modesty when the marriage contract becomes the basis of the social contract (as in *Emile, or On Education*), or by the general will underpinned by civil religion or by the categorical imperative propped up by "religion within the limits of reason alone." Girard's analysis of the bourgeois novel showed the futility of all these solutions.[125] Girard demonstrated in archaic anthropology—a state of nature as based on verifiable fact, incidentally—that not just mimesis but scapegoating and sacrifice are the matrices for both culture and religion, and even for the so-called legal institutions of civil society.[126] Then, most radically of all, Girard taught us to see how the anthropology of the Gospel and of Jesus of Nazareth not only fully diagnosed the root problem of mimetic violence, whether physical or psychological, but also manifested God's remedy for it, which is the only remedy: unconditional forgiveness of one's enemies and persecutors, commitment to helping the world's victims, loving despite unrequited love.

NOTES

1. Isomorphism refers to a similarity in the relations between two sets of terms without assuming any similarity between parallel terms.
2. See *Grace and Freedom: Operative Grace in the Thought of St Thomas Aquinas,* in Frederick E. Crowe and Robert M. Doran, eds., *Collected Works of Bernard Lonergan,* vol. 1 (Toronto: University of Toronto Press, 2000), 15–16. Lonergan speaks of

   > grasping that the idea of the supernatural is a theorem, that it no more adds to the data of the problem than the Lorentz transformation theorem puts a new constellation in the heavens. What Philip the Chancellor systematically posited was not the supernatural character of grace, for that was already known and acknowledged, but the validity of a line of reference termed nature. In the long term and in the concrete the real alternatives remain charity and cupidity, the elect and the *massa damnata*. But the whole problem lies in the abstract, in human thinking: the fallacy in the early thought had been an unconscious confusion of the metaphysical abstraction, nature, with the concrete data which do not quite correspond; Philip's achievement was the creation of a mental perspective, the introduction of a set of coordinates, that eliminated the basic fallacy and its attendant host of anomalies.

   Eric Voegelin was probably correct in holding that the decadent or derailed scholastic tradition turned this distinction between nature and supernature into a separation; as we shall see, rather than recovering the distinction in its proper meaning, he thinks it preferable to abandon it altogether.
3. Robert O. Johann, *Building the Human* (New York: Herder and Herder, 1968), 68.
4. See Bernard Lonergan, *Insight: A Study of Human Understanding* (New York: Philosophical Library, 1957), 209–11 on emergent probability and history; and 233–34 on a practical theory of history; and Eric Voegelin, "Ewiges Sein in der Zeit," and "Was ist Politische Realität?" in *Anamnesis: Zur Theorie der Geschichte und Politik* (Munich: Piper, 1966), 254–80, 283–354.
5. See Bernard Lonergan, "Mission and Spirit," in *A Third Collection: Papers by Bernard J. F Lonergan,* ed. Frederick E. Crowe (New York: Paulist Press, 1985), 23–34; "Finality, Love, Marriage," in *Collection: Papers by Bernard Lonergan, S. J.* (New York: Herder and Herder, 1964), 16–53.
6. Fred Lawrence, "The Fragility of Consciousness: Lonergan and the Postmodern Concern for the Other," in *Theological Studies* 54 , no. 1 (1993): 55–94.

7. Aristotle, *De Anima (On the Soul),* trans. J. A. Smith, in *The Basic Works of Aristotle,* ed. Richard McKeon (New York: Random House, 1941), 535–603; and Eric Voegelin, "Man in Society and History," in *Collected Works of Eric Voegelin,* vol. 11, *Published Essays 1953–1965,* ed. with an introduction by Ellis Sandoz (Columbia: University of Missouri Press, 2000), 191–92.

8. See Lonergan, *Insight,* 458–87, on genetic method and human development.

9. On meaning as constitutive, see Bernard Lonergan, *Method in Theology* (New York: Herder and Herder, 1973), 78, 178, 180, 306, 356, 362.

10. See Bernard Lonergan, "Reality, Myth, Symbol," in *Myth, Symbol, and Reality,* ed. Alan M. Olson (Notre Dame, IN: University of Notre Dame Press, 1980), 31–37.

11. Eric Voegelin, *The New Science of Politics: An Introduction* in *Modernity without Restraint,* ed. with an introduction by Manfred Henningsen (Columbia: University of Missouri Press, 1952), 112.

12. N. T Wright, *The New Testament and the People of God* (Minneapolis: Fortress Press, 1992), 280–99.

13. N. T. Wright, *Jesus and the Victory of God* (Minneapolis: Fortress Press, 1996), 95; see 95–97.

14. See Aristotle, *The Nicomachean Ethics of Aristotle* 1134b 18–1135a 25. trans. David Ross (London: Oxford University Press, 1963), 123.

15. See Henningsen, "Introduction" (sections 3 and 4), in Voegelin, *The New Science of Politics,* 98–108; and "The Greatness of Max Weber," in *Collected Works of Eric Voegelin,* vol. 31, *Hitler and the Germans,* trans., ed., and with an introduction by Detlev Clemens and Brendan Purcell (Columbia: University of Missouri Press, 1999), 257–73.

16. See Eric Voegelin, "From Political Ideas to Symbols of Experience," in *Autobiographical Reflections,* ed. with an introduction by Ellis Sandoz (Baton Rouge: Louisiana State University Press, 1989), 62–69.

17. Eric Voegelin, *Order and History,* vol. 4, *The Ecumenic Age* (Baton Rouge: Louisiana State University Press, 1974), 268–69.

18. Eric Voegelin, *The New Science of Politics,* in *Collected Works of Eric Voegelin,* vol. 5, *Modernity without Restraint: The Political Religions; The New Science of Politics; and Science, Politics, and Gnosticism,* ed. Manfred Henningsen (Columbia: University of Missouri Press, 2000), 89.

19. See Eric Voegelin, "Equivalences of Experience and Symbolization in History," in *Collected Works of Eric Voegelin,* vol. 12, *Published Essays 1966–1985,* ed. Ellis Sandoz (Baton Rouge: Louisiana State University Press, 1990), 115–33.

20. Voegelin, *Anamnesis,* 32, from a letter of 17 September 1943, to his friend and colleague Alfred Schutz.

21. Eric Voegelin, *Order and History,* vol. 2, *The World of the Polis* (Baton Rouge: Louisiana State University Press, 1957), 1, 22, 24, and passim.

22. Voegelin gives the clearest explanation I have seen of his use of "existential" in *Faith and Political Philosophy: The Correspondence between Leo Strauss and Eric Voegelin, 1934–1964,* trans. and ed. Peter Emberley and Barry Cooper (University Park, PA: Penn State University Press, 1993). The correspondence comprises pages 1–106; this is followed by part 2, which is made up of key essays by the correspondents (two apiece) on the theme announced in

the title, and part 3, made up of commentaries by seven authors. The relevant letter is Voegelin's to Strauss (Letter 27: 2 January 1950), where he says: "Ontological knowledge emerges in the process of history and biographically in the process of the individual person's life under certain conditions of education, social context, personal inclination, and spiritual conditioning. *Epistêmê* is not just a function of understanding, it is also in the Aristotelian sense, a dianoetic *aretê*. For this *non*cognitive aspect of *episteme* I use the term 'existential.'" Strauss's response (Letter 28: 14 March 1950) warns Voegelin that this usage threatens to reduce the *vita contemplativa* and its knowledge of/quest for the truth to its perhaps attendant but not necessary conditionings. See 63–66. Strauss evoked Voegelin's explanation of "existential" by tracing its genealogy as meaning "opposed to 'objective' or 'theoretical'" in the rejection of Plato and Socrates by Heidegger and Kierkegaard. See 63.

23. An important text here is the chapter titled "Schelling," in the section "Last Orientation" in *Collected Works of Eric Voegelin*, vol. 25, *History of Political Ideas, vol. 6, The New Order and Last Orientation*, ed. Jürgen Gebhardt and Thomas A. Hollweck (Columbia: University of Missouri Press, 1999), 193–242.

24. See Eric Voegelin, *Anamnesis. Zur Theorie der Geschichte und Politik* (Munich: R. Piper Verlag, 1966), 11.

25. See Strauss in the Strauss-Voegelin Correspondence, *Faith and Political Philosophy*, 89.

26. See Eric Voegelin, "Response to Professor Altizer's 'A New History and a New but Ancient God,'" in *Collected Works of Eric Voegelin*, vol. 12, 292–303; and "The Beginning and the Beyond," in *Collected Works of Eric Voegelin*, vol. 28, *What Is History? And Other Late Unpublished Writings*, ed. Thomas A. Hollweck and Paul Caringella (Baton Rouge: Louisiana State University Press, 1990), 173–232.

27. Voegelin, "Reason: The Classic Experience," in *Published Essays 1966–1985*, 270; see 265–91.

28. Voegelin commenting on Aristotle's admission of becoming *philomythoteros* in his old age, and quoting *Metaphysics* 982b 18 and 1072b 25 in *Anamnesis* 298–99.

29. Voegelin, "Schelling," in "Last Orientation," in *Collected Works of Eric Voegelin*, vol. 25, 211.

30. See Eric Voegelin, *Order and History*, vol. 1, *Israel and Revelation* (Baton Rouge: Louisiana State University Press, 1956).

31. See Eric Voegelin, *Order and History*, vol 2, *The World of the Polis* (Baton Rouge: Louisiana State University Press, 1957), 7; and vol. 3, *Plato and Aristotle* (Baton Rouge: Louisiana State University Press, 1957).

32. See Eric Voegelin, *Order and History*, vol. 4, *The Ecumenic Age* (Baton Rouge: Louisiana State University Press, 1974).

33. Voegelin, "The Beginning and the Beyond," 182.

34. Voegelin, "What Is History?" in *Collected Works of Eric Voegelin*, vol 28, 5.

35. See Eric Voegelin, "Anxiety and Reason," in *Collected Works of Eric Voegelin*, vol. 28, 52–110, see especially 53–56.

36. See Voegelin, "What is History?" in *Collected Works of Eric Voegelin*, vol. 28, 55.

37. Voegelin, "What is History?" in *Collected Works of Eric Voegelin*, vol. 28, 66.

38. Voegelin, *Ecumenic Age*, 195.

39. Voegelin, *Ecumenic Age*, 197: "The concupiscential exodus of the conqueror is a deformation of humanity, but it bears the mark of man's existential tension just as much as the philosopher's or the prophet's, or the saint's exodus. The structure of the Metaxy reaches, beyond noetic consciousness, down into the concupiscential roots of action."

40. Voegelin, *Ecumenic Age*, 301–2.

41. The key texts on this are in *Israel and Revelation*, 452–58, in the commentary on the prophet Isaiah, 450–53.

42. See the chapter of that name in Voegelin, *Ecumenic Age*, 239–60.

43. See the section entitled "The Principle of History of Effect" (*Wirkungsgeschichte*) in Hans-Georg Gadamer, *Truth and Method*, translation revised by Joel Weinsheimer and Donald G. Marshall, 2nd rev. ed. (New York: Crossroad, 1991), 300–307.

44. See the end of chapter 5, Voegelin, *Ecumenic Age*, 260–71, on egophanic deformation.

45. Voegelin, *Ecumenic Age*, 303–4.

46. Voegelin, *Ecumenic Age*, 305.

47. Voegelin, *Ecumenic Age*, 309.

48. Voegelin, *Ecumenic Age*, 326.

49. Leo Strauss, "Correspondence Concerning Modernity," exchange of letters with Karl Löwith beginning 1 October 1946, *Independent Journal of Philosophy/Revue Indépendante de Philosophie* 4 (1983): 105–19.

50. See Leo Strauss, *Leo Strauss: The Early Writings (1921–1932)*, trans. and ed. Michael Zank (Albany: State University of New York Press, 2002).

51. Leo Strauss, "Progress or Return? The Contemporary Crisis of Western Civilization," in *An Introduction to Political Philosophy: Ten Essays by Leo Strauss*, ed. with an introduction by Hilail Gildin, 2nd expanded printing (Detroit: Wayne State University Press, 1989), 249–302.

52. See Heinrich Meier, *Carl Schmitt and Leo Strauss: The Hidden Dialogue*, trans. J Harvey Lomax (Chicago: University of Chicago Press, 1995); Meier, *The Lesson of Carl Schmitt: Four Chapters on the Distinction between Political Theology and Political Theology*, trans. Marcus Brainerd (Chicago: University of Chicago Press, 1998). See also John P. McCormick, *Carl Schmitt's Critique of Liberalism: Against Politics as Technology* (Cambridge: Cambridge University Press, 1997).

53. Leo Strauss, "Comments on *Der Begriff des Politischen*," in Carl Schmitt, *The Concept of the Political*, trans., with introduction and notes, by George Schwab (New Brunswick, NJ: Rutgers University Press, 1976), 105; see 81–105.

54. See the section on Weber in Leo Strauss, "Natural Right and the Distinction between Facts and Values," in *Natural Right and History* (Chicago: University of Chicago Press, 1953), 35–80.

55. Leo Strauss, "A Giving of Accounts: Jacob Klein and Leo Strauss (1970)," in *Jewish Philosophy and the Crisis of Modernity: Essays and Lectures in Modern Jewish Thought*, ed. with an introduction by Kenneth Hart Green (Albany: State University of New York Press, 1997), 461; see 457–66. On Strauss and Weber, see Nasser Behnegar, *Leo Strauss, Max Weber and the Scientific Study of Politics* (Chicago: University of Chicago Press, 2003).

56. Leo Strauss, "An Introduction to Heideggerian Existentialism," in *The Rebirth of Classical Political Rationalism: An Introduction to the Thought of Leo Strauss: Essays and Lectures by Leo Strauss,* selected and introduced by Thomas L. Pangle (Chicago: University of Chicago Press, 1989), 27–46; on the contrast between Heidegger and Husserl in the latter's favor, see Leo Strauss, "Philosophy as a Rigorous Science and Political Philosophy," in *Studies in Platonic Political Philosophy,* ed. with an introduction by Thomas L. Pangle (Chicago: University of Chicago Press, 1983), 29–37.

57. See Leo Strauss, *Spinoza's Critique of Religion,* trans. E. M. Sinclair (New York: Schocken Books, 1965), the republication in English of a book originally written in 1925–28 and published in Germany with the more indicative title, *Die Religionskritik Spinozas als Grundlage seiner Bibelwissenschaft. Untersuchungen zu Spinozas Theologische-Politischen Traktat* (Berlin: Akademie-Verlag, 1930). The autobiographical "Preface to the English Translation," 1–32, is the most informative source on the evolution of Strauss's thought up to 1962.

58. Leo Strauss, "Esoteric Teaching," in *Rebirth of Classical Political Rationalism,* 63–71.

59. See Leo Strauss, "Persecution and the Art of Writing," in *Persecution and the Art of Writing,* reprint of 1952 edition (Chicago: University of Chicago Press, 1988), 22–37.

60. See Barry Cooper, *Eric Voegelin and the Foundations of Modern Political Science* (Columbia: University of Missouri Press, 1999), 129–30; see especially 129, n. 18.

61. Leo Strauss, "Introduction," in *The City and Man* (Chicago: University of Chicago Press, 1978), 1–12.

62. Leo Strauss, "The Problem of Socrates: Five Lectures," in *Rebirth of Classical Political Rationalism,* 103–83.

63. Leo Strauss, "Political Philosophy and History," in *What Is Political Philosophy? and Other Studies* (Chicago: University of Chicago Press, 1988; originally published 1959), 56–77.

64. Leo Strauss, "Jerusalem and Athens (1970)," in *Jewish Philosophy and the Crisis of Modernity,* 377–405. About the relationship in Strauss between philosophy as political and pure philosophy, see Heinrich Meier, *Die Denkbewegung von Leo Strauss: Die Geschichte der Philosophie und die Intention des Philosophen* (Stuttgart/Weimar: J. B. Metzler Verlag, 1996); and on the role of religion/God/faith in political philosophy and the choice of philosophy as a way of life, see Meier, *Das theologisch-politische Problem: Zum Thema von Leo Strauss* (Stuttgart/Weimar: J. B. Metzler Verlag, 1996).

65. Strauss-Voegelin Correspondence, *Das theologisch-politische Problem,* 78.

66. Robert Sokolowski, appendix to chapter 11, in *The God of Faith and Reason: Foundations of Christian Theology* (Notre Dame, IN: University of Notre Dame Press, 1982), 157–64.

67. See H. Meier's references in *Das theologisch-politische Problem: Zum Thema von Leo Strauss* to a *scriptum* used as the basis for Strauss's January 1948 lecture at Hartford Theological Seminary, Hartford, Connecticut, entitled "Reason and Revelation (1947–1948)," in the Leo Strauss Papers, Box 11, Folder 13. See page 16 and n. 3.

68. Meier notes in *Das theologisch-politische Problem,* 46, that the motto Strauss chose for his *Socrates and Aristophanes* is taken from John Calvin's *Institutio christianae religionis,* whose interdict on asking *quid sit deus?* he had referred to more than three decades earlier in his *Die Religionskritik Spinozas.* Meier also refers (47) to Luther's similar indictment.

69. Paraphrasing Meier, in his interpretation of Tertullian's expression, *credo quia absurdum* (*De carne Christi* V, in *Opera omnia,* Migne, *PL,* II 805B–807B, Paris, 1866).

70. See Ernest L. Fortin, "St. Thomas Aquinas, 1225–1274," in *History of Political Philosophy*, ed. Leo Strauss and Joseph Cropsey, 3rd ed. (Chicago: University of Chicago Press, 1987), 250–51; see 248–75.

71. See Leo Strauss, "How Farabi Read Plato's *Laws*," and "Maimonides's Statement on Political Philosophy," in *What Is Political Philosophy*, 95–169; "The Literary Character of the *Guide for the Perplexed*," and "The Law of Reason in the *Kuzari*," in *Persecution and the Art of Writing*, 38–141; see also Meier, *Das theologisch-politische Problem*, especially 25–27. See especially n. 32 on 41–42, where Meier cites two letters, one to his friend Jacob Klein and the other to (a chief interlocutor in *Philosophy and Law*) Julius Guttmann, in which Strauss speaks of his discovery that Moses Maimonides was actually "ein Philosoph."

72. Leo Strauss, *Philosophy and Law: Contributions to the Understanding of Maimonides and His Predecessors*, trans. with an introduction by Eve Adler (Albany: State University of New York Press, 1995), 38.

    Thus, the last "truth" of the alternative orthodoxy or Enlightenment is revealed as the alternative of "orthodoxy or atheism." Orthodoxy, with its hostile eye, recognized from the beginning that this is the case. Now it is no longer contested even by the enemies of orthodoxy. The situation thus formed, the present situation, appears to be insoluble for the Jew who cannot be orthodox and who must consider purely political Zionism, the only "solution of the Jewish problem" possible on the basis of atheism, as a resolution that is indeed highly honorable but not, in earnest and in the long run, adequate. This situation appears not only insoluble but actually is so, as long as one clings to modern premises. If, finally, there is in the modern world only the alternative of "orthodoxy or atheism," and if on the other hand the need for an enlightened Judaism is urgent, then one sees oneself compelled to ask whether enlightenment is necessarily modern enlightenment. Thus one sees oneself induced—provided at the outset that only new, unheard-of, ultramodern thoughts can apply for aid to the medieval Enlightenment, the Enlightenment of Maimonides.

73. See the reference to this passage in Strauss, *Natural Right and History*.

74. Strauss, *Philosophy and Law*, 45–47.

75. Strauss, *Philosophy and Law*, 35.

76. Strauss, "Political Philosophy and History," 56–57.

77. Strauss, *Philosophy and Law*, 136.

78. Strauss, *Philosophy and Law*, 136.

79. Leo Strauss, "Preface to Spinoza's Critique of Religion," in *Liberalism Ancient and Modern* (New York: Basic Books, 1968), 225.

80. Strauss, "The Three Waves of Modernity," in *An Introduction to Political Philosophy*, 81–98.

81. See Voegelin, "Was ist Politische Realität?" in *Anamnesis*, 301–11, on "pneumopathological loss of reality" and the formation of "Second Realities," borrowing a term from Robert Musil. See also "The Eclipse of Reality," in *Collected Works of Eric Voegelin*, vol. 28, 111–62; "Reason: The Classic Experience," in *Collected Works of Eric Voegelin*, vol. 12, 265–91.

82. See Eric Voegelin, "Liberalism and Its History (1960)," in *Collected Works of Eric Voegelin*, vol. 11, 83–99.

83. I have never come across any work that successfully refutes Strauss's book, *Thoughts on Machiavelli* (Seattle: University of Washington Press, 1958).

84. Niccolò Macchiavelli, *The Prince,* trans. Harvey C. Mansfield Jr. (Chicago: University of Chicago Press, 1996), chap. 15.

85. See Bernard Lonergan, "Finality, Love, Marriage," in *Collection: Papers by Bernard Lonergan,* ed. Frederick E. Crowe (New York: Herder and Herder, 1967), 116.

86. See also Strauss, "What Is Political Philosophy," in the section titled "The Modern Solutions," in *What Is Political Philosophy?* 40–55.

87. See Herbert Butterfield, *The Origins of Modern Science, 1300–1800,* rev. ed. (New York: Free Press, 1966).

88. Leo Strauss, *The Political Philosophy of Hobbes: Its Basis and Its Genesis,* trans. Elsa M. Sinclair, with a new preface (Chicago: University of Chicago Press, 1952), 88, n. 5.

89. See René Descartes, Part VI, in *Discourse on Method and Meditations,* trans. Laurence J. Lafleur (Indianapolis: Bobbs-Merrill, 1980).

90. See Thomas Hobbes, *Leviathan,* ed. Michael Oakeshott (New York: Collier-Macmillan, 1962).

91. Strauss, *Natural Right and History,* 248.

92. Jean-Jacques Rousseau, *The First and Second Discourses,* ed. Roger D. Masters, trans. Roger D. Masters and Judith R. Masters (New York: St. Martin's, 1964), 51. On the centrality of Rousseau for Strauss, see Meier, *Die Denkbewegung von Leo Strauss,* 34–41.

93. Jean-Jacques Rousseau, *On the Social Contract,* ed. Roger D. Masters, trans. Judith R. Masters (New York: St. Martin's, 1978), 46.

94. Willmoore Kendall, *Willmoore Kendall Contra Mundum,* ed. Nellie D. Kendall (New Rochelle, NY: Arlington House, 1971), 456.

95. See Immanuel Kant, "Perpetual Peace: First Supplement," in *Kant on History,* ed. Lewis White Beck (Indianapolis: Library of Liberal Arts/Bobbs-Merrill, 1977), 112; see 106–14.

96. Karl Marx, "Critique of the Gotha Program," in *Basic Writings on Politics and Philosophy: Karl Marx and Friedrich Engels,* ed. Lewis S. Feuer (New York: Doubleday Anchor, 1959), 119; see 112–32.

97. See Kojève's important critique of Strauss's *On Tyranny: An Interpretation of Xenophon's Hiero* (New York: Political Science Classics, 1948), "L'action politique des philosophes," in *Critique,* October 1950, 46–55. This was translated from French and published in the revised and enlarged edition of *On Tyranny* (Glencoe, IL: Free Press, 1963), with a foreword by Allan Bloom, under the title "Tyranny and Wisdom," 143–88. Strauss's reply (including a response to Eric Voegelin's critical review of *On Tyranny,* by Leo Strauss, *Review of Politics* 11 [1949], 241–44), which first appeared in French, together with Kojève's critical essay, in 1954, was published in full in *On Tyranny: Including the Strauss-Kojève Correspondence,* rev. and expanded ed., ed. Victor Gourevitch and Michael S. Roth (New York: Free Press, 1991).

98. Marx, "Excerpts from 'The German Ideology,'" in *Basic Writings,* 254; see 246–66.

99. Strauss, *Liberalism Ancient and Modern,* 21.

100. Strauss, *Natural Right and History,* 92.

101. Voegelin, "Das Rechte von Natur," and "Was ist Natur?" in *Anamnesis,* 117–52.

102. Allan Bloom, "Leo Strauss: September 20, 1899–October 18, 1973," in *Giants and Dwarfs: Essays 1960–1990* (New York: Simon and Schuster, 1990), 238; see 235–55.

103. Leo Strauss, "Collingwood's Philosophy of History," in *Review of Metaphysics* 5 (1952): 584; see 559–86.

104. Strauss, "The Problem of Socrates," 126.

105. Strauss, "Collingwood's Philosophy of History," 583.

106. *On the Social Contract*, ed. Roger D. Masters, trans. Judith R. Masters (New York: St. Martin's Press, 1978), Book II, ch vii, 69.

107. Strauss, "On Classical Political Philosophy," 93–94.

108. See Carnes Lord, "Thoughts on Strauss and Our Present Discontents," in *Leo Strauss, the Straussians, and the American Regime*, ed. Kenneth L. Deutsch and John A. Murley (Lanham, MD: Rowman and Littlefield, 1999), 415; see 413–17.

109. Harry V. Jaffa, "Strauss at One Hundred," in *Leo Strauss, the Straussians, and the American Regime*, 44; see 41–48.

110. For a reliable and comprehensive survey of Girard's thought, see Wolfgang Palaver, *René Girards mimetische Theorie: Im Kontext kulturtheoretischer und gesellschaftspolitischer Fragen* (Münster, Germany: LIT Verlag, 2003).

111. See René Girard, *Violence and the Sacred*, trans. Patrick Gregory (Baltimore: The Johns Hopkins University Press, 1977); *The Scapegoat*, trans. Yvonne Freccero (Baltimore: The Johns Hopkins University Press, 1986).

112. All this is stated clearly in René Girard, "Book 2: The Judeo-Christian Scriptures," in *Things Hidden since the Foundation of the World*, trans. Stephen Bann (Books 1 and 3) and Michael Metteer (Book 1), (Stanford, CA: Stanford University Press, 1987), 141–280. Besides the stories of Abel, of Joseph, and of the judgment of Solomon about the child claimed by the two prostitutes emphasized in *Things Hidden*, the Jewish prefiguring also comes up in Girard's *Job: The Victim of his People*, trans. Yvonne Freccero (Stanford, CA: Stanford University Press, 1987).

113. *Things Hidden since the Foundation of the World*, 184–90, 195, 250, 259–60.

114. See René Girard, *I See Satan Fall like Lightning*, trans. with a foreword by James G. Williams (Maryknoll, NY: Orbis Books, 2001).

115. In *The Pillar of Fire* (Garden City, NY: Doubleday Image Books, 1959), Stern writes an open "Letter to My Brother" where he recalls "the story I have recited [earlier in the text] of the Rabbi who looks through the window at the announcement of the Messiah, and says, "I see no change" (253). In the earlier version, the rabbi, looking through the window, says, "With towns and villages of innocent people bombed, with millions of innocents thrown into machines of annihilation, it simply cannot be that there was a Messiah here on earth" (174).

116. See René Girard, "The Anthropology of the Cross: A Conversation with René Girard," in *The Girard Reader*, ed. James G. Williams (New York: Crossroad, 1996), 262–88.

117. See the works that are more emphatically on literary criticism: René Girard, *Deceit, Desire, and the Novel: Self and Other in Literary Structure*, trans. Yvonne Freccero (Baltimore: The Johns Hopkins University Press, 1965); *"To Double Business Bound": Essays on Literature, Mimesis, and Anthropology* (Baltimore: The Johns Hopkins University Press,

1978); *A Theater of Envy: William Shakespeare* (New York: Oxford University Press, 1991); *Resurrection from the Underground: Feodor Dostoevsky,* trans. and foreword by James G. Williams (New York: Crossroad, 1997).

118. Girard, "The Anthropology of the Cross," 283–87.

119. I asked Girard (at an opportunity to converse informally when he was the McCarthy Lecturer at Boston College) if the descriptions of the state of nature in Hobbes and Rousseau were not examples of the mimetic process exposed by him, and he agreed without hesitation that they were.

120. Blaise Pascal, *Pensées,* trans. A. J. Krailsheimer (London: Penguin Books, 1966), #118, p. 60: "Man's greatness even in his concupiscence. He has managed to produce such a remarkable system from it and make it the image of true charity."

121. See Raymond Schwager, *Brauchen wir einen Sündenbock? Gewalt und Erlösung in den biblischen Schriften* (Munich: Kösel Verlag, 1978); *Der wunderbare Tausch: Zur Geschichte und Deutung der Erlösungslehre* (Munich: Kösel Verlag, 1986); *Jesus im Heilsdrama. Entwurf einer biblischen Erlösungslehre,* Innsbrukcer theologische Studien 29 (Innsbruck: Tyrolia Verlaganstalt, 1990).

122. Paul Caringella and Robert Hamerton-Kelly conveyed this information on the last day of our colloquium at Stanford.

123. Girard, "The Anthropology of the Cross," 268.

124. As for Strauss, so for Girard, Nietzsche is a figure of utmost importance. See Girard, "Strategies of Madness—Nietzsche, Wagner, and Dostoevsky," in *"To Double Business Bound,"* 61–83; "The Founding Murder in the Philosophy of Nietzsche," in *Violence and Truth: On the work of René Girard,* ed. P. Dumouchel (Stanford, CA: Stanford University Press, 1988), 227–46; "The Twofold Nietzschean Heritage," in *I See Satan Fall like Lightning,* 170–92; "Nietzsche versus the Crucified," in *The Girard Reader,* 243–61.

125. See Girard, *Deceit, Desire, and the Novel.*

126. See Ludwig Ecker, *Zwischen Recht und Vergebung: Der Beitrag der Theorie René Girards zur Beschreibung christlicher Existenz* (Linz, Austria: Verlagsatelier Wagner, 1999), especially "I. Prologomena: Heuristischer Rahmen einer Theorie," 19–91.

Modernity and the Jewish Question

What Leo Strauss Learned from Nietzsche

John Ranieri
Seton Hall University, South Orange, New Jersey

With the exception of Plato, no thinker had a greater influence on Leo Strauss than Nietzsche. By Strauss's own admission, "Nietzsche so dominated and bewitched me between my 22nd and 30th years, that I literally believed everything that I understood of him."[1] Nor does this influence fade with time. In his final book, *Studies in Platonic Political Philosophy,* Strauss's essay on *Beyond Good and Evil* occupies a central place. References to Nietzsche occur with some frequency throughout Strauss's writings, often at critical junctures.[2] More often than not, Strauss speaks approvingly of Nietzsche, but he can also be sharp in his criticism. According to Strauss, "no one has ever spoken so greatly and so nobly of what a philosopher is as Nietzsche," and it is Nietzsche who "transformed the deadly truth of relativism into the most life-giving truth."[3] At the same time Strauss can accuse Nietzsche of preaching "the sacred right of 'merciless extinction' of large masses of men with as little restraint as his great antagonist [Marx] had done," and of using his "unsurpassable and inexhaustible power of passionate and fascinating speech" to prepare the way "for a regime, which, as long as it lasted, made discredited democracy look again like the golden age."[4] Nonetheless, Strauss is of the belief that while "there is an undeniable kinship between Nietzsche's thought and fascism," Nietzsche, unlike Heidegger, would not have thrown in his lot with National Socialism. In the end, Strauss sees Nietzsche's relationship to

Nazism as parallel to that of Rousseau's to the French Revolution; "by interpreting Nietzsche in the light of the German revolution, one is very unjust to Nietzsche, but one is not *absolutely* unjust."[5] Even when he is not mentioned explicitly, Nietzsche's spirit hovers over Strauss's explorations.

Nowhere is this more apparent than in Strauss's treatment of the "Jewish question" and its connection to the issue of the relationship between Athens and Jerusalem. This is not simply a matter of pointing out similarities between Nietzsche and Strauss as proof of influence. Certainly these similarities are present. But the evidence for Strauss's reliance on Nietzsche is stronger than this. First, there is Strauss's acknowledged indebtedness to Nietzsche. In addition there is the fact that at critical junctures in Strauss's works, Nietzsche's authority and insights are explicitly invoked. At the start of Strauss's academic career, Nietzsche helps him to articulate what is at stake in the Jewish question, and in Strauss's last work it is Nietzsche with whom he must come to terms as he considers the incompatible claims of Athens and Jerusalem.

To introduce the thought of René Girard into this discussion is to invite the criticism that we are coming to these questions from a perspective that has little or nothing to do with that of either Strauss or Nietzsche. By bringing Girard's insights to bear on Strauss and Nietzsche, are we not seeking to impose a framework that is alien to the overriding concerns of these philosophers? Are we engaging in a reductionism of the worst sort? To answer in the affirmative would be to largely ignore the relevant connections among these thinkers. First there is the fact that both Strauss and Girard acknowledge the importance of Nietzsche for contemporary thought. Both have written on Nietzsche and both take the religious problematic to be central to his work. Perhaps most significantly, what links the thought of Girard, Nietzsche, and Strauss is their profound attempt to come to terms with the meaning of the Bible. For Strauss, the Jewish question is inseparable from a consideration of the Bible's claims; hence the manner in which this text is interpreted has profound implications for how the question is answered. I believe Nietzsche's influence is apparent both in Strauss's treatment of the Jewish question and in his interpretation of the Bible. The central question then, is who best accounts for the biblical data. The encounter between Strauss, Nietzsche, and Girard concerns the meaning of the biblical tradition and its role in civilization. All three men agree that there is no more pressing question.

"I believe I can say, without any exaggeration, that since a very, very early time the main theme of my reflections has been what is called the 'Jewish question.'"[6] To those who know Strauss primarily as a political philosopher, this assertion may seem startling. Yet from his perspective, not only is there no conflict between his work as a political philosopher and his engagement with the Jewish question but the two areas are, in fact, directly connected. He writes in the preface to his book, *Spinoza's Critique of Religion*, "From every point of view it looks as if the Jewish people were the chosen people, at least in the sense that the Jewish problem is the most manifest symbol of the human problem insofar as it is a social or political problem."[7] For Strauss, the "Jewish *question*" is inseparable from what he describes as the "Jewish *problem*." And with uncharacteristic bluntness he further informs his readers that "There is no solution to the Jewish problem."[8] What, then, is this question/problem, and why is there no solution to it?

The Jewish problem arises because throughout history there have been those who hate Jews simply because they are Jews. Confronted with this hatred and the frequent persecution and violence that accompany it, some Jews fight back, hoping for triumph over their enemies or at the very least a courageous death. Another possibility is perpetual exile, in which, deprived of a Jewish homeland, they live as a separate people within the nations in which they find themselves, faithfully adhering to their ancestral traditions. Under the conditions of exile, Jewish suffering may fuse with Jewish identity, and come to be interpreted theologically, finding its ultimate meaning within God's final plan of redemption. Finally, Jews may submerge or abandon their identity and become one with the surrounding culture. This is the way of assimilation. In the Germany of Strauss's day, many Jews held out hope that the guaranteed rights and legal protections against discrimination offered by liberal democracy might offer a permanent solution to the Jewish problem. In Strauss's view, such hopes were sadly misplaced. Liberal democracy may prohibit public, legal, and governmental discrimination against Jews and other minorities, but a liberal state cannot prevent private, social discrimination without intruding into the lives of its citizens in a way that contradicts its own commitment to freedom.[9] To abolish all discrimination it would be necessary to do away with the distinction between the public and private spheres, and the corresponding intrusion of the state into all areas of human life would be a cure far worse than the disease it is meant to alleviate.

What, then, of the Zionist response to the Jewish problem? In the 1920s and early 1930s, Strauss was a committed political Zionist, but as sympathetic as he was to the goals of the movement, within a few years his intellectual honesty led him to judge both political and cultural Zionism to be inadequate in resolving the predicament of his people. Specifically, he faults Zionist ideology for avoiding the issue that is central to Jewish tradition—belief in an omnipotent God, "belief in the creation of the world, in the reality of biblical miracles, in the absolute obligation and the essential immutability of the Law as based on the revelation at Sinai."[10] From this perspective the avowed agnosticism or atheism of political Zionism makes it incapable of resolving the *Jewish* question. Further, the answers given by political Zionism remain within the horizon of modern political thought and thereby represent a falling away from Jewish tradition, a tradition firm in its belief that the solution to the plight of the Jews lies not in the human but in the divine will. In the midst of the debates in which he was actively involved, Strauss writes:

> Tradition, according to its meaning, excludes politics, that is, "politics" understood as a will sustained by the consciousness of responsibility for the existence and dignity of a people, whereby such existence is seen as depending on purely "natural" conditions, whether human or extra-human. . . . "Apolitical" may mean: lying on a different plane than politics, and it may also mean: excluding politics. Of course I only had the second meaning in mind when speaking of the apolitical character of the Jewish tradition.[11]

Already the tension between Athens and Jerusalem begins to emerge in Strauss's thought.

Strauss respects the honest atheism of political Zionism, yet he finds the attempt by cultural Zionism to mediate between political Zionism and Orthodoxy to be deeply unsatisfactory. In contrast to political Zionism, cultural Zionism appreciates the value of Jewish religion for Jewish identity; but in Strauss's view, cultural Zionism reduces biblical religion to an expression of the spirit of the Jewish people. In so doing it is entirely unfaithful to the self-understanding of Jewish tradition, in which believers understood themselves to be addressed by God; they certainly did not see their faith as an expression of their own genius. Strauss defends the right of the atheist to regard the religion of Israel as a human creation (in fact, as a conscientious atheist he is bound to do so)—what he objects to in cultural Zionism is the superficiality of the view that takes no cognizance of the fact that understanding Jewish faith as an expression of the genius of the Jewish people is a denial of God, and that such a denial is very much at odds with the tradition.[12] Unlike political Zionism, cultural Zionism is atheism in disguise.

We are left, then, with a dilemma:

> The foundation, the authoritative layer, of the Jewish heritage presents itself, not as a product of the human mind, but as a divine gift, as a divine

> revelation. . . . When cultural Zionism understands itself, it turns into religious Zionism. But when religious Zionism understands itself, it is in the first place Jewish faith and only secondarily Zionism. It must regard as blasphemous the notion of a human solution to the Jewish problem.[13]

Neither political nor cultural Zionism can solve the Jewish problem. Both have been severely compromised by their acceptance of many of the premises of modern thought, whether in the form of political ideology or the presuppositions of a modern biblical science whose critique empties the tradition of the reality of God and undermines belief in the miraculous. A result of this modern critique has been to make return to Orthodoxy much more difficult for many Jews who have imbibed the spirit of modern culture. But even if that were not the case, the acceptance of Orthodoxy represents, for Strauss, a decision to reject the political as a means to normalize Jewish life. If, instead, Jews go the route of modern politics in an attempt to solve the Jewish problem, they threaten their identity as a people by accepting the ways of the modern nations. This is seen clearly in the effects of assimilation. What, then, are Jews to do when the choice before them seems to be preservation of their identity under conditions of permanent exile and persecution, or the normalization of Jewish existence at the expense of their distinctiveness as a people?

The problem is further complicated by the fact that the question is formulated within a context that, in Strauss's view, is already distorted by the influence of modernity. The Enlightenment critique of religion has "undermined the foundation of the Jewish tradition."[14] Reacting to this critique, some modern Jewish thinkers (e.g., Moses Mendelssohn) try to mediate "between orthodoxy and radical enlightenment," and when that proves unsuccessful the next generation (Cohen, Rosenzweig, Buber) tries to move beyond the level on which the battle has been previously fought, in order to achieve a higher synthesis of Enlightenment and Orthodoxy.[15] In both cases, Strauss detects a capitulation to modern thought, and, in the latter case in particular, an "internalization" of basic "external" claims concerning creation and miracles that is essentially a disavowal of Jewish tradition. To begin to seriously move toward a proper understanding of that tradition, modernity must be transcended. This will not be easy, because in the contemporary situation, those who would understand tradition must ascend from not one but two caves. The modern horizon constitutes a second, "unnatural" cave from which we need to be released before we can reach the level of the "natural" cave described by Plato: "To use the classical presentation of the natural difficulties of philosophizing, namely Plato's parable of the cave, one may say that today we find ourselves in a second, much deeper cave than the lucky ignorant ones Socrates dealt with"[16] How is it that we find ourselves in this second cave? Strauss notes: "the difficulty of doing philosophy is fundamentally increased, and the *freedom* of doing philosophy is fundamentally reduced, by the fact that a revelation-based tradition has stepped into the world of philosophy."[17] At first glance it might appear as if Judaism itself, as a "revelation-based tradition," is included in this charge. If so, it would make little sense for Strauss to attempt to return to a Jewish tradition that is itself constitutive of the second cave from which modern humanity needs to ascend. But to understand Strauss's point we must note his reference to a revelation-based tradition that has "stepped into the world of philosophy." For Strauss, that tradition is Christianity, not Judaism. Historically in Judaism, philosophy's status has been more precarious, because it remains in permanent tension with the Law, but Christianity, by integrating philosophy with the study of theology, also hampered philosophy's freedom.[18] Subjecting philosophy to a higher control, Christianity creates an artificial, "unnatural" condition for thought. When modern thinkers react against this control, they do so in a context that is different from that of their Greek forbears:

> In order to make philosophizing possible in its naturally difficult state, the artificial complication of philosophizing must be removed; one must fight against prejudices. Herein lies a fundamental difference between modern and Greek philosophy: whereas the latter only fights against appearance and opinion, modern philosophy begins by fighting against prejudices. Hence, in this respect, the Enlightenment wants to restore Greek freedom.[19]

In Strauss's narrative, modern philosophy, in attempting to overthrow prejudice, is only partially successful. In the course of its struggle it becomes more entangled in the tradition it seeks to overcome.[20] This entanglement is not surprising, since for Strauss, modernity is in many ways a child of Christianity and of prophetic, messianic Judaism.[21] Despite the harshness of their criticism of Christianity, Strauss finds that many important modern thinkers (including Nietzsche) remain influenced by the very tradition they attack. Thus the modern critique of "prejudice," while largely directed against the doctrines of the Christian churches, has also infected Judaism:

> That this critique made an impact on the Jewish context is illustrated historically by the fact that the Jewish tradition, insofar as it was not able to reconstruct itself with regard to this critique, succumbed to Europe's attack.

> Herein lies the decisive cause of what is known as assimilation, which therefore is Jewishly legitimate from this perspective. . . . [The] result of the critique in question is the limitation it puts on the claim to validity of tradition.[22]

By succumbing to "Europe's attack" and by allowing themselves to be affected by Enlightenment polemics, Jewish thinkers have unwittingly gotten embroiled in what is in some sense an internecine Christian quarrel.

The Jewish problem is indeed a serious one, and it compels Strauss to raise the question of "how the people is to live from now on."[23] Here we get a glimpse of the direction in which Strauss's thought will move, as the question of how *this* people is to live opens up onto the more general question of the best way to live, the *political* question. It also becomes increasingly clear why, for Strauss, "the Jewish problem is the most manifest symbol of the human problem insofar as it is a social or political problem." The Jewish people's struggle to preserve its identity in the midst of the onslaught of modernity is paradigmatic for all modern people. To deny one's identity, as the price to be paid for political and social acceptance, is to consent to one's loss of existence as a people, calling into question the very purpose of the political. The experience of modern Jews illustrates this dilemma profoundly. At a time when unbelief has permeated the fabric of Western civilization, including Jewish life, what can it mean to speak of Jewish identity, an identity traditionally understood as constituted by belief? With regard to this question, one thing at least is clear to Strauss: "It is impossible not to remain a Jew. It is impossible to run away from one's origins. . . . it is impossible to get rid of one's past."[24] But what does this mean in a context in which the only alternatives appear to be "orthodoxy or Enlightenment"? Strauss is perhaps thinking of himself when he writes:

> The present situation appears to be insoluble for the Jew who cannot be orthodox and who must consider purely political Zionism, the only "solution of the Jewish problem" possible on the basis of atheism, as a resolution that is indeed highly honorable but not, in earnest and in the long run, adequate. This situation not only appears insoluble but actually is so, as long as one clings to the modern premises.[25]

Strauss's task is to transcend the "modern premises" that distort Jewish tradition and to begin to emerge from the second cave in which modern men and women are trapped. To do this requires a more radical attempt than has previously been undertaken to shake off the influences that ensnare Jewish intellectual life and dilute Jewish identity:

> One simply cannot absorb somewhat deeper German things without absorbing along with them, among other things, a dose of specifically Christian spirit. Further, it should be kept in mind that the internal Jewish reaction to liberalism availed itself, entirely as a matter of course, of the weapons that Christian Europe had forged, during the period of restoration and even prior to it, against the spirit of the Enlightenment. Thus we see ourselves held fast on all sides in the German-Jewish world in which we have grown up spiritually. . . . it is imperative to get out of this world "*somehow*."[26]

This is quite an undertaking for "a young Jew born and raised in Germany who found himself in the grip of the theologico-political predicament," an undertaking that might be less daunting if there was someone to lead the way. Strauss finds just such a guide in Nietzsche:

> Through Nietzsche, tradition has been shaken to its roots. It has completely lost its self-evident truth. We are left in a world without any authority, any direction. Only now has the question *pous bioteon* [How are we to live?] again received its full edge. We can pose it again. We have the possibility of posing it in earnest. . . . But we cannot immediately answer on our own, for we know that we are deeply entangled in a tradition: we are even much lower down than the cave dwellers of Plato. We must rise to the origin of tradition, to the level of natural ignorance.[27]

It is from Nietzsche, "a man who stood at the opposite pole of all obscurantism and fundamentalism,"[28] that Strauss learns how to "to plumb the pre-'Christian' depths of the Jewish as well as of the Hellenic-European spirit."[29] In Nietzsche's thought, Strauss finds exhilarating possibilities for gaining access to the origins of culture, free of modern, Christianized influences.

This investigation of origins owes a great deal to Nietzsche's insight into the relativizing effects of historicism:

> According to Nietzsche, the theoretical analysis of human life that realizes the relativity of all comprehensive views and thus depreciates them would make human life itself impossible, for it would destroy the protecting atmosphere within which life or culture or action is alone possible. Moreover, since the theoretical analysis has its basis outside of life, it will never be able

> to understand life. The theoretical analysis of life is noncommittal and fatal to commitment, but life means commitment.[30]

Nietzsche writes of the "universal law" that "a living thing can be healthy, strong, and fruitful only when bounded by a horizon."[31] Strauss echoes Nietzsche's insight:

> [One] cannot behold, i.e., truly understand, any culture unless one is firmly rooted in one's own culture or unless one belongs in one's capacity as a beholder to some culture.[32]

For Strauss, Nietzsche's observations bear directly on the Jewish question, since they address in the most fundamental fashion the issue of what it means to be a people. Nietzsche "shows us that culture is possible only if men are fully dedicated to principles of thought and action which they do not and cannot question, which limit their horizon and thus enable them to have a character and a style."[33] Of course Nietzsche is well aware that this sort of blind dedication to the values of one's culture is problematic for "men of intellectual probity," who understand the relativistic consequences of historical thinking and who cannot, as a result, willfully ignore its lessons. Whether or not Nietzsche successfully overcomes this tension, Strauss believes that no one (except himself, perhaps) better articulates the direction in which a solution is to be found:

> The different values respected in different epochs had no objective support, i.e., they were human creations; they owed their being to a free human project that formed the horizon within which a culture was possible. What man did in the past unconsciously and under the delusion of submitting to what is independent of his creative act, he must now do consciously. . . . It is in this way that Nietzsche may be said to have transformed the deadly truth of relativism into the most life-giving truth. . . . We can do no more than allude here to the difficulties in which Nietzsche became involved in trying to overcome the difficulties that afflict his solution. . . . We limit ourselves here to saying that the movement of Nietzsche's thought can be understood as a movement from the supremacy of history towards the supremacy of nature, a movement that bypasses the supremacy of reason throughout or tries to replace the opposition between the subjective and the objective (or between the conventional and the natural) by the opposition between the superficial and the profound.[34]

Those familiar with Strauss's work will recognize how much "the movement of Nietzsche's thought" resembles the movement of Strauss's own thought. No issue is more important to Strauss than the recovery of "nature" in the face of historicism. An equally strong case can be made that Strauss's philosophy takes the opposition between the superficial and the profound as a central focus. Even where he and Nietzsche appear to diverge, that is, over the "supremacy of reason," we must keep in mind how Strauss's final word on Nietzsche could well be viewed as an attempt to bring the seemingly "irrational" Nietzsche much closer to the rationalism of Plato.[35] Finally, Strauss shares with Nietzsche the view that too much history is not a good thing, and that in order to be strong and healthy, a people must be confident in the rightness of the principles that constitute its horizon and give character to the "regime."[36]

In summary, Strauss finds in Nietzsche someone who reveres the genius of the particular, while simultaneously looking forward to a broader culture of excellence that does not suffer from the modern defects of leveling and homogenization. Nietzsche shows the way out of the second, deeper cave and he anticipates a culture beyond the first cave as well. For Strauss, Nietzsche is a "beholder" of cultures who raises the question of what the multiplicity of cultures could mean in light of humanity's as yet unrealized goal. Strauss cites the chapter "On the Thousand and One Goals" from *Zarathustra* and observes how "Nietzsche has a deeper reverence than any other beholder for the sacred tables of the Hebrews as well as of the other nations in question."[37] It is scarcely possible to disentangle Strauss's handling of the Jewish question from the influence of Nietzsche; especially since the years in which the question takes shape in Strauss's work largely coincide with the period during which he admits to having believed everything he read of the German philosopher. It is not the case that Strauss has a clearly formulated conception of the Jewish question and then encounters Nietzsche. Nietzsche is present in the very formulation of the question.[38]

There is a sense in which all the important themes of Strauss's later work emerge from his engagement with Nietzsche. Through his critique of Western tradition, Nietzsche clears the way for its reconstruction. In doing so he attempts to dissolve the accumulated accretions of modernity. As part of this project he levels a scathing attack against Christianity, which he believes has played a crucial role in forming the cultural, political, social, and moral horizon of modernity. Given Strauss's own concern that in imbibing "German things," Jews also absorb "a dose of specifically Christian spirit," who better to learn from than a thinker whose disgust with things German and things

Christian could not be more emphatic? In addition, by both acknowledging and challenging the hold of historicism, Nietzsche opens the possibility for a recovery of "nature." This movement of Nietzsche's thought from the "supremacy of history" to the "supremacy of nature" will inspire Strauss's own consideration of "nature" in classical philosophy. Perhaps most paradoxically, Nietzsche offers what Strauss will refer to as "an atheistic vindication of God." For those like Strauss who find it difficult to believe, yet remain convinced of the centrality of the religious question for Jewish tradition, Nietzsche's achievement is of crucial importance. Finally there is the fact that while Nietzsche despises Christianity and those aspects of Judaism conducive to slave morality, he admires much in the Old Testament and has a profound respect for the Jewish people.

To better appreciate the influence of Nietzsche on Strauss, a brief synopsis of Nietzsche's attitude toward the Bible may be helpful. For Nietzsche, "God" can often be a people's highest and most exalted creation. Conceptions of God reflect the strength or weakness of their creators. A strong, vibrant people has a correspondingly powerful and awe-inspiring God; while a slavish people worships a compassionate deity (who is anything but compassionate toward the people's enemies). In the case of the Old Testament, Nietzsche praises the Yahweh who is a reflection of the Hebrews' vitality and warlike spirit.[39] When Israel succumbs to internal dissension and external enemies, its triumphant God should disappear as well; instead, under the unfortunate influence of priests and prophets, Israel's glorious past is reinterpreted as sinful defection from the divine will, deserving of punishment by a God whose honor has been offended. A preoccupation with sin, guilt, repentance, and salvation now dominates the imagination of the Jewish people.[40] Christianity carries these Jewish tendencies to their logical conclusion. The movement from the original God of the Hebrews to the Christian God is one of sad decline. Consequently, the greatest sin ever committed by literary Europe is to have ignored this difference and to have joined the New Testament to the Hebrew Scriptures in the creation of the Bible.[41] It must be emphasized, though, that the story Nietzsche tells about the Bible and its protagonists is not a simple dichotomy between Old and New Testaments. Rather, there are two trajectories. One is that of ascending, powerful life, captured in the inspiring tales of Israel's victories and the God who made them possible. The other also begins in the Old Testament, but it is the story of declining life, reflected first in Israel's prophetic and priestly traditions, and reaching its nadir in the Christian gospel. As always for Nietzsche, the dividing line is based on the separation between that which serves or heightens life and that which weakens. This schema also governs Nietzsche's attitude to the history of the Jewish people. He complements his well-known criticism of the Jews as the originators of the slave revolt in morality with high regard for their tenacity, creativity, and ability to endure suffering. In the Europe to come, Nietzsche finds it difficult to overestimate the contribution to be made by this people which has been strengthened and steeled by centuries of persecution.[42] And despite having given birth to Christianity, Jews are also responsible for keeping alive the spirit of enlightenment and intellectual independence, especially during the Middle Ages, when the philosophical culture of the classical world was in danger of being completely Christianized.[43]

The impact of Nietzsche's narrative is apparent throughout Strauss's interpretation of Jewish tradition. With Nietzsche he shares the belief that a people's god(s) tells us much about that people's character and abilities:

> A nation is a nation by virtue of what it looks up to. In antiquity, a nation was a nation by virtue of its looking up to its gods. They did not have ideologies at that time; they did not have even ideas at that time. At the top, there were the gods. And now, our ancestors asserted *a priori*—that is to say, without looking at any of these gods—that these gods were nothings and abominations.[44]

Strauss's attitude here mirrors Nietzsche's claim that, real or not, "God" is "the holiest and mightiest of all that the world has yet owned."[45] In a 1925 review in *Judische Rundschau* of Simon Dubnow's *World History of the Jewish People*, Strauss comments:

> For example, "zeal for God" is, objectively speaking, quite an essential factor in the morale of an army, and thus of its strength, regardless of whether God exists and helps or does not. . . . the biblical sources themselves give us the possibility of arriving at a—perhaps not deep, but nevertheless accurate—conception of the beginnings of our people.[46]

In fact, Strauss characterizes Judaism as a "heroic delusion," while simultaneously expressing tremendous reverence for belief in the God who is its highest ideal and inspiration.[47] Despite his rationalist bent, Strauss, like Nietzsche, is far more concerned with the religious meaning of "God" than in philosophical proofs for God's existence. For both men, the God question runs deeper than the reach of philosophy. Strauss the rational, Platonic political philosopher can no more put aside the religious question than can Nietzsche. In their minds, "God," however conceived, has called forth some of the noblest, most self-sacrificing, and most heroic behavior in human history. Strauss considers this tremendously important in constituting Jewish identity:

> But suffering indeed, heroic suffering, suffering stemming from the heroic act of self-dedication of a whole nation to something which it regarded as infinitely higher than itself—in fact, which it regarded as the infinitely highest. No Jew can do anything better for himself today than to live in remembering this past.[48]

The Jewish past evoked by Strauss is a valorized past reminiscent of the strong-willed people of the Old Testament so admired by Nietzsche. It is a history of suffering, but it is not a history of *redemptive* suffering. Instead, Strauss consistently emphasizes the heroic virtue of the Jews in withstanding their persecutors, even when this resistance is met with defeat.[49] Strauss approves of Theodor Herzl's insight that "We are a nation—the enemy makes us a nation whether we like it or not" and "the enemy is necessary for the highest effort of the personality."[50] Elsewhere Strauss explains:

> On the premise of assimilationism, Jewish suffering—suffering for Judaism—becomes meaningless. That suffering is merely the residue of a benighted past, a residue which will cease in proportion as mankind makes further progress. . . . Our ancestors had been immune to hatred and contempt because it merely proved to them the election of Israel. The uprooted assimilated Jew had nothing to oppose to hatred and contempt except his naked self. Full social equality proved to require the complete disappearance of the Jews as Jews—a proposition which is impracticable, if for no other reason, then at least for the perfectly sufficient one of simple self-respect.[51]

In a generally critical review of Simon Dubnow's *Contemporary History of the Jewish People,* Strauss makes the following observation:

> There is, however, one viewpoint that justifies the structure of Dubnow's work, a linear enumeration of mostly very sad encounters of the Jewish people. The detailed portrayal, inspired by strong feelings, of the suffering of the Russian, Polish, and Romanian Jews has intrinsic value: as *martyrology.* No one should contest its importance. This is so because, first, it has the vital function of keeping alive in us the deep hatred that facilitates our

> existence in this world of hatred, and that takes for us the place of an army and of fortresses; and because, second, it is the cognitive preservation of an essential form of the life of our people, namely suffering as such.[52]

Strauss comes remarkably close to Nietzsche in this passage, in his understanding of the role of hatred in preserving and even heightening the existence of a people.[53] In the following passage from *Daybreak*, which Strauss knows well (and as we shall see shortly, cites approvingly), Nietzsche says of the Jewish people:

> Every Jew possesses in the history of his fathers and grandfathers a great fund of examples of the coldest self-possession and endurance in fearful situations, of the subtlest outwitting and exploitation of chance and misfortune; their courage beneath the cloak of miserable submission, their heroism in *spernere se sperni* [despising that one is despised], surpasses the virtues of all the saints. For two millennia an attempt was made to render them contemptible by treating them with contempt. . . . They themselves have never ceased to believe themselves called to the highest things, and the virtues which pertain to all who suffer have likewise never ceased to adorn them. The way in which they honor their fathers and their children, the rationality of their marriages and their marriage customs, distinguish them among all Europeans. In addition to all this, they have known how to create for themselves a feeling of power and of eternal revenge out of the very occupations left to them. . . . For our respect for ourselves is tied to being able to practice requital, in good things and in bad. At the same time however, their revenge does not easily go too far: for they all possess the liberality, including liberality of soul, to which frequent changes of residence, of climate, of the customs of one's neighbours and oppressors educates men; they possess by far the greatest experience of human society, and even in their passions they practice the caution taught by this experience.[54]

Nietzsche's attitude toward the Jews is a controversial topic that cannot be adequately discussed here. While many absolve him of any trace of anti-Semitism, I believe Nietzsche's attitude toward the Jewish people is more ambivalent. Although he stands out positively when compared to the more virulent anti-Semites of his day, he still makes use of offensive stereotypes about Jews even when he is praising them. A number of passages could be quoted (including the one just cited) to support this view. My point, however, is not to determine whether Nietzsche was anti-Semitic, but to highlight the similarities between him and Strauss on this matter. It certainly says something about the depth of Nietzsche's influence on Strauss at the time that Strauss is able to largely agree with Nietzsche's description of the Jews without giving the slightest indication that Nietzsche may be reflecting anti-Jewish stereotypes. At least in his early years, Strauss seems to be entirely under Nietzsche's spell.

Nietzsche's effect on Strauss is apparent in other ways as well. Whether he is speaking directly about Jewish suffering or not, the accent in Strauss's telling of Jewish history most often falls on examples of the very Nietzschean virtues of struggle and self-overcoming. Addressing a predominantly Jewish audience Strauss asks:

> Why should we, who have a heroic past behind and within us, which is not second to that of any other group anywhere on earth, deny or forget that past? That past is all the more heroic, one could say, since its chief characters are not the glitter and trappings of martial glory and of cultural splendor, although it does not lack even these. Assimilation proved to require inner enslavement as the price of external freedom. Or to put it somewhat differently, assimilation seemed to land the Jews into the bog of philistinism, of shallow satisfaction with the most unsatisfactory present—a most inglorious end for a people which had been led out of the house of bondage into the desert with careful avoidance of the land of the Philistines.[55]

The main threat to Jewish existence would seem to be a capitulation to the shallowness of their environment; a temptation to which Jews have not succumbed in their finest hours. Strauss echoes Nietzsche's indictment of the modern world for its superficiality, its flabbiness, and its lack of aspiration. Rather than interpreting the avoidance of the Philistines as a moving away from the idolatry and violence of a sacrificial system, Strauss makes use of this incident to express a Nietzschean disgust with mediocrity.

In some instances the connection to Nietzsche is quite explicit. This is especially clear in Strauss's comments on the just cited passage from *Daybreak* in which Nietzsche speaks of the role that Jews might one day play in Europe.[56] Strauss is tremendously impressed by Nietzsche's analysis:

> This is the most profound and most radical statement on assimilation which I have read. It does not lose any of its significance by the fact that Nietzsche has not written without irony. In other words, he had no hopes in this respect; he only thought something through. Assimilation cannot mean

> abandoning the inheritance, but only giving it another direction, transforming it. And assimilation cannot be an end, it could only be a way toward that. Assimilation is an intermediate stage in which it means distinguishing oneself in pursuits which are not as such Jewish, but, as Nietzsche would say, European, or as we would say, Western.[57]

Assimilation is acceptable to Strauss only if it is a matter of Jews drawing upon their own distinctive experience and heritage to set an example of excellence for Western civilization. Jewish struggle, endurance, and overcoming have formed a people capable of employing their own strength in the service of an overall elevation of culture—an elevation sorely needed in a modern world understood by both Nietzsche and Strauss as thoroughly mediocre. The recovery of Jewish particularity is a first step in a lengthy process of civilizational renewal to which Jews, making use of the energy and passion they have accumulated over the centuries, can make a signal contribution. As Strauss points out, though, this assimilation of Jews to Western civilization is not the final goal. The preservation of Jewish distinctiveness is essential if Western civilization is to preserve its life-giving tension between Athens and Jerusalem. Again Strauss underlines the inseparability of the particular, the Jewish question, from the wider political question of how we ought to live. For according to Nietzsche, it is the ancient Jewish God in whom all who prize human achievement will rejoice.

At the same time, Strauss's comments point to a possible source of tension in his thought, a tension that may be a consequence of his indebtedness to Nietzsche. In extolling the virtues of the Jewish people, Strauss appears to follow Nietzsche's agonistic rendering of Jewish experience with its emphasis on suffering, struggle, and triumph over one's persecutors, however spiritually conceived. Strauss is too careful a thinker to have lightly chosen the word "heroic" to describe the Jewish past. Like Nietzsche, he highlights those aspects of Jewish experience in which the Jews are brought closest to the Greeks. Elsewhere he accuses Freud of a "supreme act of assimilation" in depicting the relationship of Moses to the Jews as analogous to that of Jesus and the Gentiles;[58] but is it not the case that Strauss's own account assimilates Jewish experience to the ways of the Greeks as mediated through Nietzsche?

Assimilation in the highest sense as articulated by Nietzsche is not to be confused with the actual assimilation of Jews in the modern world. Distressed by the mediocrity around him, Strauss casts aside his usual restraint and launches into a harangue that would make Nietzsche proud:

> There exists a kind of Jewish glorification of every clever or brilliant Jewish mediocrity, which is as pitiable as it is laughable. It reminds one of the villagers who have produced their first physicist, and hail him for this reason as the greatest physicist that ever was. . . . [This] inclination to self-glorification, in things in which there is no reason for self-glorification, is a disgrace. That today we have so many outstanding Jews is due (let us not deceive ourselves about that) to the general decline, to a general victory of mediocrity. It is today very easy to be a great man.[59]

In a post-Holocaust world, assimilation is the greatest threat to Jewish identity, and Strauss seeks to strengthen his people's sense of distinctiveness and excellence. Following Nietzsche, he insists on the need for a serious horizon within which a people can test their mettle. If the Jewish community is to avoid being dissolved into liberal modernity, Jews must recover a deep sense of themselves as a people.

With this in mind, Strauss consistently downplays the universalizing tendencies within Jewish tradition. The ancient Jewish world is a closed world, one that has been destroyed by the advent of modernity.[60] Regarding Nietzsche as "the most reverent beholder of the tablets of the Hebrews," Strauss agrees with him in viewing an essential part of the specifically Hebraic genius as the veneration accorded the ancestral, and the emphasis on the law of the ancestors as an expression of the divine will.[61] Rejecting what he views as the "softening" of Judaism in neo-Orthodoxy, Strauss argues that the greatness of the tradition consists in its "rigidity."[62] The Greeks, when confronted with the multiplicity of divine codes and their manifest contradictions, pursue the way of philosophical inquiry into the fundamental principles of reality, and transcend the difficulty in the direction of abandoning the notion of a particular divine law. By contrast, the answer given by the Bible is that there is but one truly divine code, that given by God to Israel. Such an assertion, Strauss believes, entails a corresponding type of God—a creator God who is omnipotent, uncontrollable, and mysterious.[63] Strauss does not deny the important role played by notions of God's justice, mercy, and love in the biblical tradition, but he places much greater weight on God as inscrutable will and power. The biblical deity as depicted by Strauss well illustrates Nietzsche's statement that "there is no other alternative for gods: either they are the will to power, and they remain a people's gods, *or* the incapacity for power, and then they necessarily become *good*.[64] Discussing Nietzsche in a letter to Karl Lowith, Strauss remarks how the philosopher "had to wean us and himself from millennia-old pampering (softening) due to belief in creation and providence."[65] Given that Strauss acknowledges the centrality of the doctrines of creation and providence within Judaism, we can only wonder what a Judaism would look like if it held to these beliefs while resisting their "softening" effects. Strauss provides his readers with more than a hint. Power, will, heroic struggle, and a commitment to values that contribute to self-overcoming—essentially Nietzschean ideas—are the words that recur most frequently in Strauss's depiction of the Jewish people and their God. There is both Nietzschean nobility and Nietzschean hardness in his account of Jewish history. That history presents the Jewish people with the greatest challenge–either assimilation or the embrace of their unique identity. Strauss takes pride in the accomplishment of his people in establishing a Jewish homeland; a place where Jews live lives of "heroic austerity supported by the nearness of biblical antiquity."[66]

A heroic, long-suffering people serving a majestic, inscrutable God in obedience to the Law—these are the salient features in Strauss's account of biblical Judaism. There is also a noticeable neglect of the prophetic-messianic strain in the Bible. This seems to be due in part to Strauss's association of these tendencies with modern notions of universalism and progress. In "On the Argument with European Science," written during the height of his Zionist phase, Strauss asks:

> What right do we have to endanger our so fragile Jewish cohesion even further by troubling a Jewish public with comments on works that belong entirely to a European context (even though some of their authors may happen accidentally to be Jewish)? . . . Moreover, if some European fact is of European significance, it does not follow that it concerns any of us in any way as Jews, unless, of course, one shares the view of "Jewish universalism" held by a certain liberalism.[67]

Elsewhere Strauss criticizes Albert Levkowitz for maintaining that Jewish involvement in modern culture "derives from the classical universalism of Judaism."[68] Strauss also rejects Hermann Cohen's claim that the patriotism of the prophets is at bottom nothing but universalism.[69] From Strauss's perspective, Cohen naively blends Israelite prophecy with modern humanitarianism.[70] As Strauss understands the situation of contemporary Jews, "a certain liberalism" in conjunction with a vague humanitarianism has infected Jewish self-understanding and led to a misinterpretation of Jewish tradition. He does not consider that Cohen may be in fact closer to the core of Jewish tradition than Strauss himself, to the extent that Cohen grasps the importance of the prophets' anti-sacrificial, anti-mythological message and its relationship to modern efforts on behalf of victims.

Strauss is equally critical of attempts to link Judaism to modern notions of progress. In response to the question of whether the messianic hope for redemption indicates a higher regard for the future than for the past, however venerable, Strauss says that "according to the most accepted view, the Messiah is inferior to Moses."[71] The messianic future will in fact be a return to the past, to the full practice of the Torah. In "Progress or Return?" Strauss further specifies what he means: "Judaism is a concern with return; it is not a concern with progress. 'Return' can easily be expressed in biblical Hebrew; 'progress' cannot."[72] For Strauss, the notion of return presupposes the Bible's affirmation of a perfect beginning from which humankind declines, whereas the idea of progress looks back to a barbarous beginning, which humankind will overcome through its own efforts. Here Strauss's omissions are as telling as his examples. For someone concerned to understand the roots of tradition, it is noteworthy that he focuses only on the early chapters of Genesis. If the goal is to get back to the most primordial layers of Jewish self-understanding, why not begin with the liberating events of the Exodus, events considered to be constitutive of Israel's existence as a people? By establishing the contrast as he does between a biblical teaching of a perfect beginning (with "return" as the authentic response) and a modern, progressive view of the past as disorder and imperfection, Strauss diverts our attention from the fact that the position he labels progressive has an equal or perhaps even superior claim to a biblical lineage. Taking the Exodus as a paradigm, we find that in the beginning there was the house of bondage, the place of oppression, and that history, as redeemed by God, is a movement away from this condition toward a future of peace and well-being.[73] Certainly Girard's work makes us suspicious of "perfect beginnings" and reminds us of how the Bible illuminates the connection between victimization and origins. The direct line from the paradigmatic liberation depicted in Exodus to the modern concern for victims that underpins much of "progressive" politics is a dimension of the biblical story that Strauss, for the most part, disregards.

The relationship between Jewish tradition and modernity poses a problem for Strauss. The basis of his criticism of other modern Jewish thinkers is their insufficient break with the presuppositions of modern thought in appropriating their tradition. At the same time, Strauss understands modernity to be in certain respects a triumph of the biblical orientation, however much he may downplay these elements.[74] Modern Jewish thinkers interpret Judaism through a lens fashioned by modernity, but a modernity that is to some degree the child of the tradition being interpreted. Strauss seeks a way to escape this interpretive circle, and he finds an ally in Nietzsche. At this point it may be useful to recall Nietzsche's interpretation of Jewish history and his identification of its two trajectories—one representing ascending life, for example, the triumphant, self-confident nation that was ancient Israel and the persecuted yet tenacious people whose fire-tested strength is the hope of Western civilization; and the other epitomizing the destructive effects of slave morality in the forms of priestly Judaism and Christianity. Strauss develops a similar narrative: one that distinguishes between an earlier Jewish tradition distorted by modern interpreters, and the later emergence of prophetic-messianic movements. In this fashion he can argue that he is engaged in an attempt to get back to the origins of the tradition, while relegating to a secondary position those parts of the heritage he views as having contributed to the development of modernity. The question remains whether Strauss actually reaches a primordial Jewish tradition, or whether he is in fact reconstructing a tradition with the aid of tools and models supplied by Nietzsche.

Through Nietzsche, "tradition has been shaken to its roots," "it has lost its self-evident truth," and "we are left in this world without any authority, any direction." This condition opens up the most astonishing possibilities:

> We can no longer read Plato's dialogues superficially only to puzzle over how much old Plato knew about such and such; we can no longer superficially polemicize against him. Similarly with the Bible: we no longer self-evidently agree with the prophets; we ask ourselves seriously whether perhaps the kings were right. We must really begin from the very beginning. . . . tradition is utterly alien to us, utterly questionable.[75]

Any doubt as to the seriousness with which Strauss accepts Nietzsche's challenge is dispelled by this passage. To suggest the possibility that the biblical kings were right and the prophets mistaken is to move beyond the question of the relative importance of the Law and the prophets; it is, rather, an attempt to call into question the centrality of the prophetic impulse in Judaism, an impulse that, by almost any measure, is one of the constitutive elements of biblical tradition. To claim that tradition is "utterly alien to us, utterly questionable" and to say that the tradition has lost its self-evident truth is to radicalize the quest for origins. Strauss's "recovery" of the tradition is, in fact, closer to a re-creation of the tradition, a "revaluation of values." He should be taken at his word when he says we are now "without any authority, any direction." In the spirit of Nietzsche's genealogical method, Strauss is essentially deconstructing tradition in order to reconstitute it in a fashion that better accords with the exigencies of the political. The tradition thus reconstructed will be one that accords with Strauss's political philosophy, one that is compatible with the requirements of political life as he understands them. The distinctively biblical disappears, canceled out by arguments in the service of a greater "political responsibility." In some instances this will mean rendering the Bible harmless by pointing out its apolitical nature; in other cases it will involve highlighting the tension between Athens and Jerusalem; and at times it will be a matter of approximating the biblical tradition to classical philosophy. The Bible no longer serves to unmask the scapegoating that is so frequently a part of politics; instead, the biblical perspective is judged according to the requirements of political life:

> [The] theological conception of these beginnings may derive from a time in which there was no longer any political life, and therefore also no longer any political understanding. The most topical consequences depend on this. If, for example, the establishment of the kingdom under Saul was stylized as an apostasy only later, that is, in the exile; if, as the sources permit to shine through, what originally impelled the establishment of the kingdom was self-evident and elementary needs rather than the theatricality of some hysterical intoxication with normality; if the later stylization was indeed the effect of prophecy, but the effect of prophecy on a people weaned of political responsibility, then the opponents of our political Zionism, who fight us by an appeal to tradition, do not have such an easy position to defend.[76]

Written in 1925, well before his intensive study of classical political philosophy, this passage indirectly points to the major themes of Strauss's later work. In the writings of the classical thinkers, Strauss discovers a kind of moderation well-suited to the "self-evident and elementary" needs of political existence, a moderation he finds lacking in the prophetic strains of biblical thought. In addressing the Jewish question, the tension between Athens and Jerusalem comes into focus.

Ultimately Strauss comes to the Jewish question in light of his appropriation of Nietzsche's doctrines of the will to power and the eternal return. His most significant discussion of these doctrines occurs in his late essay, "Note on the Plan of Nietzsche's *Beyond Good and Evil*," which is included in *Studies in Platonic Philosophy*. Strauss deliberately chose the selections and the order for the book, which as it stands, consists of 15 chapters. He did not live to complete a proposed essay on Plato's *Gorgias* (intended as the fourth chapter), nor was he able to write the introduction to the work. An illuminating introduction has been added to the book, and the author of this introduction, Thomas Pangle, underlines the coherence of the work and the importance Strauss gives to the sequence of its chapters.[77] With this in mind, a good case can be made for the centrality of Nietzsche in *Studies in Platonic Philosophy*. The Nietzsche essay follows the chapter entitled "Jerusalem and Athens: Some Preliminary Reflections." Had Strauss completed the *Gorgias* essay, the "Jerusalem and Athens" chapter and the Nietzsche chapter would occupy chapters 8 and 9, the very center of the book. In itself, this juxtaposition would be significant, but the relationship between the two chapters is more complex than this. In "Jerusalem and Athens," the first thinker Strauss mentions is Nietzsche. Nietzsche is introduced as an exemplary figure for his handling of the implications of historicism, and as an unsurpassed "beholder of the tablets of the Hebrews." The remainder of the first part of the essay is taken up with Strauss's exegesis of the first several chapters of Genesis. The second part of "Jerusalem and Athens," titled "On Socrates and the Prophets," begins with a critical (even dismissive) assessment of Cohen's understanding of the relationship between Plato and the prophets, and concludes with a comparison between Socrates and the prophets that seems to suggest the superiority of Socratic prudence and moderation over the more confrontational style of the prophets in dealing with wayward political leaders.[78] In the Nietzsche essay, Strauss identifies the religious issue as central to the philosopher's thought, and at the heart of *Beyond Good and Evil* he detects the conflict between Athens and Jerusalem: "the rule of philosophy over religion or the rule of religion over philosophy."[79] The essay concludes with Strauss's reflections on Nietzsche's problematic recovery of "nature" and its relationship to the will to power and the eternal return. If we take these two chapters together, Nietzsche gets both the first and the last word; he frames and in a sense resolves the problem of Athens and Jerusalem.[80] In particular, Nietzsche's teaching enables Strauss to deal with the thorny issue, central to the Jewish question, of how one can be a person of intellectual probity, even an atheist, and still remain a Jew. Given its centrality in the structure of the book, Strauss's discussion of Nietzsche in *Studies in Platonic Philosophy* takes on particular weight as an indication of his own mind.

In Strauss's account, the doctrine of the will to power is Nietzsche's atheistic vindication of God, the true foundation of that unbounded Yes to life that transcends nihilism in the direction of a new form of religiosity. In Nietzsche's hands, "God" becomes the key to a world-affirming rather than a world-denying form of life. The old God, the God of the Bible, is sacrificed to the Nothing, but "the adoration of the Nothing proves to be the indispensable transition from every kind of world-denial to the most unbounded Yes: the eternal Yes saying to everything that was and is."[81] From this perspective,

> The transformation of the world-denying way of thinking into the opposite ideal is connected with the realization or divination that the stone, the stupidity, the Nothing to which God is being sacrificed, is in its "intelligible character" the will to power.[82]

Strauss then concludes that "in a manner the doctrine of the will to power is a vindication of God, if a decidedly non-theistic vindication of God."[83] In Strauss's reading, eternal return is inseparable from the will to power. The doctrine of the will to power reflects a convergence between the intellectual probity that realizes that "human life is utterly meaningless and lacking support," and Nietzsche's effort to recover "nature." Intellectual probity rejects the soothing, progressive "cover story" of modernity, while the recovery of a genuine understanding of "nature" begins with the recognition that, as moderns, we are indeed inhabitants of the second, deeper, "unnatural" cave. Few have the courage or ability to face this truth and to commit themselves to the onerous task of "making natural" (*Vernatuerlichung*). Those who are up to the task stand at the summit of the natural hierarchy of rank that modernity has done so much to destroy. Rank among human beings must be recognized and fostered. Humanity needs to be made "natural" for the first time.[84] In Strauss's understanding, this implies an acceptance of eternal return:

> We are natural beings who live and drink under unnatural conditions—we must recall our natural being in order to remove the unnatural conditions by thought. . . . Yet to be sure, the eternal return, or more exactly the willingness to endure it, is the *conditio sine qua non* for a truly natural morality.[85]

Modern mastery over nature contributes to the formation of a society in which the abolition of natural differences can be overcome, a society that fosters equality and seeks an end to suffering. This movement must be tempered if human excellence (and consequently the natural emergence of rank among human beings) is to be made possible. But this means having the fortitude to will the conditions that would enable this to occur:

> As we have observed, for Nietzsche nature has become a problem and yet he cannot do without nature. Nature, we may say, has become a problem owing

> to the fact that man is conquering nature and there are no assignable limits to that conquest. As a consequence, people have come to think of abolishing suffering and inequality. Yet suffering and inequality are the prerequisites of human greatness (aph. 239 and 257). Hitherto suffering and equality have been taken for granted, as "given," as imposed on man. Henceforth they must be willed. That is to say, the gruesome rule of non-sense and chance, nature, the fact that almost all men are fragments, cripples and gruesome accidents, the whole present and past is itself a fragment, a riddle, a gruesome accident unless it is willed as a bridge to the future (cf. Zarathustra, "Of Redemption"). While paving the way for the complementary man, one must at the same time say unbounded Yes to the fragments and cripples. Nature, the eternity of nature, owes its being to a postulation, to an act of the will to power on the part of the highest nature.[86]

With these insights in mind, let us consider the following remarks by Strauss concerning the plight of the Jewish people:

> Judaism is not a misfortune but, let us say, a "heroic delusion." In what does this delusion consist? The one thing needful is righteousness or charity; in Judaism these are the same. This notion is not defensible if the world is not the creation of a just and loving God, the holy God. . . . The Jewish people and their fate are the living witness for the absence of redemption. This, one could say, is the meaning of the chosen people; the Jews are chosen to prove the absence of redemption. . . . What is a delusion? We also say a "dream." No nobler dream was ever dreamt. It is surely nobler to be a victim of the most noble dream than to profit from a sordid reality and to wallow in it.[87]

Earlier we remarked that Strauss is sympathetic to the view that Nietzsche "had to wean us and himself from millennia-old pampering (softening) due to belief in creation and providence." If that is so, and if righteousness and charity are only defensible if the world is "the creation of a just and loving God, the holy God," then it would seem that for Strauss, a commitment to righteous and charity has no basis in the order of things. To persist in such a commitment may be entirely noble, but it is also entirely hopeless. Yet Strauss seems reluctant to abandon this heroic delusion, and he attempts to find meaning in it in light of Nietzsche's atheistic religiosity:

> [The] peculiarity of Old Testament theology in contradistinction especially to Greek theology is the conception, the creation of the holy God (cf. *Dawn*

> *of the Morning* aph. 68). For Nietzsche "the great style" (of certain parts of) the Old Testament shows forth the greatness, not of God, but of what man once was: the holy God no less than the holy man are creatures of the human will to power. Nietzsche's vindication of God is then atheistic, at least for the time being. . . . There was a time when theism was possible or necessary. But in the meantime "God died" (*Thus Spoke Zarathustra,* Zarathustra's Prologue Nr. 3). This does not merely mean that men have ceased to believe in God, for men's unbelief does not destroy God's life or being. It does mean, however, that even while God lived he never was what the believers in him thought him to be, namely deathless. Theism as it understood itself was therefore always wrong. Yet for a time it was true, i.e. powerful, life-giving.[88]

It would be difficult to find a better explication of the meaning of "heroic delusion." A God who lives but has no existence, a will to power that seems unable to do without some form of transcendence—as a Jew who finds it difficult to believe, Strauss appears to be drawn to the paradoxes of Nietzsche's religious atheism. Like Nietzsche, Strauss admires the spirit of his people and he sees in their heroic delusion testimony to the greatness of "what man once was." With Nietzsche he spurns the mediocrity he attributes to modernity and bemoans the inroads modern thinking has made in Jewish belief. But no more than Nietzsche does Strauss affirm the reality of the living God of the Hebrew Bible. What Strauss regrets is the loss in the modern world of a kind of courageous excellence, fatalistic in outlook, that accepts the absence of redemption while continuing to honor the powerful, life-giving, and noble dream inspired by *belief* in the holy God. Strauss shares Nietzsche's *amor fati,* and with reference to the plight of Jews throughout history he says: "One must not run away from one's place, from one's fate, but accept it, and even love it and praise it."[89]

As with Nietzsche, there is in Strauss a deep ambivalence in his relationship to the biblical God. The possibility of an "atheistic religiosity" compels both men to consider how such a notion could make sense, and leads them both to reflect on the meaning of the eternal. For both men, the notion of an eternal return functions as a substitute sacred in place of the God of the Bible. Giles Fraser makes the following point about Nietzsche, a point easily extended to Strauss:

> The doctrine of the eternal recurrence is, in a sense, the atheistic rendition of the desire to experience with joy all that comes one's way. . . . The eternal recurrence is principally a test of one's capacity for *amor fati.* It is in loving

> who we are that we are redeemed. . . . Whereas before God's death the weight of divine judgement bore down upon each and every human choice, the felt presence of heaven and hell rendered human decision making of ultimate significance, freedom from divine judgement means that what human beings choose to do no longer carries the same significance. What is required by Nietzsche is some way of generating gravity, of introducing judgement, without returning to divine judgement or divine weight. This is the purpose of the eternal recurrence. The thought of eternal recurrence sets out to become a moral centrifuge, a way for the self to generate its own gravity.[90]

Like Nietzsche, Strauss wishes to place human life within a serious horizon, to "generate gravity" within a modern context seen as lacking in nobility and heroism. The notion of eternal recurrence provides the ground upon which such an attempt can be understood as meaningful:

> There will always be men who will revolt against a state which is destructive of humanity or in which there is no longer a possibility of noble action and of great deeds. . . . Someone may object that the successful revolt against the universal and homogeneous state could have no other effect than that the identical historical process which has led from the primitive horde to the final state will be repeated. But would such a repetition of the process—a new lease of life for man's humanity—not be preferable to the indefinite continuation of the inhuman end? Do we not enjoy every spring although we know the cycle of the seasons, although we know that winter will come again?[91]

In his correspondence with Karl Lowith, Strauss is quite explicit about the origin and purpose of the doctrine and its role as a substitute for biblical faith:

> The eternal return is discovered in the search for a strong and courage-producing myth. . . . It is asserted convulsively by Nietzsche only because he had to wean us and himself from millennia-old pampering (softening) due to belief in creation and providence.[92]

A willingness to persevere in noble ideals despite the absence of signs that would warrant hope in an ultimate redemption; an embrace of one's fate without the consolation of belief in a benign Providence—Strauss's interpretation of Jewish existence echoes Nietzsche's own troubled religiosity:

> "What more has Israel to offer the world than eternal patience?" This sentence indeed calls for a long commentary. One sentence must here suffice: what is called "eternal patience" is that fortitude in suffering, now despised as "ghetto mentality" by shallow people who have surrendered wholeheartedly to the modern world, or who lack the intelligence to consider that a secession from this world might again become necessary for Jews and even for Christians.[93]

Strauss speaks eloquently of the suffering of Jews. He also chooses his language carefully. His people are not to hope for redemption; rather, they are to embrace their fate with eternal patience. For Strauss, as for Nietzsche, this is a life-affirming choice. Equipped with his understanding of Nietzsche's atheistic religiosity and his doctrine of the eternal return, Strauss is able to speak meaningfully of why Jews ought to remain Jews. In affirming their identity as Jews, they give themselves over to the noblest of dreams. For those whose intellectual probity bars the way to traditional belief, the doctrine of the eternal return functions as a type of a-theistic transcendence. Commenting on what it could mean to commit oneself to this noble dream, Strauss says:

> Dream is akin to aspiration. And aspiration is a kind of divination of an enigmatic vision. And an enigmatic vision in the emphatic sense is the perception of the ultimate mystery. The truth of the ultimate mystery—the truth that there is an ultimate mystery, that being is radically mysterious—cannot be denied even by the unbelieving Jew of our age.[94]

It may be well to note that when Strauss speaks of ultimate mystery, he refers not to the God known through the revelatory traditions of his people but to the experienced *permanence of problems* against which the human intellect inevitably runs in trying to understand the world. Strauss's "unbelieving Jew" and the classical philosopher stand in a similar relationship to ultimate mystery. Those who wish to reconcile what Strauss says about ultimate mystery with those traditions that emphasize the continuity between philosophical wonder and biblical revelation need to recall that for Strauss, one is *either* a philosopher *or* a theologian.[95] Even when he describes philosophy as "the quest for the eternal order," and assumes "that there is an eternal and immutable order within which history takes place, and which remains entirely unaffected by history," he never claims that philosophy attains this order. Strauss is and remains more of a skeptic than any of his classical philosophical models; in this he is far closer to Nietzsche than to Plato.[96] Strauss's deep and ongoing appreciation for Lucretius and Thucydides supports this view.[97] Strauss does hesitate to critique Plato from a Thucydidean perspective, comparing the former's "comforting message" (that is, noble lie) with the latter's "somber wisdom."[98] Again it may be pertinent to emphasize that Strauss came to the classics after his appropriation of Nietzsche; if he is drawn to Thucydides it is because the teaching of the Greek thinker resembles that of the author of *The Birth of Tragedy* and not vice versa. In a post-Holocaust world, Strauss's fatalistic skepticism may be understandable, but the question remains whether the embrace of a noble dream, that is, the "divination of an enigmatic vision," can take the place of faith in the God of Israel.

Against the backdrop of a profoundly mysterious and fateful reality, the doctrine of eternal return, in Strauss's eyes, can give meaning to Jewish existence. In affirming their identity as Jews, they may invite further suffering at the hands of those who hate them, but, as Nietzsche teaches, suffering is the precondition for human greatness. The crucial difference is that in the midst of modernity and its leveling effects, suffering must now be *willed*. For Strauss as for Nietzsche, this is not masochism but a matter of being able to act nobly and in freedom. It is an acknowledgment of the truth of the doctrine of the will to power, with its affirmation that life develops and is strengthened only when it is able to encounter and overcome resistance. It is also an acceptance of the eternal return, to the extent that willing in the face of resistance and suffering entails a willing of the conditions that provide the resistance out of which human excellence can emerge. To choose assimilation in exchange for comfort and security is to conform to a civilization that knows little of human excellence.

Strauss is troubled by Judaism as Nietzsche was by Christianity. Nietzsche's torment is far more apparent, manifest in the increasingly shrill denunciations of Christianity that mark his later work. Yet Strauss's reticence cannot disguise the problematic relationship he has with the faith of his birth. Nowhere is he less convincing than in his attempt to sustain Jewish identity by substituting a fatalistic acceptance of suffering for the biblical hope of redemption. There is pathos to be found in the philosophizing of both Strauss and Nietzsche, who at some level seem to understand that their exhortations to human fortitude and nobility require a ground that renders such efforts meaningful. A doctrine such as the eternal return represents an attempt to provide that ground. But the false transcendence of the eternal return falls back upon itself and masks the real problem. That problem is the one from which philosophy diverts its eyes, captivated by the seeming profundity of its own smoke screen. The philosophical appropriation of the eternal return is yet another covering thrown over the violent sacred.

Philosophy's hesitancy in directly addressing the presence of the violent sacred may explain why the reality of violence seldom becomes the explicit theme of Strauss's philosophizing. The same cannot be said for his treatment of religion. Strauss shares with Girard an awareness of the importance of religion's role in culture, as well as a belief that the problematic animating Nietzsche's thought is essentially a religious one. For all three thinkers, the central issues revolve around the role of the Bible in Western civilization. However, the very aspects of the Bible held up by Nietzsche and Strauss as the inspiring and life-affirming message of the text are the very tendencies from which, in Girard's view, the Bible is freeing itself. According to Girard, the Bible's teaching unfolds in a way that moves away from a reliance on the sacrificial mechanisms that sustain culture, and in this process the role of the victim becomes increasingly clear. Nietzsche would agree that the Bible tends in this direction, but he would judge this development to be a falling away from the robust faith of ancient Israel. Likewise, he acknowledges the fact that the modern concern for victims is a direct byproduct of biblical revelation—and he condemns a good part of the Bible for fostering this concern. By contrast, Strauss rarely criticizes the Bible directly, nor does he denounce the biblical concern for victims. Nonetheless we find in Strauss the same focus on struggle, overcoming, and power, the same affirmation of a God who embodies the heroic strength of his people.

The omnipotent, even arbitrary, God of the Bible, as described by Strauss, bears traces of the sacrificial. In Strauss's telling of Jewish history there is ample discussion of suffering, but almost nothing on the victim as victim and the possible implications of this insight. Strauss largely neglects those biblical texts that highlight compassion and concern for victims; and from his reactions to Cohen's thought one gets the impression that Strauss believes reading the Bible in this way is an imposition of modern ideas onto the biblical text. In Strauss's estimation, the "extreme" tendencies within the Bible, for example, its emphasis on charity and compassion, have, through the mediation of prophetic-messianic Judaism and especially Christianity, been absorbed by modern thought and interpreted as the central tenets of biblical tradition.[99] We must recall that, for Strauss, the reconstruction of Jewish tradition involves serious consideration as to whether the prophets are mistaken and the kings are right.

In light of the historical persecution of the Jews, with fear of the disappearance of the Jewish people through assimilation, and with great concern that the leveling tendencies of modernity will only accelerate these trends, Strauss tends to be wary of the process of globalization occurring in the contemporary world. On the basis of personal experience and political conviction, he fears that the breaking down of differences anticipates the coming of "the universal and homogeneous state." The realization of such a state would, in his opinion, spell the end, not only of the Jews as an identifiable people but of all human distinctiveness and excellence, including the practice of philosophy. Societies, in order to survive and flourish, need clear boundaries, and they require for their cohesion certain shared and unquestionable beliefs. In this sense, every healthy society is, for Strauss, a closed society:

> Classical political philosophy opposes to the universal and homogeneous state a substantive principle. It asserts that the society natural to man is the city, that is, a closed society. . . . it asserts that every political society that ever has been or ever will be rests on a particular fundamental opinion which cannot be replaced by knowledge and hence is of necessity a particular or particularist society.[100]

Strauss believes modern liberalism is antagonistic toward the idea of a closed society; instead, it aims "at the greatest possible approximation to the universal and homogeneous state." Liberals may defend the values of the Western tradition, but "they are not sufficiently concerned with the fact that that tradition is ever more being eroded by the very changes in the direction of One World which they demand or applaud."[101] Once the universal and homogeneous state comes into existence, there is no escape. Fear of the masses, and of the political leaders that do their bidding, and concern that increasing globalization means the loss of strong communal identity and of the possibilities for human excellence fuel Strauss's critique of liberalism. The very questions that motivate his critique also lead him to reflect on its possible relationship to the Jewish question:

> Not much familiarity with political life is needed in order to see that it is particularly difficult for a nonorthodox Jew to adopt a critical posture toward liberalism. . . . In what sense or to what extent is Judaism one of the roots of liberalism? Are Jews compelled by their heritage or their self-interest to be liberals? Is liberalism necessarily friendly to Jews and Judaism? Can the liberal state claim to have solved the Jewish problem? Can any state claim to have solved it?[102]

Strauss's critique of liberalism helps us to understand his resistance to universalistic, humanitarian interpretations of the Bible. He reads the biblical text and approaches Jewish tradition in a way that supports his preference for closed societies. Jerusalem, as Strauss describes it, is a city formed by unquestioning obedience to the Law given by an inscrutable God. In a letter to Carl Schmitt, Strauss explains how closed societies serve human well-being:

> If I have correctly understood your opinion . . . it leads precisely to the conclusion that there is a *primary* tendency in human nature to form *exclusive groups*. . . . Because man is by nature evil, he therefore needs *dominion*. But dominion can be established, that is men can be unified, only in a unity *against*—against other men. Every association of men is *necessarily* a separation from other men.[103]

As with every human group, Jewish identity is formed in opposition to its environment. Nietzsche teaches the benefits of struggle; through their trials, Jews will cohere as a people. One might ask, then, whether the dreaded "universal and homogeneous state" might not be the most salutary for Jews, since it would maximize their need for such a purifying struggle and thereby make them stronger as a people. Strauss anticipates this question, and as noted earlier, he sees in Nietzsche's doctrine of the eternal return a meaningful response to the advent of the "One World" of the last man. Yet it seems as if for Strauss, Jews would fare best in a liberal state that best approximates the best features of a closed society. This would be a strong society, confident in its fundamental values and little given to self-doubt or self-criticism. Such a society would offer freedom to Jews while at the same time resisting the slide toward the universal and homogeneous state. Since no society can solve the Jewish problem, Jews would still have to struggle in order to retain their identity. But as envisioned by Strauss, such a society would embody the principles of true liberalism, that is, a liberalism drawing upon the best of the classical tradition in political philosophy.[104] In such a society, the tension between Athens and Jerusalem, the very lifeblood of the West, would be kept alive. In living out that tension, Jews would be compelled to reflect upon their identity and in so doing they would position themselves to fulfill their role in the revival of Western civilization foreseen for them by Nietzsche and embraced by Strauss.

Strauss's fear of the universal and homogeneous state allows him to overlook the dangers associated with a closed society. Strauss's ideal would seem to be a moderate, robustly patriotic regime, protective of the benefits of liberal freedoms without the tendencies toward globalization and universalism. He does not seem to appreciate the fact that the tendencies he despises are byproducts of the same process that accounts for the modern commitment to the protection of individuals and minorities. Based upon his insight into the emerging consciousness of victimization moving forward in the modern world, Girard takes a rather different view:

> The gradual loosening of various centers of cultural isolation began in the Middle Ages and has now led into what we call "globalization," which in my view is only secondarily an economic phenomenon. The true engine of progress is the slow decomposition of the closed worlds rooted in victim mechanisms. This is the force that destroyed archaic societies and henceforth dismantles the ones replacing them, the nations we call "modern."[105]

Girard undermines any attempt to romanticize the world of the closed society by pointing to the hidden mechanism that generates its unity. Strauss the philosopher works to hide this truth from view, contrasting the moderation and prudence of the ancient city to the excesses of a biblically inspired modernity. From Girard's perspective, such an interpretation does not do justice to the Judaeo-Christian scriptures, because it remains mired, however unwittingly, in the sacrificial stance that the Bible seeks to undermine. Strauss's philosophical sanitizing of the classical ideal does not break sufficiently with culture-founding violence:

> Whatever may be the essence of Christianity, no misinterpretation could be more complete than to assimilate it to the religions of difference. The way of thinking that believes it has thus understood Christianity is in fact always understood by it, for this way of thinking is located inside the city and perceives poorly or not at all how the latter's closure is achieved through constant recourse to the expulsion of the Other. Christianity breaks free of the ancient city whose closure it rejects[106]

Strauss's thought remains proudly within the city, and this is the source of its blindness. As with Nietzsche (but without his ferocity), Strauss resists the cultural effects of the biblical revelation of the victim because he views these effects as contributing to the modern horrors from which he wishes to escape. What Girard understands, in a way that Nietzsche and Strauss do not, is that despite the excesses that accompany the progress of biblical revelation, the gravest threat to civilization comes from those who would stifle the biblical voice. Girard is well aware that

> Hitler's genocide flagrantly contradicts the thesis . . . that the Western world, and now effectively the entire planet, is dominated by the concern for victims. This contradiction should compel me to change my views or to make it the basis of my entire interpretation of genocide. The second solution is the good one, I believe.[107]

The modern world is most prone to imbalance when it obscures or abandons its biblical legacy. Strauss accepts this to a certain degree; his retrieval of the meaning of Jerusalem is intended as a contribution to the strengthening of Western society. His reliance on Nietzsche, however, leads him to appropriate the biblical tradition in a way that accords only secondary importance to the very aspects of the tradition that account for modernity's increasing sensitivity toward victims and also provide the most effective bulwark against the kind of totalitarian threats he fears. Taking Nietzsche as a model, Strauss suffers from similar oversights.

Is Strauss a Nietzschean? At the risk of being evasive, I would say the answer depends on how one defines a Nietzschean. It seems accurate to say of Strauss that

> He was a Nietzschean in line with everything he thought he understood of Nietzsche. But Strauss's Nietzsche would not be recognizable as the Nietzsche presented in most contemporary scholarship. To take but one example, the postmodernist Nietzsche, Strauss could not have cared less about who was more "metaphysical," Nietzsche or Heidegger. . . . Nor would Strauss have accepted the view that at the heart of Nietzsche's thought lay only the will of an esoteric nihilist. Strauss's Nietzsche intended a paradoxical "return" to Nature, not the customarily announced metaphysical emancipation from it. And perhaps even more iconoclastic, Strauss's Nietzsche was a "Platonist."[108]

The only part of this assessment to which I would take exception is that Strauss is in line with "*everything* he understood of Nietzsche." Strauss certainly understands Nietzsche's polemical and rhetorical use of language, and he rejects it as unacceptable and dangerous, if understandable given the circumstances in which Nietzsche found himself.[109] Laurence Lampert takes Strauss's criticism of Nietzsche as "irresponsible and damaging," and he believes it is intended mainly for the edification of Strauss's audience, a rhetorical "descent to the people" offering "a pious denunciation of the impious Nietzsche." Lampert also argues that Strauss is ultimately too cautious to follow Nietzsche's teaching unreservedly; in the end Strauss embraces the moderation of Plato.[110]

Unlike Lampert, I believe Strauss's indictment of Nietzsche's rhetoric is meant seriously, and his turn to Plato does not indicate a failure of nerve but is the result of a deep understanding of the potential dangers of Nietzsche's style, if not his teaching. According to Strauss:

> The essential difficulties of Nietzsche's teaching are created by its polemical character, and immediately disappear when one distinguishes between polemical approach and the teaching itself. . . . It is not sufficient to simply stop where Nietzsche is no longer right; rather one must ask whether or not Nietzsche himself became untrue to his intention to repeat antiquity, and did so as a result of his confinement within modern presuppositions or in polemics against these.[111]

From Strauss's perspective, even Nietzsche was unable to free himself entirely from the second cave; he remained to some degree contaminated by the modern thought he sought to overcome. In his polemical, politically irresponsible language, Nietzsche is too much a product of modernity, a modernity that has inherited from the Bible a commitment to pursue and to speak the truth with boldness. As in his criticism of Machiavelli, Strauss finds Nietzsche's proclamation of the deadly truth to be unsettling, in that it undermines the opinions upon which society must rely in order to be confident and cohesive. Nietzsche is too truthful for society's good. To truly revive antiquity, we must recover the classical genius for understanding the requirement of moderation that accompanies political speech.

Strauss shares with Plato an apprehension that there are certain truths about the city that need to remain hidden. This explains in part why Plato becomes the primary model for Strauss's political philosophy. However, while Platonic prudence may be more appropriate than Nietzschean excess, this does not mean that Nietzsche is left behind. Strauss does not oppose Nietzsche as much as he sees himself as correcting and completing Nietzsche's work. From Strauss's perspective, Nietzsche has not freed himself sufficiently from the holy God of the Bible—his prophetic manner of speaking undermines the effectiveness of his teaching. Strauss's turn to classical political philosophy can be seen as an attempt to fulfill Nietzsche's project of reversing the modern triumph of the biblical. Strauss, in his recovery of the ancients, understands his own task as completing the project that Nietzsche was unable to finish, due to the latter's inability to completely free himself from the biblically influenced horizon of modernity. There is certainly evidence for this claim. Reflecting on his own work, Strauss wonders whether the attempt to restore classical social science is not perhaps utopian, "since it implies that the classical orientation has not been made obsolete by the triumph of the biblical orientation."[112] In similar fashion, Strauss remarks to Karl Lowith that "there can be no doubt that our usual way of feeling is conditioned by the biblical tradition," even while he refuses to rule out the possibility of correcting that feeling.[113] Strauss resembles Nietzsche in his desire to dethrone the "biblical orientation" from its current place in the modern world. This accounts for Strauss's distinction between Nietzsche's teaching (with which Strauss often agrees) and Nietzsche's manner of speech (which Strauss views as irresponsible). For example, in announcing the necessity of sacrifice, Nietzsche may be speaking the truth, but it is a truth that should never be spoken out loud. That is why it is much more difficult to identify explicit indications of sacrificial thinking in Strauss. Yet even a cursory reading of Strauss's Nietzsche essay reveals repeated references to Dionysus, sacrifice, and cruelty, all set within the context of a discussion of philosophy, the will to power, and the eternal return. Strauss, like Nietzsche, seems to have a profound awareness of the fact that the problem of the sacralization of order does not disappear with the abandonment of biblical faith. Like Girard, Strauss appreciates the importance of the sacred and its relationship to culture in Nietzsche's thought. Yet no more than Nietzsche does Strauss seem able to free himself from the challenge posed by biblical thought, and much like Nietzsche he realizes that philosophy cannot do without some form of the sacred. We have already made reference to the centrality of the essays on Athens and Jerusalem and *Beyond Good and Evil* in *Studies in Platonic Political Philosophy*. That book also contains the essay "Preliminary Observations on the Gods in Thucydides' Work," which begins with a statement referring the reader back to Strauss's treatment of Thucydides in *The City and Man*.[114] There Strauss ends the chapter on Thucydides (and the book itself) with an expression of gratitude to Fustel de Coulanges for calling attention to the Greek understanding of religion, the "remote or dark side of the city" that has been neglected by philosophers.[115] In addition, Strauss's penultimate work, *The Argument and the Action of Plato's Laws,* begins with Avicenna's remark that "the treatment of prophecy and the Divine law is contained in the *Laws*," followed by Strauss's own observation that the *Laws* is Plato's most political and most pious work.[116]

That Strauss has some awareness of the sacrificial underpinnings of culture is evident from his treatment of the doctrine of eternal return. Observing how, for Nietzsche, the decay of institutional religion coincides with an increase in religiosity, Strauss asks, "Could atheism belong to the free mind as Nietzsche conceives of it while a certain kind of non-atheism belongs to the philosopher of the future who will again worship the god Dionysos . . . ?" The religion of the future envisioned by Nietzsche may have some resemblance to Vedanta philosophy, but Strauss argues that Nietzsche anticipates "a more Western, a sterner, more terrible and more invigorating possibility: the sacrificing from cruelty, i.e. from the will to power turning against itself, of God which prepares the worshipping of the stone, stupidity, heaviness (gravity), fate, the Nothing. He anticipates in other words that the better among contemporary atheists will come to know what they are doing."[117] The sacrifice of God (the old God of the Bible) leaves in its wake a nihilistic scenario in which the religious impulse veers wildly in its pursuit of a new sacred (the stone, stupidity, fate, and so on) culminating in worship of the Nothing. But Strauss denies that this is Nietzsche's final word on the problem:

> Nietzsche does not mean to sacrifice God for the sake of the Nothing, for while recognizing the deadly truth that God died he aims at transforming it into a life-inspiring one or rather to discover in the depth of the deadly truth its opposite.[118]

The sacrifice of the biblical God and the resulting nihilism is but a stage on the way to a new form of the sacred, one that must be willed in the interest of society: "The adoration of the Nothing proves to be the indispensable transition from every kind of world-denial to the most unbounded Yes: the eternal Yes-saying to everything that was and is." Strauss says of Nietzsche's atheism that it "is not unambiguous, for he had doubts whether there can be a world, any world whose center is not God."[119] To make this unbounded Yes requires an act of will; hence the coming religion will be a reflection of the life-serving will to power:

> Nietzsche brings out the fact that in a manner the doctrine of the will to power is a vindication of God, if a decidedly non-theistic vindication of God. . . . [The] vindication of God is only the inversion of the sacrificing of God to stupidity, to the Nothing, or at any rate presupposes that sacrificing. What is it that suddenly, if after a long preparation, divinizes the Nothing? Is it the willing of eternity which gives to the world, or restores to it its worth which the world-denying ways of thinking had denied it? Is it the willing of eternity that makes atheism religious?[120]

The trajectory of Nietzsche's thought on religion and the sacred, as described by Strauss, has remarkable similarities to Girard's presentation of the logic of aphorism 125 from *The Gay Science* (however much Girard and Strauss differ in their ultimate evaluation of Nietzsche).[121] Girard points out that Nietzsche speaks clearly of the ritual murder of God, while Strauss uses the equally violent language of sacrifice; neither commentator is taken in by the idea that Nietzsche intended God's death to be understood as a natural and peaceful process. In Girard's reading, the first announcement of the murder of God precipitates the sacrificial crisis that follows as humanity careens about in search of its sacred bearings. Strauss describes the crisis in terms of humanity's impulse to find something to worship in place of the biblical God, whether stone, fate, or the Nothing. "What ceremonies of atonement, what sacred games shall we have to invent?" asks Nietzsche's Madman, and Girard, like Strauss, believes Nietzsche found his answer in the doctrine of the eternal return. Nietzsche's appropriation of the doctrine serves his philosophy well, since it has deep roots in sacrificial religion:

> Sacrifice takes place when sacred violence takes charge of the victim; it is the death that produces life, just as life produces death, in the uninterrupted circle of eternal recurrence common to all the great theological views that are grafted upon sacrificial practices—those that do not acknowledge the demystifying effect of the Judaeo-Christian tradition. It is not by chance that Western philosophy begins, and up to a certain point ends, in the "intuition" of the Eternal Recurrence that the pre-Socratics and Nietzsche hold in common. This is the sacrificial intuition *par excellence*.[122]

The ambiguity Girard detects in aphorism 125 is that in linking the eternal return to the collective murder that is its engine, the doctrine's effectiveness is damaged. As long as the murder remains hidden, the sacrificial mechanism can accomplish its work with little resistance. Once it is exposed, its functioning is seriously impaired. In order to exorcize the murder, the veil of philosophy must be thrown over it.[123] Girard argues that this is precisely what Heidegger did with Nietzsche, and I would maintain that the same can be said of Strauss.[124] His sensitivity to Nietzsche's use of the language of religious sacrifice and its relationship to the eternal return is especially noteworthy in this regard, although, as is so often the case with Strauss, his own view is not easily distinguished from what he offers to the reader in his role as commentator.[125] Of course, the very indirection of such speech is symptomatic of the obfuscating role of philosophical discourse. Strauss's language constantly hovers around Nietzsche's grimmest thoughts, allowing Nietzsche's insights to surface without Strauss the prudent Platonic political philosopher ever identifying himself explicitly with them. In this way, Nietzsche is simultaneously kept at a distance and brought closer to the classical thought that Strauss so admires. Written as a comment on Nietzsche, the following remarks by Girard are equally applicable to Strauss:

> By taking up the eternal recurrence in a philosophical perspective, one may tangle the problem up to one's heart's desire. . . . One seeks to give the impression that fathomless depths lie hidden here, infinitely superior to the linear vision of history or to Judaeo-Christian "simple-mindedness."[126]

The value of a Girardian critique is that it enables us to get past the philosophical cover-up of violence. Not only does this help in detecting traces of the violent sacred in philosophical texts, but it forces us to ask how conscious the authors were themselves of the need to keep this knowledge hidden. Girard believes Nietzsche understood well how frequently myth and ritual center on the expulsion or killing of victims, and how this process is essential for the preservation of culture. Nor, in Girard's view, did Nietzsche ever shy away from the violent aspects of the Dionysian.[127] More specifically, Girard finds that Nietzsche "is very close to seeing the mechanisms and the effects of the surrogate victim, and above all to seeing that the gospels see them and, seeing them, discredit and derail them."[128] The question remains whether Strauss shares Nietzsche's degree of awareness in these matters. Inspired by the example of Plato, Strauss practices a kind of philosophy that is much more prudent with regard to the disturbing truths announced by Nietzsche. But in his choice for Plato, Strauss cannot pretend that he has not encountered Nietzsche. Nor can he ignore Nietzsche's teaching on the connection between violence and the sacred. Contrary to the impression that some may have of his thought, Strauss is well aware that there can be no return to the classical horizon. Classical wisdom must be brought to bear on *modern* problems, and that means dealing with the unpleasant truths that Nietzsche stated so recklessly. These truths, once announced, severely damage the mechanism upon which societies rely for their cohesion and stability. Strauss must confront the problem of whether the ugly truth unearthed by Nietzsche can be effectively reburied.

The resulting tension in Strauss's thought shows itself in the way his essay on *Beyond Good and Evil* revolves around the contest between Plato and

Nietzsche, the two philosophers Strauss holds in highest esteem. Nietzsche had boldly highlighted the importance of the religious and the sacrificial, and challenged the philosophers of the future to come to terms with these realities in a world freed from the power of the biblical God. Strauss accepted this challenge. If Nietzsche can be brought closer to Plato, then his ideas can be encompassed by Platonic moderation and thereby be mediated to the world in a seemingly less toxic form. This would explain what might otherwise seem a strange positioning of Strauss's Nietzsche essay at the very center of *Studies in Platonic Political Philosophy.* Nietzsche's outrageous rhetoric can be sincerely denounced, while his insights can be modified (not repudiated) and incorporated into the prudent wisdom of the classical authors. Yet if Girard is correct, any attempt to reconstitute the sacred in a world where the biblical orientation has triumphed will be extraordinarily difficult, since the mechanism on which the sacred depends for its effectiveness, once exposed by biblical revelation, cannot be easily revived. The strain of trying to do so cost Nietzsche dearly. The more prudent Strauss returns to his classical models to learn how to hide the unsettling truth from view. Nietzsche's overt references to sacrificial violence must be philosophically transfigured, and the violent origins of culture must be submerged. There is a sense in which this is precisely what occurs in Strauss's thought.

Writing in honor of his departed colleague Kurt Riezler, Strauss observes:

> For man's being is revealed by the broad character of his life, his deeds, his works, by what he esteems and reveres not in word but in deed—by the stars for which his soul longs if it longs for any stars. . . . In pondering over Riezler's highest aspiration, I had to think more than once of Thucydides—of Thucydides' quiet and manly gentleness which seeks no solace and which looks in freedom, but not in indifference, at the opposites whose unity is hidden; which does not attempt to reduce one opposite to the other.[129]

I cannot help but think that this description reveals as much about Strauss as it does about Thucydides. Seeking no solace in the face of death, standing before a reality constituted by opposition without end, and unable to penetrate its mystery—this is the voice of Leo Strauss. It is also Nietzsche's.[130] Is not Strauss's claim that the fundamental opposition between Athens and Jerusalem constitutes the vitality of Western civilization in fact a reflection of the eternal return, where life is generated through an unending conflict of opposites? Is it merely a coincidence that Strauss begins an essay on

Thucydides by emphasizing the "antagonistic principles" of Greek wisdom and biblical piety, and concludes with a reminder that Thucydides' wisdom consists in his embrace of the Heraclitean insight that war is the father of all things?[131] In Strauss's thought, the violent sacred is once again reinstalled at the heart of culture, transformed into the unending conflict of the two pillars of Western civilization. Strauss defends Jerusalem because he wishes to keep this tension alive. No more than Nietzsche does he desire a triumph of the "biblical orientation."

However, the problem posed by the biblical message, whether articulated as the Jewish question, the nature of modernity, or the conflict between Athens and Jerusalem, refuses to disappear. This presents an awkward dilemma for philosophy, which would rather avoid the uncomfortable truth about the victim at the heart of biblical anthropology. In this regard there is an interesting, if cryptic, passage in Strauss's Nietzsche essay. Following his discussion of the sacrifice of God in Nietzsche's thought, Strauss goes on to say:

> There is an important ingredient, not to say the nerve, of Nietzsche's "theology" of which I have not spoken and shall not speak since I have no access to it. It has been worthily treated by Karl Reinhardt in his essay "Nietzsche's Klage der Ariadne."[132]

What is peculiar in this passage is Strauss's identification of an "important ingredient, not to say the nerve, of Nietzsche's 'theology,'" followed by his refusal to speak about it because he has no access to it. If he truly has no access to it, how and why is he able to speak of it at all? How does he judge this ingredient to be the "nerve" of Nietzsche's theology? And how does he know that it is worthily treated by Reinhardt? Perhaps Strauss's remark is nothing more than a reminder of his lack of expertise in theology. That is unlikely however, since Karl Reinhardt is no theologian either, and that does not prevent him from treating Nietzsche's "theology" worthily. What we have here is Strauss the political philosopher calling attention to something about which philosophy cannot or will not speak. Yet it must be something of such centrality to Nietzsche's thought that it cannot be omitted. Could that which is to remain unspoken have something to do with the violent sacred? And what could that possibly have to do with philosophy? In fact, Reinhardt argues for the centrality of the figure of the god Dionysos throughout Nietzsche's thought, and for the importance of the opposition between Dionysos and the Crucified.[133] It could be that Strauss passes over this "important ingredient" of Nietzsche's "theology" because he deems it irrelevant to the central issues of political philosophy. Strauss's silence may also indicate that he understands Nietzsche all too well.

NOTES

1. Karl Lowith and Leo Strauss, "Correspondence," *Independent Journal of Philosophy* 5, no. 6 (1988): 183.
2. It would be very difficult to make the case that Strauss's involvement with Nietzsche is simply a youthful encounter that fades with time. In addition to the references to Nietzsche throughout his work, Strauss taught courses on Nietzsche at the University of Chicago in 1952, 1956, 1959, 1962, and 1967. Strauss also offered a course on Nietzsche during his time at St. John's College (1971–1973). Clearly Nietzsche remained a focal point of Strauss's concern throughout his career.
3. Leo Strauss, "Relativism" and "Introduction to Heideggerian Existentialism," in *The Rebirth of Classical Political Rationalism: Essays and Lectures by Leo Strauss,* selected and introduced by Thomas Pangle (Chicago: University of Chicago Press, 1989), 40, 26.
4. Leo Strauss, "What Is Political Philosophy?" in *What Is Political Philosophy?* (Chicago: University of Chicago Press, 1959), 54–55.
5. Strauss, "Introduction to Heideggerian Existentialism," 31; Leo Strauss, "German Nihilism," *Interpretation: A Journal of Political Philosophy* 26, no. 3 (Spring 1999): 372.
6. Leo Strauss, "Why We Remain Jews," in Leo Strauss, *Jewish Philosophy and the Crisis of Modernity: Essays and Lectures in Modern Jewish Thought,* ed. Kenneth Hart Green (Albany: State University of New York Press, 1997), 312.
7. Strauss, "Preface to *Spinoza's Critique of Religion,*" in Strauss, *Jewish Philosophy and the Crisis of Modernity,* 143.
8. Strauss, "Why We Remain Jews," 317.
9. Strauss, "Preface to *Spinoza's Critique of Religion,*" 144.
10. Leo Strauss, *Philosophy and Law,* trans. Eve Adler (Albany: State University of New York Press, 1995), 23.
11. Leo Strauss, "Comment on Weinberg's Critique," in *Leo Strauss: The Early Writings (1921–1932),* trans. and ed. Michael Zank (Albany: State University of New York Press, 2002), 119.
12. Leo Strauss, "Sigmund Freud, *The Future of an Illusion,*" in *Leo Strauss: The Early Writings,* 203.
13. Leo Strauss, "Cohen's Analysis of Spinoza's Bible Science," in *Leo Strauss: The Early Writings,* 143.
14. Strauss, *Philosophy and Law,* 23.
15. Strauss, *Philosophy and Law,* 23–24.
16. *Leo Strauss: The Early Writings,* 30; Strauss, *Philosophy and Law,* 136.

17. *Leo Strauss: The Early Writings*, 31.

18. "The precarious status of philosophy in Judaism as well as in Islam was not in every respect a misfortune for philosophy. The official recognition of philosophy in the Christian world made philosophy subject to ecclesiastical supervision. The precarious position of philosophy in the Islamic-Jewish world guaranteed its private character and therewith its inner freedom from supervision. The status of philosophy in the Islamic-Jewish world resembled in this respect its status in classical Greece." Leo Strauss, *Persecution and the Art of Writing* (Chicago: University of Chicago Press, 1952), 21.

19. *Leo Strauss: The Early Writings*, 31.

20. *Leo Strauss: The Early Writings*, 31.

21. See Clark A. Merrill, "Leo Strauss's Indictment of Christian Philosophy," *Review of Politics* 62, no. 1, (2000): 77–105; and John Ranieri, "The Bible and Modernity: Girardian Reflections on Leo Strauss," *Contagion: Journal of Violence, Mimesis, and Culture* 11 (Spring 2004).

22. Leo Strauss, "On the Argument with European Science," in *Leo Strauss: The Early Writings*, 108.

23. Strauss, "Sigmund Freud, *The Future of an Illusion*," 202.

24. Strauss, "Why We Remain Jews," 317, 320.

25. Strauss, *Philosophy and Law*, 38.

26. Leo Strauss, "Response to Frankfurt's 'Word of Principle,'" in *Leo Strauss: The Early Writings*, 69.

27. *Leo Strauss: The Early Writings*, 32–33.

28. Leo Strauss, "The Problem of Socrates," *Interpretation: A Journal of Political Philosophy* 22, no. 3 (Spring 1995): 324.

29. Leo Strauss, "The Holy," in *Leo Strauss: The Early Writings*, 76.

30. Leo Strauss, *Natural Right and History* (Chicago: University of Chicago Press, 1950), 26. See also Leo Strauss, "Relativism," in Strauss, *The Rebirth of Classical Political Rationalism*, 24–26. This book and the essay date from 1950 and 1961 respectively. I mention this in support of my contention that the influence of Nietzsche on Strauss does not lessen over the course of Strauss's career.

31. Friedrich Nietzsche, *Untimely Meditations*, trans. R. J. Hollingdale (Cambridge: Cambridge University Press, 1997), 63.

32. Leo Strauss, "Jerusalem and Athens: Some Preliminary Reflections," in *Studies in Platonic Political Philosophy* (Chicago: University of Chicago Press, 1983), 147–48.

33. Strauss, "Relativism," 25.

34. Strauss, "Relativism," 25–26.

35. Leo Strauss, "Note on the Plan of Nietzsche's *Beyond Good and Evil*," in *Studies in Platonic Political Philosophy*, 174–91.

36. Leo Strauss, "The Crisis of Our Time," and "The Crisis of Political Philosophy," in *The Predicament of Modern Politics*, ed. Harold J. Spaeth (Detroit: University of Detroit Press, 1964), 41–54, 91–103.

37. Strauss, "Jerusalem and Athens," 148.

38. Much the same can be said of the relationship of Nietzsche to Strauss's recovery of the Greeks. Strauss comes to his study of classical political philosophy after his encounter with Nietzsche, and while there is little doubt that this study influences him deeply and enables him in some sense to critique Nietzsche, it remains the case that Nietzsche is the often unacknowledged guide in Strauss's reappropriation of classical thought.

39. Friedrich Nietzsche, *The Antichrist,* in *The Portable Nietzsche,* ed. and trans. Walter Kaufmann (New York: Penguin Books, 1959), sections 16,17, 25, 26; Nietzsche, *Daybreak,* trans, R. J. Hollingdale, ed. Maudmarie Clark and Brian Leiter (Cambridge: Cambridge University Press, 1997), section 475; Nietzsche, *Beyond Good and Evil,* in *Basic Writings of Nietzsche,* trans. Walter Kaufmann (New York: The Modern Library, 1967), sections 52, 250; Nietzsche, *The Gay Science,* trans. Walter Kaufmann (New York: Vintage Books, 1974), section 136.

40. Nietzsche, *The Antichrist,* 24–27; *Beyond Good and Evil,* 195; *Daybreak,* 38, 68; *The Gay Science,* 135, 137.

41. Nietzsche, *The Antichrist,* 17, 24–27; *Beyond Good and Evil,* 52.

42. Friedrich Nietzsche, *Human, All Too Human,* trans. Marion Faber with Stephen Lehmann (Lincoln: University of Nebraska Press, 1984), section 475; *The Antichrist,* 24; *Beyond Good and Evil,* 251; *Daybreak,* 205.

43. Nietzsche, *Human, All Too Human,* 475.

44. Strauss, "Why We Remain Jews," 321.

45. Nietzsche, *The Gay Science,* section 125.

46. Leo Strauss, "Biblical History and Science," in *Leo Strauss: The Early Writings,* 135.

47. Unlike cultural Zionists, Strauss rejects the identification of God with the "creative genius of the Jewish people." God may in fact be the highest creation of the human spirit, but this in no way suggests that the human creators of this idea understood it in this way. Cultural Zionism is a form of reductionism that simply ignores this distinction. Strauss, like Nietzsche, is interested in the role that "God" plays in human life, whether such a being exists or not. Both men are very much concerned with the cultural effects of the loss of belief, and both are very much interested in the "religious" and its relationship to philosophy. This may explain in part Strauss's remark that even for one who finds religious belief impossible it is advisable to "enter into this mysterious belief" to appreciate something of what believers are talking about—even if such an encounter leaves one's own unbelief intact. At the very least, such an encounter will expand one's understanding of a dimension of human life in which one does not share. For reasons such as these Strauss says, "I believe by simply replacing God by the creative genius of the Jewish people, one gives away, one deprives oneself—even if one does not believe—of a source of *human* understanding" ("Why We Remain Jews," 345). This view is entirely consistent with Strauss's oft repeated warnings about trying to understand authors better than they understood themselves. In this case, cultural Zionism falls into just this error by blurring the distinction between its own understandings of theological language as nothing more than a reflection of the people's genius and the self-understanding of biblical Judaism with its belief that theological language, however inadequate, has a referent in the living God.

48. Strauss, "Why We Remain Jews," 323.

49. Strauss, "Why We Remain Jews," 322–23.

50. Strauss, "Preface to *Spinoza's Critique of Religion,*" 142.

51. Leo Strauss, "Progress or Return?" in Leo Strauss, *Jewish Philosophy and the Crisis of Modernity: Essays and Lectures in Modern Jewish Thought*, ed. Kenneth Hart Green (Albany: State University of New York Press, 1997), 91–92.

52. Leo Strauss, "Sociological Historiography?" in *Leo Strauss: The Early Writings*, 104.

53. Perhaps the best known passage to this effect is in section 8 of the first essay in *The Genealogy of Morals*: "[From] the trunk of that tree of vengefulness and hatred, Jewish hatred—the profoundest and sublimest kind of hatred, capable of creating ideals and reversing values . . . there grew something equally incomparable, *a new love*" (*Basic Writings of Nietzsche*, 470). Consider also the following passage from *The Antichrist*: "[The] Jewish people are a people endowed with the toughest vital energy, who placed in impossible circumstances, voluntarily and out of the most profound prudence of self-preservation, take sides with all the instincts of decadence—not as mastered by them, but because they divined a power in these instincts with which one could prevail against 'the world'" (*The Portable Nietzsche*, 593).

54. Nietzsche, *Daybreak*, 205.

55. Strauss, "Progress or Return?" 92.

56. Nietzsche, *Daybreak*, section 205. The passage reads in part:

> *Of the people of Israel*.—Among the spectacles to which the coming century invites us is the decision as to the destiny of the Jews of Europe. That their die is cast, that they have crossed their Rubicon, is now palpably obvious: all that is left for them is either to become the masters of Europe or to lose Europe as they once a long time ago lost Egypt. . . . In Europe they have gone through an eighteen century schooling such as no other nation of this continent can boast of—and what they have experienced in this terrible time of schooling has benefited the individual to a greater degree than it has the community as a whole. As a consequence of this, the psychological and spiritual resources of the Jews are extraordinary. . . . Every Jew possesses in the history of his fathers and grandfathers a great fund of examples of the coldest self-possession and endurance in fearful situations, of the subtlest outwitting and exploitation of chance and misfortune; their courage beneath the cloak of miserable submission, their heroism in *spernere se sperni* [despising that one is despised], surpasses the virtues of all the saints. For two millennia an attempt was made to render them contemptible by treating them with contempt. . . . They themselves have never ceased to believe themselves called to the highest things, and the virtues which pertain to all who suffer have likewise never ceased to adorn them. The way in which they honor their fathers and their children, the rationality of their marriages and their marriage customs, distinguish them among all Europeans. In addition to all this, they have known how to create for themselves a feeling of power and of eternal revenge out of the very occupations left to them. . . . For our respect for ourselves is tied to being able to practice requital, in good things and in bad. At the same time however, their revenge does not easily go too far: for they all possess the liberality, including liberality of soul, to which frequent changes of residence, of climate, of the customs of one's neighbours and oppressors educates men; they possess by far the greatest experience of human society, and even in their passions they practice the caution taught by this experience. . . . They themselves know best that a conquest

of Europe, or any kind of act of violence, on their part is not to be thought of: but they also know that at some future time Europe may fall into their hands like a ripe fruit if they would only just extend them. To bring that about they need, in the meantime, to distinguish themselves in every domain of European distinction and to stand everywhere in the first rank: until they have reached the point at which they themselves determine what is distinguishing. Then they will be called the inventors and signposts of the nations of Europe and no longer offend their sensibilities. And whither shall this assembled abundance of grand impressions which for every Jewish family constitutes Jewish history, this abundance of passions, virtues, decisions, renunciations, struggles, victories of every kind—whither shall it stream out if not at last into great men and great works! Then, when the Jews can exhibit as their work such jewels and golden vessels as the European nations of a briefer and less profound experience could not and cannot produce, when Israel will have transformed its eternal vengeance into an eternal blessing for Europe: then there will again arrive that seventh day on which the ancient Jewish God may *rejoice* in himself, his creation and his chosen people—and let us all, all of us, rejoice with him!

57. Strauss, "Why We Remain Jews," 325.

58. Leo Strauss, "Freud on Moses and Monotheism," in Strauss, *Jewish Philosophy and the Crisis of Modernity*, 295–96.

59. Strauss, "Why We Remain Jews," 326.

60. Strauss, "Response to Frankfurt's 'Word of Principle,'" 69.

61. *The Portable Nietzsche*, 171.

62. Strauss, "Comment on Weinberg's Critique," 121.

63. "Only the biblical authors understand what omnipotence really means, because only if God is omnipotent can one particular code be the absolute code. But an omnipotent God who is in principle perfectly knowable to man is in a way subject to man, insofar as knowledge is in a way power. Therefore a truly omnipotent God must be a mysterious God" (Strauss, "Progress or Return?" 119). See also John Ranieri, "Leo Strauss on Jerusalem and Athens: A Girardian Analysis," *Shofar: An Interdisciplinary Journal of Jewish Studies* 22, no. 2 (Winter 2004): 85–104; and John Ranieri, "Athens, Jerusalem and the Good Society: Girardian Thoughts on Leo Strauss," *Budhi: A Journal of Ideas and Culture* 7, no. 3 (2004): 1–34.

64. Nietzsche, *The Antichrist*, section 16.

65. Lowith and Strauss, "Correspondence," 183, 190.

66. Leo Strauss, "Letter to the Editor: The State of Israel," in *Jewish Philosophy and the Crisis of Modernity*, 413.

67. "On the Argument with European Science," 107–8.

68. "Review of Albert Levkowitz, *Contemporary Religious Thinkers*," in *Leo Strauss: The Early Writings*, 107.

69. Leo Strauss, "Introductory Essay to Hermann Cohen, *Religion of Reason Out of the Sources of Judaism*," in *Jewish Philosophy and the Crisis of Modernity*, 277. See also *Leo Strauss: The Early Writings*, 112–13, 156–57.

70. Commenting on Cohen's criticism of Spinoza, Strauss notes how the idea that Judaism

has as its goal the establishment of a Jewish state is viewed by Cohen as a satanic notion. Strauss then goes on to add: "he [Cohen] certainly would not have considered it satanic but divine if someone said that the sole end of the religion of Judaism is the establishment and preservation of the socialist state" (*Leo Strauss: The Early Writings*, 144).

71. Strauss, "Progress or Return?" 88. The footnote accompanying this statement holds the "most accepted view," in Strauss's opinion, to be that of Maimonides. Whether Maimonides' is in fact the most accepted view on this question or whether Strauss's is the most accepted view of Maimonides is beyond the scope of this article.

72. Strauss, "Progress or Return?" 88.

73. See Michael Walzer, *Exodus and Revolution* (New York: Basic Books, 1985). The following description by Walzer of the influence of the Exodus identifies the very things that Strauss associates with modern notions of progress: "Exodus is a model for messianic and millenarian thought, and it is also a standing alternative to it—a secular and historical account of 'redemption,' an account that does not require the miraculous transformation of the material world but sets God's people marching through the world toward a better place within it" (17).

74. See Leo Strauss, *On Tyranny: Including the Strauss-Kojève Correspondence*, ed. Victor Gourevitch and Michael S. Roth, rev. and expanded ed. (New York: Free Press, 1991), 177–78; Karl Lowith and Leo Strauss, "Correspondence Concerning Modernity," *Independent Journal of Philosophy* 4 (1983): 111.

75. *Leo Strauss: The Early Writings*, 32–33.

76. Strauss, "Biblical History and Science," 135.

77. Strauss, *Studies in Platonic Political Philosophy*, 1–26.

78. Strauss, "Jerusalem and Athens," 167–73.

79. Strauss, "Note on the Plan of Nietzsche's *Beyond Good and Evil*," 176. For a detailed discussion of Strauss's essay, see Laurence Lampert, *Leo Strauss and Nietzsche* (Chicago: University of Chicago Press, 1996).

80. Hermann Cohen, who, for Strauss, is an example (perhaps *the* example) of Jewish thought's capitulation to modern ideology, does not fare well in *Studies*. As noted, Strauss criticizes him first in "Jerusalem and Athens" and then devotes the entire last chapter of the book to further, more pointed criticism. One could argue that the chapters that follow the Nietzsche essay (chapters 9–15) have, from the perspective of Straussian political philosophy, the character of a descent. We move from the estimable medieval Jewish rationalism of Maimonides through Machiavelli and other moderns, and end with Cohen, who embodies the confusion of modern thought with Jewish tradition.

81. Strauss, "Note on the Plan of Nietzsche's *Beyond Good and Evil*," 180.

82. Strauss, "Note on the Plan of Nietzsche's *Beyond Good and Evil*," 181.

83. Strauss, "Note on the Plan of Nietzsche's *Beyond Good and Evil*," 181.

84. Strauss, "Note on the Plan of Nietzsche's *Beyond Good and Evil*," 188–90.

85. Lowith and Strauss, "Correspondence," 184, 189.

86. Strauss, "Note on the Plan of Nietzsche's *Beyond Good and Evil*," 190.

87. Strauss, "Why We Remain Jews," 328.

88. Strauss, "Note on the Plan of Nietzsche's *Beyond Good and Evil*," 179.

89. Strauss, "Freud on Moses and Monotheism," 286.

90. Giles Fraser, *Redeeming Nietzsche* (London: Routledge, 2002), 110, 115–16.

91. Strauss, *On Tyranny: Including the Strauss-Kojève Correspondence*, ed. Gourevitch and Ross, 209.

92. Lowith and Strauss, "Correspondence," 183.

93. Leo Strauss, "Perspectives on the Good Society," in *Jewish Philosophy and the Crisis of Modernity*, 440.

94. Strauss, "Why We Remain Jews," 328.

95. Strauss, "Progress or Return?" 117.

96. See Victor Gourevitch, "Philosophy and Politics II," *Review of Metaphysics* 22, no. 2, (1968): 292–99, 325.

97. Leo Strauss, "Notes on Lucretius," in *Liberalism, Ancient and Modern* (Chicago: University of Chicago Press, 1968), 76–135. Here too Nietzsche's influence weighs heavily, as Strauss ponders the Lucretian notion that "nothing lovable is eternal or sempiternal" and that "the eternal is not lovable" (preface to *Liberalism: Ancient and Modern*, x). For Strauss's treatment of Thucydides, see Leo Strauss, "Thucydides: The Meaning of Political History," in *The Rebirth of Classical Political Rationalism: Essays and Lectures by Leo Strauss*, selected and introduced by Thomas Pangle (Chicago: University of Chicago Press, 1989); Leo Strauss, "Preliminary Observations on the Gods in Thucydides' Work," in *Studies in Platonic Political Philosophy*, 89–104; Leo Strauss, *The City and Man* (Chicago: University of Chicago Press, 1964), 139–241. Elsewhere I have suggested that Strauss assimilates the biblical God to this understanding of mystery; the eternal God of the Bible, as depicted by Strauss, is inscrutable, omnipotent, and mysterious—the emphasis is hardly on God as especially loving or lovable. See Ranieri, "Leo Strauss on Jerusalem and Athens: A Girardian Analysis," 85–104; and Ranieri, "Athens, Jerusalem and the Good Society: Girardian Thoughts on Leo Strauss," 1–34.

98. Strauss, "Thucydides: The Meaning of Political History," 101.

99. Strauss, *Philosophy and Law*, 135–36. This also seems to be the basis for much of Strauss's criticism of Spinoza, who, Strauss believes, rejects the most characteristic features of Jewish tradition in favor of a modernized, that is, Christianized version of Judaism.

100. Strauss, *Liberalism, Ancient and Modern*, x.

101. Strauss, *Liberalism, Ancient and Modern*, viii–ix.

102. Strauss, *Liberalism, Ancient and Modern*, x–xi.

103. Heinrich Meier, *Carl Schmitt and Leo Strauss: The Hidden Dialogue*, trans. J. Harvey Lomax (Chicago: University of Chicago Press, 1995), 124–25.

104. Preface to *Liberalism, Ancient and Modern*, vii–xi. Specifically, Strauss sometimes cites Churchill's England as a society that has been able to adapt modern ideals to contemporary circumstances in ways that are prudent, moderate, and never lose contact with the classical political tradition. In a 1941 lecture, he praises the English for "defending the eternal principles of civilization" and adds that "it is the English, and not the Germans, who *deserve* to be, and to *remain*, an *imperial* nation . . . for only the English, and not the

Germans, have understood that in order to *deserve* to exercise imperial rule . . . one must have learned, for a very long time to spare the vanquished and to crush the arrogant." See Strauss, "German Nihilism," 372.

105. René Girard, *I See Satan Fall like Lightning,* trans. James G. Williams (Maryknoll, NY: Orbis Books, 2001), 164–65.

106. René Girard, *Oedipus Unbound* (Stanford, CA: Stanford University Press, 2004), 89–90.

107. Girard, *I See Satan Fall like Lightning,* 170–71.

108. Gregory Bruce Smith, "Athens and Washington: Leo Strauss and the American Regime," in *Leo Strauss, the Straussians, and the American Regime,* ed. Kenneth L. Deutsch and John A. Murley (Lanham, MD: Rowman and Littlefield, 1999), 105.

109. "He opposed the possibility of a planetary aristocracy to the alleged necessity of a universal classless and stateless society. Being certain of the tameness of modern western man, he preached the sacred right of 'merciless extinction' of large masses of men with as little restraint as his great antagonist had done. He used much of his unsurpassable and inexhaustible power of passionate and fascinating speech for making his readers loathe, not only socialism and communism, but conservatism, nationalism and democracy as well. After having taken upon himself this great political responsibility, he could not show his readers a way toward political responsibility. He left them no choice except that between irresponsible indifference to politics and irresponsible political options. He thus prepared a regime, which, as long as it lasted, made discredited democracy look again like the golden age." In Strauss, "What Is Political Philosophy?" 54–55. See also Strauss, "German Nihilism," 360–63, 370–72.

110. Lampert, *Leo Strauss and Nietzsche,* 9, 184–86. Lampert's own perspective is on full display in his criticism of Strauss. After citing Strauss's remark that Nietzsche "preached the sacred right of 'merciless extinction' of large masses of men with as little restraint as his great antagonist [Marx]," Lampert notes that "the sacred here can hardly refer to Dionysos, the dancing god to whom alone Nietzsche would submit as a disciple. . . . the hardness and cruelty characteristic of Dionysos are not the preached extinctions of whole populations that entered our history as pious acts of followers of the jealous God" (9).

111. Lowith and Strauss, "Correspondence," 183–84.

112. Leo Strauss, *On Tyranny: Including the Strauss-Kojève Correspondence,* ed. Gourevitch and Ross, 177–78.

113. Karl Lowith and Leo Strauss, "Correspondence Concerning Modernity," *Independent Journal of Philosophy* 4 (1983): 111.

114. Strauss, "Preliminary Observations on the Gods in Thucydides' Work," 89–104; *City and Man,* 139–241.

115. "For what is 'first for us' is not the philosophic understanding of the city but that understanding that is inherent in the city as such, in the pre-philosophic city, according to which the city sees itself as subject and subservient to the divine in the ordinary understanding of the divine or looks up to it. Only by beginning at this point will we be open to the full impact of the all-important question which is coeval with philosophy although the philosophers do not frequently pronounce it—the question *quid sit deus.*" *City and Man,* 241.

116. Leo Strauss, *The Argument and the Action of Plato's Laws* (Chicago: University of Chicago Press, 1975), 1–2.

117. Strauss, "Note on the Plan of Nietzsche's *Beyond Good and Evil*," 179–80.

118. Strauss, "Note on the Plan of Nietzsche's *Beyond Good and Evil*," 180.

119. Strauss, "Note on the Plan of Nietzsche's *Beyond Good and Evil*," 180–81.

120. Strauss, "Note on the Plan of Nietzsche's *Beyond Good and Evil*," 181.

121. René Girard, "The Founding Murder in the Philosophy of Nietzsche," in *Violence and Truth: On the Work of René Girard* (Stanford, CA: Stanford University Press, 1988), 227–46.

122. René Girard, *Things Hidden since the Foundation of the World*, trans. Stephen Bann and Michael Metteer (Stanford, CA: Stanford University Press, 1987), 226.

123. Girard, "The Founding Murder in the Philosophy of Nietzsche," 239, 245.

124. "Heidegger fought on the same side as Nietzsche, no doubt, the side of the old sacred, but on positions less exposed, less forward, less dangerous and revealing than Nietzsche's. He has succeeded, at least for a while, in neutralizing the 'imprudence' of Nietzsche in the domain of religion." René Girard, *The Girard Reader* (New York: Crossroad, 1996), 255.

125. Strauss, "Note on the Plan of Nietzsche's *Beyond Good and Evil*," 177–81.

126. Girard, "The Founding Murder in the Philosophy of Nietzsche," 241.

127. *The Girard Reader*, 247.

128. Girard, "The Founding Murder in the Philosophy of Nietzsche," 244.

129. Leo Strauss, "Kurt Riezler," in *What Is Political Philosophy?* (Chicago: University of Chicago Press, 1959), 260.

130. Strauss's reference to the soul's longing for a star is almost certainly meant to evoke Nietzsche's *Zarathustra*: "Alas the time is coming when man will no longer give birth to a star . . . What is love? What is creation? What is longing? What is a star? Thus asks the last man, and he blinks." *The Portable Nietzsche*, 129.

131. Strauss, "Thucydides: The Meaning of Political History," 72, 101.

132. Strauss, "Note on the Plan of Nietzsche's *Beyond Good and Evil*," 181.

133. Karl Reinhardt, "Nietzsche's 'Ariadne's Complaint,'" *Interpretation*. 6 no. 3 (1977): 207–24.

The Straussian Moment

Peter Thiel
President, Clarium Capital Management

For I dipt into the future, far as human eye could see,
Saw the Vision of the world, and all the wonder that would be;
Saw the heavens fill with commerce, argosies of magic sails,
Pilots of the purple twilight dropping down with costly bales;
Heard the heavens fill with shouting, and there rain'd a ghastly dew
From the nations' airy navies grappling in the central blue;
Far along the world-wide whisper of the south-wind rushing warm,
With the standards of the peoples plunging thro' the thunder-storm;
Till the war-drum throbb'd no longer, and the battle-flags were furl'd
In the Parliament of man, the Federation of the world.
There the common sense of most shall hold a fretful realm in awe,
And the kindly earth shall slumber, lapt in universal law.

—Alfred, Lord Tennyson, "Locksley Hall"

The twenty-first century started with a bang on September 11, 2001. In those shocking hours, the entire political and military framework of the nineteenth and twentieth centuries, and indeed of the modern age, with its emphasis on deterrent armies, rational nation-states, public debates, and international diplomacy, was called into question. For how could mere talking or even great force deter a handful of crazy, determined, and suicidal persons who seemingly operated outside of all the norms of the liberal

West? And what needed now to be done, given that technology had advanced to a point where a tiny number of people could inflict unprecedented levels of damage and death?

The awareness of the West's vulnerability called for a new compromise, and this new compromise inexorably demanded more security at the expense of less freedom. On the narrow level of public policy, there needed to be more x-ray machines at airports; more security guards on airplanes; more identification cards and invasions of privacy; and fewer rights for some of the accused. Overnight, the fundamentalist civil rights mania of the American Civil Liberties Union (ACLU), which spoke in the language of inviolable individual rights, was rendered an unviable anachronism.

Even as the debate over freedom and security gathered strength, whatever military force could be mustered was used to track down those responsible for the violence of September 11. Despite rapid mobilization, those efforts met with limited success. America's antiquated military was not suited to fight such an enemy, for the enemy needed to be pursued not only in America, or in a handful of terrorist camps in Afghanistan, but to the very ends of the Earth. Even worse, like the Hydra, the enemy proliferated, so that for every slain jihadist, ten more arose to seek martyrdom in perverse emulation.

On the broader level of international cooperation and development, September 11 called for wholly different arrangements. The issue of unilateralism, and of the institutions designed to provide a cover for unilateralism, could be raised publicly by serious people for the first time since 1945. Much has been said elsewhere about the relative roles of the United States and the United Nations in the political sphere, but the underlying debates extend to even more fundamental issues.

For present purposes, it is worth drawing attention to one such fundamental issue, the twentieth-century policy debate about the containment of violence. Following World War II, the centrist consensus on international development called for enormous wealth transfers from the developed to the developing world. Under the aegis of the World Bank, the International Monetary Fund, and an array of other organizations, hundreds of billions of dollars were funneled (in cheap loans or outright grants) to Third World governments, thereby, as the theory went, fostering economic growth and prosperity. But was this consensus right? Are economic incentives in fact powerful enough to contain violence?

Ex ante, wealth transfers made a certain amount of sense in the late 1940s. Those who had taken Marx seriously and were haunted by the specter of communist revolution hoped the wealth transfer apparatus would help win the Cold War and bring about world peace. For the Rockefellers to keep their fortunes (and their heads), it was perhaps prudent for them to give some of what they had to the wretched of the Earth and make them a little bit less wretched.

But *ex post*, one wonders how policymakers could have been so naïve. Let us set aside the inconvenient fact that the wealth transfer apparatus never worked as advertised, so that the West's wealth was largely squandered on white elephant projects, no real economic development took place, and even in the best of cases the money simply circulated back to the West, ending up in Swiss bank accounts held by Third World dictators. As recent events have illustrated vividly, the real problem with the theory goes much deeper. For when the long-expected blow finally came, it did not come from the *favelas* of Rio de Janeiro, or from starving peasants in Burkina Faso, or from Tibetan yak herders earning less than a dollar a day. On the contrary, it came from a direction none of the modern theories had predicted: the perpetrators were upper-middle-class Saudi Arabians, often with college degrees and with great expectations. Their mastermind, Osama bin Laden, had inherited a fortune now worth an estimated $250 million, mostly made during the Saudi oil boom of the 1970s. Had he been born in America, bin Laden could have been a Rockefeller.

In this way, the singular example of bin Laden and his followers has rendered incomplete the economically motivated political thought that has dominated the modern West. From *The Wealth of Nations* on the right to *Das Kapital* on the left, and to Hegel and Kant and their many followers somewhere in between, the brute facts of September 11 demand a reexamination of the foundations of modern politics. The openly intellectual agenda of this essay is to suggest what that reexamination entails.

The Question of Human Nature

From the Enlightenment on, modern political philosophy has been characterized by the abandonment of a set of questions that an earlier age had deemed central: What is a well-lived life? What does it mean to be human? What is the nature of the city and humanity? How does culture and religion fit into all of this? For the modern world, the death of God was followed by the disappearance of the question of human nature.

This disappearance had many repercussions. If humans can be approximated as rational economic actors (and, ultimately, even Adam Smith and

Karl Marx agree on this point), then those who seek glory in the name of God or country appear odd; but if such odd people are commonplace and capable of asserting themselves with explosive force, then the account of politics that pretends they do not exist needs to be reexamined.

There is, of course, an older Western tradition, a tradition that offered a less dogmatically economic view of human nature. That older account realized that not all people are so modest and lacking in ambition that they will content themselves, like Voltaire's Candide, with cultivating their gardens. Instead, it recognized that humans are potentially evil or at least dangerous beings; and, while there are vast differences between the Christian virtues of Augustine and the pagan virtues of Machiavelli, neither thinker would have dared lose sight of the problematic nature of humanity.[1]

The most direct method for comprehending a world in which not all human beings are *homo economicus* would therefore appear to involve a return to some version of the older tradition. However, before we try to embark on that return, there is another mystery we must confront: Why did the older tradition fail in the first place? After all, it seemed to ask some obvious and important questions. How could these questions simply be abandoned and forgotten?

On a theoretical level, the older tradition consisted of two radically incompatible streams symbolized by Athens and Jerusalem. An enormous gulf separates Athens from Jerusalem. Pierre Manent summarizes this division in *The City of Man:*

> In the eyes of the citizen, what value is there to the mortification of the Christian, when what matters is not to fall on one's knees but to mount one's horse, and the sins one ought to expiate or rather correct are not the sins one commits against chastity and truth, but military and political errors? In the eyes of the Christian, what value is there to the political and military endeavors of the citizen, when he believes that, victory or defeat, whatever the regime, this world is a vale of tears ravaged by sin and that states are nothing more and better than vast bands of robbers? To each of the two protagonists, the sacrifices the other calls for are vain.[2]

For a long time, in the Middle Ages and thereafter, the West tried to gloss over these conflicts and instead to build on the many things these traditions had in common, but in the long term, like two giant millstones grinding against one another, "city and church . . . wore each other down as they went from conflicts to conciliations. Each one's efforts to return to its original truth had strangely wrought its own defeat."[3] Neither side ever could win decisively, but in the long term, each side could decisively discredit the other, thus giving rise to the modern "individual" who defines him- or herself by rejecting all forms of sacrifice: "Since the city and the church reproach one another with the vanity of their sacrifice, the individual is the man who rejects each form of sacrifice and defines himself by this refusal."[4]

In practice, this dialectic was never simply or even primarily intellectual. For when one takes these questions seriously, they have serious repercussions, and the same holds for the modern and inverse movement that involved their abandonment.

The early modern era of the West—the sixteenth and seventeenth centuries—was characterized by the disintegration of these two older traditions and by ever more desperate attempts to force everything back together into some functioning whole. Where agreement over questions of virtue, the good life, and the true religion was unraveling, the immediate attempt involved forging such an agreement through force. This force escalated in the periods of the Reformation and Counter Reformation, and culminated in the paroxysm of the Thirty Years' War, which remains perhaps the most deadly period in the history of Europe. By some estimates, in Germany, the locus of the conflict, well over half the population was eradicated.

However, at the end of this process, agreement had become more elusive than ever, the differences greater than ever. The violence had failed to create a new unity. This failure was formalized in the Peace of Westphalia, so that 1648 can be fixed as the single year that dates the birth of the modern era. Questions of virtue and the true religion henceforth would be decided by each sovereign. The sovereigns would agree to disagree. Inexorably, questions of virtue and religion became private questions; polite and respectable individuals learned not to talk about them too much, because they could lead to nothing but unproductive conflicts.

For the modern world, questions about the nature of humanity would be viewed on par with the struggle among the Lilliputians about the correct way to cut open an egg. Hobbes, the first truly modern philosopher, boasted of how he deserted and ran away from fighting in a religious war; a cowardly life had become preferable to a heroic but meaningless death.[5] *Dulce et decorum est pro patria mori* had been an important part of the old tradition; henceforth, it would be seen as nothing more than an old lie.

And so, the Enlightenment undertook a major strategic retreat. If the only way to stop people from killing one another about the right way to open an egg involved a world where nobody thought about it too much, then the intellectual cost of ceasing such thought seemed a small price to pay. The question of human nature was abandoned because it is too perilous a question to debate.

John Locke: The American Compromise

The new science of economics and the practice of capitalism filled the vacuum created by the abandonment of the older tradition. That new science found its most important proponent in John Locke and its greatest practical success in the United States, a nation whose conception owed so much to Locke that one exaggerates only slightly to describe him as its definitive founder.

We must return to the eighteenth century to appreciate the tremendous change Locke wrought. Revolutionary America was haunted by the fear of religious war and the fanatical imposition of virtue on the entire state. The Declaration of Independence's evocation of "the right to life, liberty, and the pursuit of happiness" had a counterpoint in the older tradition, in which the first two had not existed and the pursuit of happiness would have seemed inferior to (and certainly much more subjective than) the virtuous life. When one fast-forwards to the America of the 1990s, the larger context of the Founding had been forgotten: America had proved so successful in shaping the modern world that most Americans could no longer recognize the originality and strangeness of its founding conception.

Locke's personal example is instructive of the subtle path toward the liberalism of the American Revolution. Locke's argument proceeds in an understated manner; he does not wish to inflame passions by taking sides in the contentious debates of the sixteenth and seventeenth centuries. But since it would be offensive to suggest that the things that matter most to people are silly or irrelevant, he also must avoid inflaming passions by openly denigrating all those who do take sides. In no place is there a greater need for sensitivity than on the question of religion. Religious passions had led to religious wars, but a passionate repudiation of religion (and of Christianity in particular) did not promise peace. Locke did not need the examples of the French or Russian Revolutions to know this.

And so the philosopher takes a seemingly moderate path. In *The Reasonableness of Christianity,* the philosopher sets out to denounce those "justly decried" atheists who have openly questioned the importance of the rules set for mortals by the deity.[6] But in the process of this denunciation, we learn many new things about those rules. Locke teaches us that the command for children to honor their parents does not apply if the parents have been "unnaturally careless."[7] Marriage remains an important compact, but "the Wife has, in many cases, a Liberty to separate from [the husband],"[8] and "[t]he first and strongest desire God planted in men" is not love of God or others but a healthy concern with one's self-preservation.[9] Unfortunately, the state of nature is an "ill condition," so that those living in it are "needy and wretched"; the escape from nature, however, provides the path to self-preservation and happiness.[10] It follows from this that humans are not stewards of nature (for God has provided very little to start with), but are themselves the creators of wealth and property: "[L]abor makes the far greatest part of the value of things we enjoy in this world."[11] From there, the stretch to capitalist basics is modest. Avarice is no longer a mortal sin, and there is nothing wrong with the infinite accumulation of wealth;[12] it follows quite naturally that "the law of God and nature" says that government "must not raise taxes on the property of the people without the consent of the people, given by themselves, or their deputies."[13]

As for the person of Christ, Locke informs us that Jesus's words were not to be taken plainly. If Jesus had told people exactly what he was up to, the Jewish and Roman authorities "would have taken away his life; at least they would have . . . hindered the work he was about," for his teachings would have threatened the civic order and functioning of government. And so Christ concealed his meaning so that he might live and teach.[14] Locke's conception of Christ is a world removed from that of the medieval passion plays or *The Passion* of Mel Gibson; still, the character Locke attributes to Christ comports rather well with the character that one reasonably might attribute to Locke himself and the passionless world he set out to create.

Over time, the country founded by Locke would do away with Christian religiosity even as it maintained many outward appearances of it. The United States eventually would become more secular and materialist, though most of its citizens would continue to call themselves "Christians."[15] There would be no catastrophic war against religion of the sort one had in France or Russia, but there would be no counterrevolution either. Only occasionally would conservative moralists express their perplexity at how a nation ostensibly founded on Christian principles ever could have drifted so far from its original conception; never would it cross their minds to think that this process of gradual drift had been a part of that original conception.

* * *

In a capitalist world, violent debates about truth—whether they concern questions of religion and virtue or questions about the nature of humanity—interfere with the productive conduct of commerce. It is therefore best for such questions to be eliminated or obscured. Thus, in Hobbes, all human complexity is reduced to the desire for power:

> The passions that most of all cause the difference of wit, are principally, the more or less desire of power, of riches, of knowledge, and of honour. All which may be reduced to the first, that is, desire of power. For riches, knowledge, and honour, are but several sorts of power.[16]

In Locke's *Essay Concerning Human Understanding*, the author elaborates the conception of power, while stripping it even further of anything that is specifically human: the will is the power to prefer one action over another; liberty is the power to act on this preference; the understanding is a power; a substance is merely the power to produce certain empirical effects, but these effects tell us nothing of the nature of the underlying substance.[17]

Once again, Locke proceeds cautiously. He does not directly tell us that human nature does not exist or that the older tradition of Aristotle or Aquinas is definitively wrong; he does not seek that clear a break with the past,[18] but he undermines the older tradition relentlessly, for when we observe things (and these things include other people), we can see only their secondary effects as manifested by their various powers.[19] We cannot know anything about their true natures or substances; it is an irreducible part of the human condition for humans to be limited, so that they can never know anything about the nature of humanity.[20] To ask a question about human substance, or the teleology of humanity's power, leads to debates as meaningless as "whether the best Relish were to be found in Apples, Plumbs, or Nuts."[21]

In the place of human nature, Locke leaves us with an unknowable "X."[22] This awareness of ignorance provides the low but solid ground on which the American Founding takes place. The human "X" may have certain wants and preferences, but nobody is in an authoritative position from which to challenge those desires.[23] And so, in a somewhat paradoxical manner, the unknowability of "X" leads to classic liberalism and the very strong assertion of the different rights that belong to that unknowable "X": the freedom of religion, for we cannot ever know what people are truly thinking in the temple of their minds; the freedom of speech, for we cannot irrefutably criticize the way people express themselves; the right to property and commerce, for we cannot second-guess what people will do with the things they possess.[24] "Capitalism," concludes Nobel laureate Milton Friedman, "is simply what humans do when they are left alone."

Of course, there are all sorts of hard boundary cases. One might wonder about what a libertarian framework has to say about the rights of children or criminals or insane people, or the limits of commodification (extortionate interest rates, indentured servitude, prostitution, sale of body parts, and so forth). But for Locke and the other American founders, these exceptional cases could be deferred for later consideration; in any event, the general principle of the unknowability of the human "X" would encourage a gradual expansion, over time, of the field of human freedom.[25]

There is one especially important category of boundary cases, and that concerns the question of origins. We shall return to that broader question later, but here it is worth noting one specific variant: even though we should not interfere with people disposing of their property as they see fit, how do we know that the property was acquired justly in the first place? The great importance of strong property rights would seem to force us to ask some hard questions about the origins of the property itself.

Once again, however, Locke urges us not to worry too much: there is very little value in the state of nature, and most value has been added by human work or intellect.[26] As a result, we need not reflect on the past and can focus on the future: Most new wealth will be created by the strong enforcement of property rights going forward and will be enjoyed by those who play by the capitalist rules.[27] Those who acquired their property through violence will not be capable of growing their fortunes, and in time will possess only a small and uninfluential fraction of the world's wealth. Locke would dismiss out of hand Balzac's sweeping and subversive notion that "behind every great fortune there lies a crime." We need not heed Brecht's call for more inspectors and inquisitors. Nothing should stop us from enjoying the prosperous tranquility of the capitalist paradise we have built for ourselves.

* * *

Since September 11, our peace has been broken. For there remains another very important boundary whose existence the American people had forgotten. They had forgotten about the rest of the world and its deep division from the West. The non-Western world had not yet seen the Peace of Westphalia. The progress of the Enlightenment has occurred at different rates in different parts of the world. And in that world outside the West, questions of religion and the purpose of humanity remained central; even in 2001 the greatest fear was not the fear of a painful death but the fear of what would happen to one in the life after that death.

And so, a religious war has been brought to a land that no longer cares for religious wars. Even President Bush, who styles himself a religious conservative, cannot bring himself to believe that it is religion that really matters: "[T]his great nation of many religions understands our war is not against Islam or against the faith practiced by the Muslim people."[28]

Where Bush downplays the differences, bin Laden emphasizes them, contrasting the world of pure Islam and the world of the decadent West in the most extreme way imaginable: "[T]he love of this world is wrong. You should love the other world . . . die in the right cause and go to the other world."[29]

Unfortunately, bin Laden is not simply an irrelevant crackpot of the sort that one might find screaming at the bemused spectators in Hyde Park. For bin Laden, unlike Locke, hard questions of morality and conduct need no postponement; their answers are clear and resolution cannot be delayed. Bin Laden is a passionate man of wealth and power, so that his personal example reminds us of the boundary cases Locke so readily dismissed.

Indeed, the oil industry, the source of bin Laden's wealth, presents one of the most glaring examples that run counter to Locke's felicitous generalizations. For most of the value of oil exists simply in nature, so that the "labor" that humans add by extracting and refining this oil is proportionately quite small. At the same time, however, economies rise and fall on the price of crude oil, so that it represents a significant share of the world's wealth. Indeed, the original expropriation of that oil built as many as half of the greatest fortunes of the twentieth century. And so the development of the oil industry, presided over by autocrats and despots from Asia to the Middle East and Africa, is the not-so-hidden story of crime on a scale so grand that the proceeds of that crime sufficed to purchase respectability and almost everything else. In helping to craft the post–World War II centrist economic policy consensus, the Rockefellers had forgotten their own family history.

Of course, in the long run, it may well be that power and prosperity go to those who follow Locke's capitalist rules, so that in the long run, the religious fanatics who have so violently and suddenly interposed themselves will eventually lack the wealth and the technology needed to threaten the nonreligious world the Enlightenment has built in the West; but none of this will matter if we are all dead in the short run.

Today, mere self-preservation forces all of us to look at the world anew, to think strange new thoughts, and thereby to awaken from that very long and profitable period of intellectual slumber and amnesia that is so misleadingly called the Enlightenment.

Carl Schmitt: The Persistence of the Political

But why should one return to the older tradition, when the newer world of commerce and capitalism at every point seems so much simpler and happier and more pragmatic? The German legal scholar Carl Schmitt offers an extreme alternative to Locke and all the thinkers of the Enlightenment. He concedes with the signatories of Westphalia that there never will be any agreement on the most important things, on questions of religion and virtue and the nature of humanity.[30] But where Locke says that it is in humanity's nature to know nothing about the nature of humanity, Schmitt responds that it is equally a part of the human condition to be divided by such questions and to be forced to take sides.[31]

Politics is the field of battle in which that division takes place, in which humans are forced to choose between friends and enemies. "The high points of politics," declares Schmitt, "are the moments in which the enemy is, in concrete clarity, recognized as the enemy."[32] The enemy is the one whose very presence forces us to confront the foundational questions about human nature anew; "the enemy is our own question as a figure."[33] Because of the permanence of these always contentious questions, one cannot unilaterally escape from all politics; those who attempt to do so are suffering from moments of supreme self-delusion; these include the signatories of the Kellogg Pact of 1928, which outlawed all war.[34]

Indeed, it is even worse: "[I]f a part of the population declares that it no longer recognizes enemies, then, depending on the circumstance, it joins their side and aids them."[35] There is no safety in unilateral disarmament. When one chooses not to decide, one still has a made a choice—invariably a mistaken choice, which implicitly assumes that humankind is fundamentally good or unproblematic.[36] For Schmitt, "it is a symptom of the political end":

> In Russia, before the Revolution, the doomed classes romanticized the Russian peasant as a good, brave, and Christian muzhik. . . . The aristocratic society of France before the Revolution of 1789 sentimentalized "man who is by nature good" and the virtue of the masses. . . . Nobody scented the revolution; it is incredible to see the security and unsuspiciousness with which these privileged spoke of the goodness, mildness, and innocence of the people when 1793 was already upon them—*spectacle ridicule et terrible*.[37]

Absent an invasion by aliens from outer space, there never can be a world state that politically unites all of humanity. It is a logical impossibility:

> The political entity cannot by its very nature be universal in the sense of embracing all of humanity and the entire world. If the different states, religions, classes, and other human groupings on earth should be so unified that a conflict among them is impossible and even inconceivable and if civil war should forever be foreclosed in a realm that embraces the globe, then the distinction of friend and enemy would also cease.[38]

In the medieval Catholic tradition, Schmitt sees the permanent political division of humanity as a pale reflection of an "eschatologically conceived state of historicity," which ultimately forces people to follow or reject Christ.[39] He connects the political and the religious by declaring himself against the "neutralizers, aesthetic inhabitants of Cockaigne, abortionists, cremationists and pacifists."[40] Just as pacifists believe that the political decision can be avoided in this world, so cremators reject the physical resurrection and the religious decision that needs to be made for the next world.

In this way, politics serves as a constant reminder to a fallen humanity that life is serious and that there are things that truly matter, and so Schmitt cites with great approval the Puritan Oliver Cromwell's speech denouncing Spain:

> Why, truly, your great Enemy is the Spaniard. He is the natural enemy. He is naturally so; he is naturally so throughout, by reason of that enmity that is in him against whatsoever is of God. "Whatsoever is of God" which is in you, or which may be in you.[41]

When bin Laden declares war on "the infidels, the Zionists, and the crusaders," Schmitt would not counsel reasoned half-measures. He would urge a new crusade as a way to rediscover the meaning and purpose of our lives, perhaps borrowing the exhortation from Pope Urban II at the Council of Clermont, who urged his eager listeners on to the First Crusade back in 1096: "Let the army of the Lord, when it rushes upon his enemies, shout but that one cry, '*Dieu le veult! Dieu le veult!*'"

* * *

Whatever its shortcomings, Schmitt's account of politics captures the essential strangeness of the unfolding confrontation between the West and Islam. This strangeness consists of the radical difference between the way the confrontation itself is viewed by the two sides. Perhaps never before in history has there been such a radical difference. The Islamic side retains a strong religious and political conception of reality; it views its struggle with the West as a matter more important than life and death, because Allah will judge his followers in the afterlife by how they performed in that struggle. Bin Laden would quote with approval the speeches of Cromwell and Urban II, requiring almost no changes at all. The language still resonates and motivates heroic self-sacrifice.

By contrast, on the Western side (if it can even be called a side), there is great confusion over what the fighting is for, and why there should be a civilizational war at all. An outright declaration of war against Islam would be unthinkable; we much prefer to think of these measures as police actions against a few unusual criminal sociopaths who happen to blow up buildings. We are nervous about considering a larger meaning to the struggle, and even the staunchest Western partisans of war know that we no longer believe in the existence of a *Gott mit uns* in heaven.

And then one encounters Schmitt's troubling challenge. A side in which everyone, like Hobbes, values this earthly life more than death is a side where everyone will run away from fighting and confrontation; but when one runs away from an enemy that continues to fight, one is ultimately going to lose—no matter how great the numerical or technological superiority may appear at the outset. Schmitt's solution to this impending defeat demands an affirmation of the political in the West. Here, however, one must confront an alternative and perhaps even more troubling conclusion. For let us assume that it is possible, somehow, to turn back the clock and set aside our uncertainties; that we can return to the faith of Cromwell and Urban II; that we understand Islam as the providential enemy of the West; and that we can then respond to Islam with the same ferocity with which it is now attacking the West. This would be a Pyrrhic victory, for it would come at the price of doing away with everything that fundamentally distinguishes the modern West from Islam.

A dangerous dynamic lurks in Schmitt's division of the world into friends and enemies. It is a dynamic that destroys the distinction and that altogether escapes Schmitt's clever calculations: one must choose one's enemies well, for one will soon be just like them.

* * *

If one agrees with Schmitt's starting assumptions, then the West must lose the war or lose its identity. One way or the other, the persistence of the political spells the doom of the modern West; but for the sake of completeness, we must consider also the inverse possibility, indirectly hinted at in the margins of Schmitt's own writings. For while it may well be that the political guarantees the seriousness of life and that, so long as the political exists, the world will remain divided, there is no guarantee that the political itself will survive.[42]

Let us grant that unilateral disarmament is impossible, at least for those who value survival, but is it not perhaps possible for everyone to disarm at once, and for everyone to reject politics at the same time? There can be no worldwide political entity, but there is a possibility of a worldwide abandonment of politics.

The Hegelian Alexandre Kojève believed that the end of history would be marked by the definitive abandonment of all the hard questions. Humanity itself would disappear, but there would no longer be any conflict:

> If Man becomes an animal again, his acts, his loves, and his play must also become purely "natural" again. Hence it would have to be admitted that after the end of History, men would construct their edifices and works of art as birds build their nests and spiders spin their webs. . . . "The *definitive annihilation* of Man *properly so-called*" also means the definitive disappearance of human Discourse (*Logos*) in the strict sense. Animals of the species *Homo sapiens* would react by conditioned reflexes to vocal signals or sign "language," and thus their so-called "discourses" would be like what is supposed to be the "language" of bees. What would disappear, then, is not only Philosophy or the search for discursive Wisdom, but also that Wisdom itself.[43]

Schmitt echoes these sentiments, albeit with rather different conclusions. In such a unified world, "what remains is neither politics nor state, but culture, civilization, economics, morality, law, art, entertainment, etc."[44] The world of "entertainment" represents the culmination of the shift away from politics. A representation of reality might appear to replace reality: instead of violent wars, there could be violent video games; instead of heroic feats, there could be thrilling amusement park rides; instead of serious thought, there could be "intrigues of all sorts," as in a soap opera. It is a world where people spend their lives amusing themselves to death.

Schmitt does not reject the possibility of such a world out of hand, but believes that it will not happen in an entirely autochthonous manner:

> The acute question to pose is upon whom will fall the frightening power implied in a world-embracing economic and technical organization. This question can by no means be dismissed in the belief that everything would

> then function automatically, that things would administer themselves, and that a government by people over people would be superfluous because human beings would then be absolutely free. For what would they be free? This can be answered by optimistic or pessimistic conjectures, all of which finally lead to an anthropological profession of faith.[45]

Such an artificial world requires a "religion of technicity" that has faith in the "unlimited power and dominion over nature . . . [and] in the unlimited potential for change and for happiness in the natural this-worldly existence of man."[46] For Schmitt the political theologian, this "Babylonian unity" represents a brief harmony that prefigures the final catastrophe of the Apocalypse.[47] Following the medieval tradition, Schmitt knows and fears that this artificial unity can be brought about only by the shadowy figure of the Antichrist.[48] He will surreptitiously take over the entire world at the end of human history by seducing people with the promise of "peace and security":

> God created the world; the Antichrist counterfeits it. . . . The sinister magician recreates the world, changes the face of the earth, and subdues nature. Nature serves him; for what purpose is a matter of indifference—for any satisfaction of artificial needs, for ease and comfort. Men who allow themselves to be deceived by him see only the fabulous effect; nature seems to be overcome, the age of security dawns; everything has been taken care of, a clever foresight and planning replace Providence.[49]

The world where everything seems to administer itself is the world of science fiction, of Stephenson's *Snow Crash,* or of *The Matrix* for those who choose not to take their red pills. But no representation of reality ever is the same as reality, and one must never lose sight of the larger framework within which the representation exists. The price of abandoning oneself to such an artificial representation is always too high, because the decisions that are avoided are always too important.[50] By making people forget that they have souls, the Antichrist will succeed in swindling people out of them.[51]

Leo Strauss: Proceed with Caution

We are at an impasse.

On the one hand, we have the newer project of the Enlightenment, which never became comprehensive on a global scale, and perhaps always came at too high a price of self-stultification. On the other hand, we have a return to the older tradition, but that return is fraught with far too much violence. The incredibly drastic solutions favored by Schmitt in his dark musings have become impossible after 1945, in a world of nuclear weapons and limitless destruction through technology.

What sort of coherent intellectual or practical synthesis is then possible at all? The political philosopher Leo Strauss attempted to solve this central paradox of the postmodern world. The challenge of that task is reflected in the difficulty of Strauss's own writings, which are prohibitively obscurantist to the uninitiated. A representative and not entirely random passage can serve as an illustration: "The unity of knowledge and communication of knowledge can also be compared to the combination of man and horse, although not to a centaur."[52]

Indeed, there is little in Strauss that is more clear than the need for less transparency. Unchecked philosophizing poses great risks to philosophers (as well as the cities they inhabit), as in even the most liberal or open-minded regimes there exist certain deeply problematic truths.[53] Strauss is convinced that he is not the first to have discovered or rediscovered these truths. The great writers and philosophers of the past also had known of these matters but, in order to protect themselves from persecution, these thinkers used an "esoteric" mode of writing in which their "literature is addressed, not to all readers, but to trustworthy and intelligent readers only."[54]

As a thought experiment, Strauss invites us to consider the position of a "historian living in a totalitarian country, a generally respected and unsuspected member of the only party in existence."[55] As a result of his studies, this historian comes "to doubt the soundness of the government-sponsored interpretation of the history of religion."[56] On an exoteric level, this historian will make a passionate defense of the state-sponsored view,[57] but esoterically, between the lines, "he would write three or four sentences in that terse and lively style which is apt to arrest the attention of young men who love to think."[58] It would be enough for the attentive reader, but not enough for the invariably less intelligent government censors.[59] Alternately, our writer might even state "certain truths quite openly by using as mouthpiece some disreputable character. . . . There would then be good reason for our finding in the greatest literature of the past so many interesting devils, madmen, beggars, sophists, drunkards, epicureans, and buffoons."[60]

Strauss summarizes the benefits of such a strange mode of discourse:

> It has all the advantages of private communication without having its greatest disadvantage—that it reaches only the writer's acquaintances. It has all

> the advantages of public communication without having its greatest disadvantage—capital punishment for the author.[61]

Because there are books (and perhaps other writings) that "do not reveal their full meaning as intended by the author unless one ponders over them 'day and night' for a long time," cultural relativism and intellectual nihilism are not the final word.[62] Strauss believes that there exists a truth about human nature, and that this truth can in principle be known to humanity. Indeed, the great writers of the past are in far more agreement about this truth than their exoteric disagreements would lead the superficial reader to believe, "for there were more great men who were stepsons of their time or out of step with the future than one would easily believe."[63] These writers only *appeared* to conform to the diverse cities they inhabited. Strauss alludes to the dangers they faced, by reminding us of the warning Goethe had Faust deliver to his assistant: "The few who understood something of men's heart and mind, who were foolish enough not to restrain their full heart but to reveal their feeling and their vision to the vulgar, have ever been crucified and burned."[64]

* * *

There are no short cuts in Strauss. The philosopher practices what he preaches, and so one will search in vain in Strauss's writings for a systematic statement of the hidden truth. Perhaps Strauss's only incremental concession to the would-be philosopher lies in the fact that his writings are transparently esoteric and hard to understand, in contradistinction to the past writers who wrote seemingly straightforward books whose truly esoteric nature was therefore even more obscured. "The open agenda of the Straussians," declares Harvard government professor Harvey Mansfield (and himself a Straussian), is limited to "reading the Great Books for their own sake," and does not include offering dumbed-down summaries.[65]

Nevertheless, certain themes emerge and recur—the question of the city and humanity, the issues of founding and origins, and the relation between religion and the best regime. To generalize a bit more, even if one does not take one's bearings entirely from the exceptional case (as do Machiavelli and Schmitt), it is a case that must not be forgotten. An account of politics that speaks only of the smooth functioning of the machinery of government is incomplete, and one also must consider the circumstances in which this machinery is built or created in the first place—and, by extension, where it might be threatened or modified and reconstructed.[66]

When one widens the aperture of one's investigations, one will find that there are more things in heaven and Earth than dreamt of in the modern world of Locke or Montaigne. The fact that these things are hidden does not mean that they do not exist or that they are unknowable. On the problematic question of origins, for instance, Strauss notes the surprising convergence, at least on the level of factual detail, in the Roman myth of the founding of the greatest city of the ancient world and in what the book of Genesis says about the founding of the first city in the history of the world.[67]

Does Strauss then believe that "there cannot be a great and glorious society without the equivalent of the murder of Remus by his brother Romulus?"[68] At first, he seems to suggest that America is the one exception in all of history to this rule, quoting with approval the patriotic Thomas Paine: "[T]he Independence of America [was] accompanied by a Revolution in the principles and practice of Governments. . . . Government founded on a moral theory, on a system of universal peace, on the indefeasible hereditary Rights of Man, is now revolving from west to east by a stronger impulse than the Government of the sword revolved from east to west."[69] But within a few pages, we find that even in the case of the American Founding, this patriotic account is not necessarily the whole truth, and the reader is informed that perhaps "America owes her greatness not only to her habitual adherence to the principles of freedom and justice, but also to her occasional deviation from them."[70] Moreover, we are told that there exists a "mischievous interpretation of the Louisiana Purchase and of the fate of the Red Indians."[71] Indeed, the philosopher's decision to write esoterically reminds us that even in America, the most liberal regime in history, there remain politically incorrect taboos.[72]

In reminding us of the permanent problems, the political philosopher agrees with the political theologian's exhortation to seriousness and also joins the latter in rejecting as illusory the notion that "everything has been taken care of." But because the philosopher does not share all the theologian's hopes and fears, there is more freedom in steering a middle course between "the Scylla of 'absolutism' and the Charybdis of 'relativism.'"[73] As Strauss puts it, "[t]here is a universally valid hierarchy of ends, but there are no universally valid rules of action."[74]

Strauss illustrates this claim by reminding us of "an extreme situation in which the very existence or independence of a society is at stake."[75] Such an extreme situation is represented by war. What a decent society will do during war "will depend to a certain extent on what the enemy—possibly an absolutely unscrupulous and savage enemy—forces it to do."[76] As a result, "[t]here are no limits which can be defined in advance, there are no assignable limits to what might become just reprisals."[77] And moreover: "Considerations which apply to foreign enemies may well apply to subversive elements within society."[78] The philosopher ends with a plea to "leave these sad exigencies covered with the veil with which they are justly covered."[79]

* * *

Let us recapitulate. The modern West has lost faith in itself. In the Enlightenment and post-Enlightenment period, this loss of faith liberated enormous commercial and creative forces. At the same time, this loss has rendered the West vulnerable. Is there a way to fortify the modern West without destroying it altogether, a way of not throwing the baby out with the bathwater?

At first sight, Strauss seems to offer such a moderate middle course, but his path too is fraught with peril. For as soon as the theoretical esotericism of the philosopher is combined with some sort of practical implementation, self-referential problems abound: the awareness of the problematic nature of the city makes the unreflective defense of the city impossible. In this way, Strauss's recovery of the permanent problems paradoxically might make their resolution all the more difficult. Or, to frame the matter in terms of Schmitt's eschatology, the Straussian project sets out to preserve the *katechon,* but instead becomes a "hastener against its will."[80] No new Alexander is in sight to cut the Gordian knot of our age.

Moreover, a direct path forward is prevented by America's constitutional machinery. By "setting ambition against ambition" with an elaborate system of checks and balances, it prevents any single ambitious person from reconstructing the old Republic. America's founders enjoyed a freedom of action far surpassing that of America's subsequent politicians. Eventually, ambitious people would come to learn that there is little one can do in politics and that all merely political careers end in failure. The intellectual paralysis of self-knowledge has its counterpoint in the political paralysis embedded in our open system of government.

Still, there are more possibilities for action than first appear, precisely because there are more domains than those enumerated by the conventional legal or juridical system. Roberto Calasso reminds us of the alternative thread in *The Ruin of Kasch:*

> The period between 1945 and the present could conceivably be rendered in two parallel histories: that of the historians, with its elaborate apparatus of parameters, discussing figures, masses, parties, movements, negotiations,

> productions; and that of the secret services, telling of murders, traps, betrayals, assassinations, cover-ups, and weapons shipments. We know that both accounts are insufficient, that both claim to be self-sufficient, that one could never be translated into the other, and that they will continue their parallel lives. But hasn't this perhaps always been the case . . . ?[81]

Strauss also reminds us of the exceptional framework needed to supplement the American regime: "The most just society cannot survive without 'intelligence,' i.e., espionage," even though "[e]spionage is impossible without a suspension of certain rules of natural right."[82] Again, there is no disagreement with Tennyson on ends, but only on means. Instead of the United Nations, filled with interminable and inconclusive parliamentary debates that resemble Shakespearean tales told by idiots, we should consider Echelon, the secret coordination of the world's intelligence services, as the decisive path to a truly global *pax Americana*.

Liberal critics who disagree with the philosopher also tend to dislike the philosopher's politics. Just as there appears to be something shaky and problematic about a theoretical framework that is not subject to the give and take of open debate, so there appears to be something subversive and immoral about a political framework that operates outside the checks and balances of representative democracy as described in high school textbooks; but if American liberalism is decisively incomplete, then its critique is no longer quite so decisive. For the Straussian, there can be no fundamental disagreement with Oswald Spengler's call for action at the dramatic finale of *Der Untergang des Abendlandes:*

> Für uns aber, die ein Schicksal in diese Kultur und diesen Augenblick ihres Werdens gestellt hat, in welchem das Geld seine letzten Siege feiert und sein Erbe, der Cäsarismus, leise und unaufhaltsam naht, ist damit in einem eng unschriebenen Kreise die Richtung des Wollens und Müssens gegeben, ohne das es sich nicht zu leben lohnt. Wir haben nicht die Freiheit, dies oder jenes zu erreichen, aber die, das Notwendige zu tun oder nichts. Und eine Aufgabe, welche die Notwendigkeit der Geschichte gestellt hat, *wird* gelöst, mit dem einzelnen oder gegen ihn.
>
> *Ducunt fata volentem, nolentem trahunt.*[83]

René Girard: The End of the City of Man

In spite of the inspiring sweep of the Straussian project, there remains a nagging suspicion that perhaps it is missing something fundamental altogether. And if the French literary theorist René Girard is even partially correct in his extraordinary account of the history of the world, then the Straussian moment of triumph may prove to be brief indeed.

In important ways, the Girardian analysis of the modern West echoes some of the themes already discussed. As with Schmitt and Strauss, Girard also believes that there exists a disturbing truth about the city and humanity, and that the whole issue of human violence has been whitewashed away by the Enlightenment. Moreover, there will come an hour when this truth is completely known: "No single question has more of a future today than the question of man."[84] The possibility of moving beyond the unknowable human "X" of John Locke and the eighteenth-century rationalists had already been implicit in the entire project of evolutionary science during the nineteenth century.[85] Just as Darwin's *The Origin of Species* transformed the natural sciences, some other writer's *The Origin of Religions* will provide the logical and chronological sequel and one day transform the sciences of humanity.[86]

For Girard, this post-Darwinian account must somehow combine the gradualism of Darwinian evolution with the essentialism of the pre-Darwinians, stressing both the continuity and discontinuity of humanity with the rest of the natural order. This more comprehensive account of human nature will be centered on an insight already contained in Aristotelian biology: "Man differs from the other animals in his greater aptitude for imitation."[87] Here one has both a difference of kind and one of degree, which can provide the basis for a synthesis between Aristotle and Darwin. Such a synthesis and relationship was already hinted at in the time of Shakespeare, when the word "ape" already meant both "primate" and "to imitate."

However, the new science of humanity must drive the idea of imitation, or mimesis, much further than it has in the past. According to Girard, all cultural institutions, beginning with the acquisition of language by children from their parents, require this sort of mimetic activity, and so it is not overly reductionist to describe human brains as gigantic imitation machines. Because humanity would not exist without imitation, one cannot say that there is something wrong with imitation per se or that those humans who imitate others are somehow inferior to those humans who do not. The latter group, according to Girard, simply does not exist—even though it remains the most cherished myth of a diverse array of modern ideologies to celebrate an utterly fictional human self that exists independent of everyone else.

Nevertheless, the necessity of mimesis does not render it unproblematic. Conventionally, one tends to think of imitation as primarily representational, as in the learning of language and the transmission of various cultural institutions, but nothing prevents mimesis from extending into the acquisitive realm, or stops people from emulating the desires of others. In the process of "keeping up with the Joneses," mimesis pushes people into escalating rivalry. This disturbing truth of mimesis may explain why the knowledge about mimesis remains rather suppressed, in an almost unconscious way. Of all the mortal sins of medieval Catholicism, envy is the one closest to mimetic rivalry, and it is the one mortal sin that still remains a cultural taboo even in the most *avant garde* postmodern circles.

And finally: because the mimetic ability is more advanced in humans than in other animals, there exist in us no instinctual brakes that are strong enough to limit the scope of such rivalry. Thus, at the core of the mimetic account, there exists a mystery: What exactly happened in the distant past, when all the apes were reaching for the same object, when the rivalry between mimetic doubles threatened to escalate into unlimited violence?

* * *

For the philosophers of the Enlightenment, the war of all against all would culminate in a recognition by the warring parties of the irrationality of such a war. In the midst of the crisis, the warring parties would sit down, have a sober conversation, and draw up a social contract that would provide the basis for a peaceful society. Because Girard rightly views this account as preposterous, he considers the social contract to be the fundamental lie of the Enlightenment—a lie so brazen that none of the advocates of the social contract theory, from Hobbes to Rousseau, themselves believed it to be the case that an actual contract had ever been signed.

In Girard's alternative account of these matters, the war of all against all culminates not in a social contract but in a war of all against one, as the same mimetic forces gradually drive the combatants to gang up on one particular person. The war continues to escalate and there is no rational stopping point, at least not until this person becomes the scapegoat whose death helps to unite the community and bring about a limited peace for the survivors.[88]

That murder is the secret origin of all religious and political institutions, and is remembered and transfigured in the form of myth.[89] The scapegoat, perceived as the primal source of conflict and disorder, had to die for there to be peace. By violence, violence was brought to an end and society was born. But because society rests on the belief in its own order and justice, the founding act of violence must be concealed—by the myth that the slain victim was really guilty. Thus, violence is lodged at the heart of society; myth is merely discourse ephemeral to violence. Myth sacralizes the violence of the founding murder: myth tells us that the violence was justified because the victim really was guilty and, at least in the context of archaic cultures, truly was powerful.[90] Myth transfigures the murdered scapegoats into gods, and religious rituals reenact the founding murder through the sacrifice of human or animal substitutes, thereby creating a kind of peace that is always mixed with a certain amount of violence.[91] The centrality of sacrifice was so great that those who managed to defer or avoid execution became the objects of veneration. Every king is a sort of living god, and therein lies the true origin of monarchy:

> There is no culture without a tomb and no tomb without a culture; in the end the tomb is the first and only cultural symbol. The above-ground tomb does not have to be invented. It is the pile of stones in which the victim of unanimous stoning is buried. It is the first pyramid.[92]

That is how things used to work. But we now live in a world where the cat is out of the bag, at least to the extent that we know that the scapegoat really is not as guilty as the persecuting community claims. Because the smooth functioning of human culture depended on a lack of understanding of this truth of human culture, the archaic rituals will no longer work for the modern world.

As in Hegel, the owl of Minerva spreads its wings only at dusk. The unveiling of the mythical past opens toward a future in which we no longer believe in any of the myths; in a dramatic rupture with the past, they will have been deconstructed and thereby discredited.[93] But unlike Hegel, our knowledge of our hidden history—of the "things hidden since the foundation of the world"—does not automatically bring about a glorious final synthesis.[94] Because these founding myths also served the critical role of distinguishing between legitimate and illegitimate violence, their unraveling may deprive humanity of the efficacious functioning of the limited and sacred violence it needed to protect itself from unlimited and desacralized violence.

For Girard, this combination of mimesis and the unraveling of archaic culture implies that the modern world contains a powerfully apocalyptic dimension. From a Girardian perspective, the current political debates remain inadequate for the contemporary world situation to the extent that, across the spectrum, there remains a denial of the founding role of the violence caused by human mimesis and, therefore, a systematic underestimation of the scope of apocalyptic violence. Nuclear weapons pose a horrific dilemma, but one could (just barely) imagine a nuclear standoff in which a handful of states remain locked in a cold war. But what if mimesis drives others to try and acquire these same weapons for the mimetic prestige they confer, so that the technological situation is never static, but instead contains a powerful escalatory dynamic?

One may define a "liberal" as someone who knows nothing of the past and of this history of violence, and still holds to the Enlightenment view of the natural goodness of humanity. And one may define a "conservative" as someone who knows nothing of the future and of the global world that is destined to be, and therefore still believes that the nation-state or other institutions rooted in sacred violence can contain unlimited human violence. The present risks a terrible synthesis of the blind spots in that doctrinaire thinking, a synthesis of violence and globalization in which all boundaries on violence are abolished, be they geographic, professional (for example, civilian noncombatants), or demographic (for example, children). At the extremes, even the distinction between violence inflicted on oneself and violence inflicted on other people is in the process of evaporating, in the disturbing new phenomenon of suicide-murderers. The word that best describes this unbounded, apocalyptic violence is "terrorism."

Indeed, one may wonder whether any sort of politics will remain possible for the exceptional generation that has learned the truth of human history for the first time. It is in this context that one must remember that the word apocalypse originally meant unveiling. For Girard, the unveiling of this terrible knowledge opens a catastrophic fault line below the city of man: "[I]t is truly the end of the world, the Christian apocalypse, the bottomless abyss of the unforgettable victim."[95]

History and Knowledge

In the debate between Strauss and Girard, perhaps the key issue of contention can be reduced to a question of *time*. When will this highly disturbing knowledge burst upon general awareness, render all politics impossible, and finally bring the city of man to an end?

If there is something prophetic about Girard's announcement of the founding murder, then Strauss might note that his situation also resembles the plight faced by Nietzsche's madman announcing the death of God to an unbelieving world:

> I come too early . . . my time has not come yet. This tremendous event is still on its way, still wandering—it has not yet reached the ears of man. Lightning and thunder require time, the light of the stars requires time, deeds require time even after they are done, before they can be seen and heard. This deed is still more distant from them than the most distant stars—and yet it is they who have done it![96]

For Strauss as for Nietzsche, the truth of mimesis and of the founding murder is so shocking that most people, in all times and places, simply will not believe it. The world of the Enlightenment may have been based on certain misconceptions about the nature of humanity, but the full knowledge of these misconceptions can remain the province of a philosophical elite. The successful popularization of such knowledge would be the only thing to fear, and it was in this context that the Straussian, Pierre Manent, launched a ferocious attack on Girard's theory: "If human 'culture' is essentially founded on violence, then [Girard] can bring nothing other than the destruction of humanity in the fallacious guise of non-violence."[97] Girard, in turn, would counter that salvation is no longer to be found in philosophical reticence, because there will come a day when there is no esoteric knowledge left:

> I do think it is necessary for us to engage in the discourse we have been pursuing here. But if we had chosen otherwise, others would have taken up this discourse. And there will be others, in any case, who will repeat what we are in the process of saying and who will advance matters beyond what we have been able to do. Yet books themselves will have no more than minor importance; the events within which such books emerge will be infinitely more eloquent than whatever we write and will establish truths we have difficulty describing and describe poorly, even in simple and banal instances. They are already very simple, indeed too simple to interest our current Byzantium, but these truths will become simpler still; they will soon be accessible to anyone.[98]

For Girard, the knowledge of the founding murder is driven by the historical working of the Judeo-Western revelation. The revelation may be slow (because it contains a message that humans do not wish to hear), but it is not reversible. For this reason, the decisive difference between Girard and Strauss (or Nietzsche) centers on the question of historicism.

On the level of the individual, even at the end there will still remain a choice of sorts between Jerusalem and Athens. We have Sir Thomas More, a Christian saint, as a helper in making that choice. In his *Dialogue of Comfort Against Tribulation,* More declares:

> [T]o prove that this life is no laughing time, but rather the time of weeping, we find that our savior himself wept twice or thrice, but never find we that he laughed so much as once. I will not swear that he never did, but at the least wise he left us no example of it. But, on the other side, he left us example of weeping.[99]

The saint knew that the opposite had been true of Socrates, who left us no example of weeping, but left us example of laughter.[100]

* * *

But the world has not yet come to an end, and there is no easy telling how long the twilight of the modern age will endure. What then must be done, by the Christian statesman or stateswoman aspiring to be a wise steward for our time?

The negative answers are straightforward. There can be no return to the archaic world or even to the robust conception of the political envisioned by Carl Schmitt. There can be no real accommodation with the Enlightenment, since so many of its easy bromides have become deadly falsehoods in our time. But also there cannot be a decision to avoid all decisions and to retreat into studying the Bible in anticipation of the Second Coming, for then one will have ceased to be a statesman or stateswoman.

The Christian statesman or stateswoman must diverge from the teachings of Strauss in one decisive respect. Unlike Strauss, the Christian statesman or stateswoman knows that the modern age will not be permanent, and ultimately will give way to something very different. One must never forget that one day all will be revealed, that all injustices will be exposed, and that those who perpetrated them will be held to account.

And so, in determining the correct mixture of violence and peace, the Christian statesman or stateswoman would be wise, in every close case, to side with peace. There is no formula to answer the critical question of what constitutes a "close case"; that must be decided in every specific instance. It may well be that the cumulative decisions made in all those close instances will determine the destiny of the postmodern world. For that world could differ from the modern world in a way that is much worse or much better—the limitless violence of runaway mimesis or the peace of the kingdom of God.

NOTES

1. Leo Strauss, *Thoughts on Machiavelli* (Glencoe, IL: Free Press, 1958), 9–10.
2. Pierre Manent, *The City of Man*, trans. Mark A. LePain (Princeton, NJ: Princeton University Press, 1998), 27.
3. Manent, *The City*, 27.
4. Manent, *The City*, 35.
5. Leo Strauss, *Natural Right and History* (Chicago: University of Chicago Press, 1953), 197.
6. John Locke, *Atheism*, in *John Locke: Political Essays*, ed. Mark Goldie, 2nd ed. (New York: Cambridge University Press, 1999), 245–46.
7. John Locke, *First Treatise of Government*, in *Two Treatises of Government*, ed. Peter Laslett, 2nd ed. (Cambridge: Cambridge University Press, 2003), 214.
8. Locke, *Second Treatise of Government*, in *Two Treatises of Government*, 321.
9. Locke, *First Treatise*, 216.
10. Locke, *Second Treatise*, 294 and 352.
11. Locke, *Second Treatise*, 297.
12. Locke, *Second Treatise*, 300.
13. Locke, *Second Treatise*, 362.
14. John Locke, *The Reasonableness of Christianity, with A Discourse of Miracles, and part of A Third Letter Concerning Toleration*, ed. abridged, and with an introduction by I. T. Ramsey (Stanford, CA: Stanford University Press, 2002), 38.
15. Egon Mayer, Barry A. Kosmin, and Ariela Keysar, *The City University of New York American Religious Identification Survey, http://www.gc.cuny.edu/faculty/research_briefs/aris/key_findings.htm* (noting that 76.5 percent of Americans identify themselves as "Christian").
16. Manent, *The City*, 113 (citation and quotation omitted).
17. John Locke, *Essay Concerning Human Understanding*, ed. Alexander Campbell Fraser (Cambridge: Cambridge University Press, 1959), 313–21.
18. Manent, *The City*, 123–24.
19. Manent, *The City*, 169–71.
20. Locke, *Essay*, 391–95.

21. Manent, *The City,* 130 (citation and quotation omitted).

22. Manent, *The City,* 126.

23. Manent, *The City,* 135–36.

24. Manent, *The City,* 126–28.

25. Manent, *The City,* 139–40.

26. Manent, *The City,* 148–49.

27. Manent, *The City,* 141.

28. George W. Bush, "Remarks by the President in Town Hall Meeting with Citizens of Ontario," *www.whitehouse.gov/news/release/2002/01/20020105–3.html* (accessed 15 March 2007).

29. Charles Krauthammer, "They Hate Civilization," *New York Post,* 16 October 2001, quoting Osama bin Laden, *www.mideasttruth.com/nyp1.html* (accessed 15 March 2007).

30. Heinrich Meier, *The Lesson of Carl Schmitt: Four Chapters on the Distinction between Political Theology and Political Philosophy,* trans. Marcus Brainard (Chicago: University of Chicago Press, 1998; citation and quotation omitted).

31. Meier, *The Lesson,* 41–42.

32. Carl Schmitt, *The Concept of the Political,* 2nd ed., trans. and with an introduction by George Schwab (Chicago: University of Chicago Press, 1996), 67.

33. Meier, *The Lesson,* 1.

34. Schmitt, *The Concept,* 50.

35. Schmitt, *The Concept,* 51.

36. See Schmitt, *The Concept,* 50–51.

37. Schmitt, *The Concept,* 68.

38. Schmitt, *The Concept,* 53.

39. Meier, *The Lesson,* 49 (emphasis omitted).

40. Carl Schmitt, *Glossarium—Aufzeichnungen der Jahre 1947–1951* (Berlin: Duncker and Humblot, 1988), 165.

41. Schmitt, *The Concept,* 68 (quotation omitted).

42. Meier, *The Lesson,* 43–44.

43. Alexandre Kojève, *Introduction to the Reading of Hegel,* ed. Allan Bloom, trans. James H. Nichols Jr. (New York: Basic Books, 1969), 159–60 (emphases in the original).

44. Schmitt, *The Concept,* 53.

45. Schmitt, *The Concept,* 57–58.

46. Heinrich Meier, *Carl Schmitt and Leo Strauss: The Hidden Dialogue,* trans. J. Harvey Lomax, foreword by Joseph Cropsey (Chicago: University of Chicago Press, 1995), 47–48.

47. Meier, *Carl Schmitt,* 47.

48. Meier, *Carl Schmitt,* 47–48.

49. Meier, *Carl Schmitt,* 48.

50. Meier, *The Lesson*, 46.
51. Meier, *Carl Schmitt*, 48.
52. Strauss, *Thoughts*, 290.
53. Leo Strauss, *Persecution and the Art of Writing* (Glencoe, IL: Free Press, 1952), 25.
54. Strauss, *Persecution*, 22–23.
55. Strauss, *Persecution*, 24.
56. Strauss, *Persecution*, 24.
57. Strauss, *Persecution*, 36.
58. Strauss, *Persecution*, 36.
59. Strauss, *Persecution*, 25.
60. Strauss, *Persecution*, 36.
61. Strauss, *Persecution*, 25.
62. Strauss, *Persecution*, 174.
63. Strauss, *Persecution*, 174.
64. Strauss, *Persecution*, 174 (citation and quotation omitted).
65. Harvey Mansfield, "Straussianism Democracy and Allan Bloom II: Democracy and the Great Books," in *Essays on the Closing of the American Mind*, ed. Robert L. Stone (Chicago: Chicago Review Press, 1989), 112. Mansfield's essay is itself a summary and critique of Allan Bloom's *The Closing of the American Mind*.
66. Strauss, *Thoughts*, 13–14.
67. Strauss, *Thoughts*, 204.
68. Strauss, *Thoughts*, 14.
69. Strauss, *Thoughts*, 13 (citation and quotation omitted).
70. Strauss, *Thoughts*, 14.
71. Strauss, *Thoughts*, 14.
72. Strauss, *Thoughts*, 14.
73. Strauss, *Natural Right*, 162.
74. Strauss, *Natural Right*, 162.
75. Strauss, *Natural Right*, 160.
76. Strauss, *Natural Right*, 160.
77. Strauss, *Natural Right*, 160.
78. Strauss, *Natural Right*, 160.
79. Strauss, *Natural Right*, 160.
80. Meier, *The Lesson*, 165 (citation omitted).
81. Roberto Calasso, *The Ruin of Kasch*, trans. William Weaver (Cambridge, MA: Belknap Press of Harvard University Press, 1994), 253.

82. Strauss, *Natural Right,* 160.

83. Oswald Spengler, *Der Untergang des Abendlandes* (Munich: C. H. Beck Verlag, 1969), 1194–95. "For us, however, whom a Destiny has placed in this Culture and at this moment of its development our direction . . . willed and obligatory at once, is set for us within narrow limits, and on any other term life is not worth the living. We have not the freedom to reach to this or to that, but the freedom to do the necessary or to do nothing. And a task that historic necessity has set *will* be accomplished *with* the individual or against him" (emphases in the original).

84. René Girard, *Things Hidden since the Foundation of the World,* trans. Stephen Bann and Michael Metteer (Stanford, CA: Stanford University Press, 1987).

85. Girard, *Things Hidden,* 3.

86. Girard, *Things Hidden,* 3.

87. Girard, *Things Hidden,* 1.

88. Girard, *Things Hidden,* 80.

89. Girard, *Things Hidden,* 25.

90. Girard, *Things Hidden,* 82.

91. Girard, *Things Hidden,* 82.

92. Girard, *Things Hidden,* 83.

93. Jean-Pierre Dupuy, "Totalization and Misrecognition," in *Violence and Truth: On the Work of René Girard,* ed. Paul Dumouchel; essay translated by Mark R. Anspach (Stanford, CA: Stanford University Press, 1988), 93 (citation and quotation omitted).

94. Girard, *Things Hidden,* 138.

95. René Girard, "The Founding Murder in the Philosophy of Nietzsche," in *Violence and Truth: On the Work of René Girard,* ed. Paul Dumouchel (Stanford, CA: Stanford University Press, 1988), 246.

96. Girard, *Things Hidden,* 135 (citation and quotation omitted).

97. Dupuy, "Totalization and Misrecognition," 92.

98. Girard, *Things Hidden,* 135.

99. Leo Strauss, *The City and Man* (Chicago: University of Chicago Press, 1978), 61 (citation and quotation omitted).

100. Strauss, *The City,* 61.

Understanding in Quest of Faith

The Central Problem in Eric Voegelin's Philosophy

Stefan Rossbach

Center for the Study of Politics and Spirituality (CSPS), University of Kent, UK

I.

Although *The Collected Works of Eric Voegelin* can hardly be considered a critical edition, the 34 volumes will undoubtedly make Eric Voegelin's writings more accessible than ever.[1] In addition, Voegelin's correspondence with contemporaries such as Leo Strauss, Robert Heilman, and Alfred Schütz is now also available in book form,[2] while Voegelin's original correspondence files, typescripts, notes, and unpublished lectures can easily be accessed in the Hoover Archives at Stanford University. This primary material plus Geoffrey Price's *International Bibliography (1921–2000)* of works by and on Voegelin appear to give Voegelin's oeuvre an availability and unity that afford us the opportunity to reflect on the thinker's contribution as a whole rather than to discuss selected ideas in isolation.[3] The present essay aims to initiate such a reflection.

The "unity" of Voegelin's work, however, should not be taken for granted as an a priori assumption of our reflection; whether or not such unity can be found has to be established empirically with reference to the above-mentioned materials. Moreover, the very notion of the unity of the work may need clarification. What exactly are we looking for when we look for unity? A theme? A question? A project? A problématique? Or, indeed, a life? Or a lifework?

This essay assumes that we can identify a thinker's characteristic approach to reality—his or her "fingerprints"—in the gaps, errors, and "loose ends" he or she leaves in the work. Every thinker has a characteristic configuration of loose ends, and this configuration is the key index to the thinker's lifework. In some sense, therefore, I am proposing that it is more instructive to characterize the work according to its failures rather than according to its achievements, though this statement makes sense only if the term "failure" is properly qualified.

First, it is important to appreciate that the identification of loose ends and failures cannot be based on the work's reception, because audiences always bring their own contexts, backgrounds, expectations, and issues to the work in question. An idea that is controversial or unconvincing at the time of publication does not necessarily represent a loose end or a failure. For the purposes of this essay, the primary standard for the identification of failures must be the thinker's self-assessment. Any thinker of rank is usually aware of the unresolved issues in his or her work, and it is precisely because of this awareness that the loose ends are not so much failures but evidence of directed, sustained creativity. The loose ends are concepts, ideas, encounters, and experiences to which the thinker needs to return again and again because, in the thinker's own self-understanding, he or she remains dissatisfied with his or her own efforts to articulate the underlying problems and/or their solution. This "failure," therefore, is at the same time the very basis for the achievements that unfold from the thinker's creative efforts to pursue and master the loose ends that continue to trouble the thinker. The unity of the work is closely related to the loose ends and the "failure" they reflect because they motivate the thinker to move beyond past accomplishments and problems of reception, and they thereby give the work its uniqueness and identity. Accordingly, although I focus on loose ends, gaps, and errors, this essay is not an exercise in criticism but an exercise in reconstruction.

In order to be able to understand the configuration of loose ends, it is crucial that in our reading of the work we let ourselves be guided by the thinker. In other words, an internal reading of the work is required, a reading that not only absorbs the work itself but also absorbs the author's comments and reflection on the work. If available, unpublished documents, letters, notebook entries, transcripts of unpublished lectures and interviews, prefaces, especially prefaces to second editions, and similar material can help indicate where a thinker sees the weaknesses and loose ends in his or her work, and how the thinker intends to improve on his or her present understanding of the relevant issues. In Voegelin's case, for example, it is important that throughout his life he sent first drafts of his work to friends and colleagues for feedback. One carbon copy of every new installment of the *History of Political Ideas* went to Friedrich Engel-Janosi, and the resulting exchange between Voegelin and Engel-Janosi reveals—at least occasionally—how the former assessed various aspects of his own work. The exchanges with Alfred Schütz and, to a lesser extent, Robert Heilman are also important.

An internal reading of the work tends to be biased toward the thinker's late work because the late work often includes a reflective element. This may be because the late work simply has the luxury of later insight, of being able to look back at earlier efforts and their consequences and implications. The reflective element may also be provoked in response to the reception of the work. "Success" usually means that the work is read, that reviews are written, and that the work is critically appraised by a growing audience, thereby providing opportunities for the author to respond to both criticism and praise and to return to his or her earlier work. However, success can also imply that the author becomes distracted by the concerns of his or her audience, and that indeed the demands of managing success override independent questioning in importance. Finally, the nearness of death can provide a further impetus toward self-reflection.

II.

Voegelin's published writings do not facilitate an internal reading, because throughout his life, Voegelin was extremely reluctant to characterize his work in terms of "positions" outside of the context of the historical investigation he was engaged in at the time. In his first book, *On the Form of the American Mind,* he accepts the academic convention that authors should talk about their methods only with many reservations. In the introduction to the book, Voegelin confidently refuses to "engage in arguments concerning methodology" and declares apodictically that he would "neither accept nor refute theories about the purity of methods, the correlation of method and object, and a ban on methodological syncretism." Although he admits that "of necessity something will have to be said concerning the method employed here," he appears to betray such a sense of professional discipline a few sentences later, when he proclaims that it was "almost too much to say that rules were *followed.*"[4] Rather, the rules, principles, or criteria that he did accept were found during the course of the investigation; they emerged from—rather than preceded—the enquiry.

In other words, Voegelin tried to extract "the instruments of interpretation as well as the meaning from the material itself."[5]

This paradoxical rule—the rule that no rules should be followed—seems to imply that the materials suggest their own method of interpretation and that the author's creative imagination is unnecessary to reveal their meaning. This denial of the responsibility of authorship remained a constant in Eric Voegelin's life. As late as 1983, when asked whether there was anything in *Anamnesis* that he would deny 17 years after its publication, he replied by repeating a by then well-known formula:

> No. I rarely have something to deny because I always stick close to the empirical materials and do not generalize beyond them. So when I generalize, I have to generalize because of the materials.[6]

Not unlike Michel Foucault, who once admitted that he wrote "in order to have no face,"[7] Voegelin could easily become impatient with his readers' attempts to find *him*—*his* position, *his* method, *his* approach, *his* viewpoint—behind the materials. According to his self-understanding, Voegelin did not have positions, viewpoints, or approaches; only ideologists did.[8] He had his own strategies for dealing with readers and listeners who wanted "to nail him down" as the representative of a position:

> I frequently have to ward off people who want to "classify" me. When somebody wants me to be a Catholic or a Protestant, I tell him that I am a "pre-Reformation Christian." If he wants to nail me down as a Thomist or Augustinian, I tell him I am a "pre-Nicene Christian." And if he wants to nail me down earlier, I tell him that even Mary the Virgin was not a member of the Catholic Church. I have quite a number of such stock answers for people who pester me after a lecture; and then they get talked around as authentic information on my "position."[9]

"Positions," he explained, were the unfortunate side effects of the tendency to "dogmatize a result of empirical analysis," and his reputation and self-understanding as a scholar depended on his continuous openness towards empirical reality. His work, therefore, did not express positions but the "present state of science in the matter at hand."[10]

III.

Against this background of denials, it is remarkable that there is *one* positive affirmation of a label for his work, even though this was not reported by Voegelin himself. As Gregor Sebba reports:

> To me Eric Voegelin has always been an exemplary representative of rationality in the Greek sense, but when I argued that against a statement calling him a mystic philosopher he wrote back: "This will shock you, but I *am* a mystic philosopher." [11]

This important admission reflects Voegelin's understanding "of the function of mysticism in a time of social disorder."[12] Voegelin considered mysticism as a solution to the problems that arise when "the limits of doctrinal expression of truth [become] visible," a condition that is both cause and effect of social and spiritual disorder.[13] Jean Bodin, the man "about whom [he] knew the most,"[14] was Voegelin's great model of a "spiritualist" who, at a time when there were eight religious civil wars in France,

> recognized that the struggle between the various theological truths on the battlefield could be appeased only by understanding the secondary importance of doctrinal truth in relation to mystical insight.[15]

Voegelin fully agrees with Bodin on the crucial significance of mystical insight in times of ideological conflict. When the path of rational debate has long been left behind, the only way forward is a form of detachment, a negative way, that allows us to look beyond the "dogmatomachy of the time" toward the experiences that engendered, as their symbolic expression, those very doctrines and dogmas. The key to the resolution of the deadlock of doctrinal conflict, therefore, is to appreciate that doctrines are secondary, contingent phenomena; they are indices of experiences and by the time that they are considered to be absolutes, they have effectively become separated from their engendering experiences. Fighting over doctrines—be they theological or ideological—is a form of idolatry and thus a spiritual problem, which requires a spiritual solution, a return to the "true experience" that symbols and dogma were once meant to safeguard against oblivion.

In the *Lettre à Jan Bautru*—identified by Voegelin as "one of the most important documents to affect [Voegelin's] thought"[16]—Bodin defines the essence of the "true religion" as a "proper turning to God [*conversio*] with a purified spirit." In Voegelin's understanding, this detachment and purification is precisely the function of the mystical *via negativa*, for it is through negation that we pierce through the cloud of unknowing formed by multiple layers of doctrinal encrustation. Mysticism represents a "revolt of a personal experience" against dogmatizations and therefore can help the individual regain his "freedom" [*Freiheit*].[17]

In Voegelin's understanding, therefore, mysticism is the key to an "understanding of order in times of spiritual disorder,"[18] and the fact that he was happy to be called a "mystic philosopher" sheds considerable light on his self-understanding and the kind of contribution he intended to make. The following three quotations will show in more detail how this rather unique appreciation of the social and political significance of mysticism—a constant in his life and work—can itself be traced back further to Voegelin's understanding of the very nature of reality:

A. What collapses is a historical stage of concretization and the corresponding institutions; for the individual today, as much as for the individual in the fifth and fifteenth century, there remains the socially indestructible position of the *theologia negativa;* for the individual undergoes a crisis only if he insists on finding his absolute coordinates in his nation, as a Marxist, as a Liberal etc.[19]

B. Every mystic is in a way an "atheist" inasmuch as he knows there is a time when symbols become "unbelievable," in personal life as well as in history, when they must be renewed and recast through recourse to the experiences from which they emerge.[20]

C. The experience of divine presence, when symbolized, is burdened with the historical concreteness of the symbols. No symbolization is adequate to the ineffability of the divine Beyond. Hence, when you are a believer on the level of symbols, you become an "infidel" to the ineffable truth of divine reality; and when your faith is constituted by your relation to the ineffably divine, you become an "infidel" on the level of the symbols. Again in Western language, the problem looks to me very much like that of the *fides quaerens intellectum,* of the faith on the level of imaginative symbolism moving beyond its acceptance of the symbols, through meditative contemplation, towards the understanding of the experiences which endow the symbols with their sense.[21]

Voegelin's statements show how his understanding of the nature of reality—of Reality—was closely related to the problem of "social destruction" as in (A), of dissolution of order. The destruction of order implied the destruction of "absolute coordinates" in which beliefs were expressed. The mystic in (B) will look at believers with a mixture of skepsis—for they too will have to live the death of their absolute coordinates—and longing for the innocence they still have. As Nietzsche noted, "when skepticism mates with longing, mysticism is born."[22] For this mystic, therefore, the experience of Reality is an experience of transcendence, of reality transcending itself. Reality is a process of transfiguration, a continuous movement beyond its own structure.[23] Voegelin speaks of the "paradox of reality" and the "exodus within reality."[24]

The pragmatic background of this understanding of reality transcending itself is characterized by the rise, the expansion, the decline, and the collapse of empires. The successive destruction of traditional community order under the pressure of imperial expansion correlates with "spiritual outbursts," which generate new "saving tales" showing people how to overcome the death of reality, how to "immortalize" their souls at a time when their surrounding realities die. Empires function as the "graveyard[s] of societies."[25] As a result of the dissolution of order, the old, traditional symbols become unbelievable as humanity's existential unrest intensifies. The splendor of the old gods becomes derivative as a horizon of new divinities is introduced beyond the old gods, eventually leading to the distinction between false and true gods. According to Voegelin, this succession of old and new, of falsehood and truth, eventually becomes thematic in Plato, who introduces the symbol of the absolute beyond (*epekeina*)—the Beyond—which has no further beyond from where new divinities could appear. In Voegelin's reading of Plato, therefore, *epekeina* is the ineffably divine that cannot be undermined by further dissolutions of order; it is the divine abyss that can never become derivative.

The Beyond, as the horizon of reality's movement beyond its own structure, is experienced not "directly" but "only" indirectly through the negation of symbols that, at least for some time, posed as "terminal" symbols. The Beyond itself, therefore, must remain an "unknown God," an infinite depth, a darkness, a formless and nameless abyss, and it can be glimpsed as such in moments of dissolution when our former beliefs become "unbelievable," when we live the death of our absolute coordinates. Plato's *epekeina,* as understood by Voegelin, is precisely the mysterious darkness that is progressively being revealed as concrete history stumbles from one dissolution to the next.

Voegelin is adamant that no belief is immune to the fate of social destruction. Whoever wants to aim higher and become immune to the loss of self through social destruction must envision himself or herself in nonsymbolic terms, without absolute coordinates. In practice, this can be accomplished through the hyper-absoluteness of the *via negativa,* of an inner movement that preserves a "reflective distance" from the symbols and coordinates that it uses to refer to itself. Accordingly, these symbols are never to be taken as terminal symbols, as endpoints, but only as "indices" of the reflectively distancing movement. Given Voegelin's biographical background—his courageous attempts at preserving his moral and intellectual integrity in Nazi Germany and Nazi Austria, culminating in his dramatic break with his father and his escape to the United States via Switzerland—it is not difficult to see how Voegelin's appreciation of the *via negativa* was both an intellectual and a deeply personal concern.

IV.

Any plausible account of the unity of Voegelin's lifework must be able to determine the extent to which his concern with *gnosis* and Gnosticism was indeed central to the unfolding of his philosophy. In his Charles R. Walgreen Lectures, delivered at the University of Chicago in early 1951 and later published as *The New Science of Politics* (*NSP*), Voegelin argued (i) that "the growth of Gnosticism" was "the essence of modernity" and (ii) that there was a historical continuity linking the Gnosticism of late antiquity to modern ideological movements such as "progressivism, positivism, Marxism, psychoanalysis, communism, fascism, and national socialism."[26] At least biographically, there can be little doubt that the success of *NSP* was a crucial turning point in Voegelin's career. The book quickly turned Voegelin into a political science celebrity, even provoking a five-page feature article on *NSP*'s argument in *Time* magazine.[27] As Eugene Webb has pointed out, "Eric Voegelin is probably best known, especially among many who have not actually read him, for his denunciations of something called 'gnosticism.'"[28] Along similar lines, Murray Jardine observed that Eric Voegelin is still "probably best known to the current generation of American political theorists from his unrelenting critique of modernity in *The New Science of Politics*."[29]

Thus, if we were to take the reception of Voegelin's work as a guide, we would immediately be led to Gnosticism as one of his central concerns. However, as we noted above, Voegelin's own assessment of the significance of *NSP* for the development of his thought is far more significant for our purposes than issues of reception. In fact, it is highly significant that, chronologically, Voegelin's Chicago lectures preceded—and in an important sense initiated—his later philosophical work including *Order and History* and *Anamnesis.*

Throughout his life, Voegelin reflected on these lectures as a "breakthrough," crucially positioned between the unpublished and unfinished work on the *History of Political Ideas* and the published yet equally unfinished *Order and History* series.[30]

Why was the mystic philosopher Eric Voegelin preoccupied with Gnosticism? Voegelin's interest in Gnosticism was sparked by a genuine reading experience. In several letters to various addressees, Voegelin explained how he "ran across the problem for the first time" and his explanations are consistent throughout his correspondence. For example, in a 1959 letter to Carl J. Friedrich, he wrote:

> Well, if you attribute to me, as is frequently done, the great discovery of the problem of modern Gnosis and its continuity with antiquity, I must decline the honor and humbly disavow that stroke of genius. I ran across the problem for the first time in Balthasar's *Prometheus* of 1937. Then I ascertained that he was right, through the study of Jonas' *Gnosis* of 1934, and through the reading of mountains of materials on medieval sectarianism. For the modern application, I found this view confirmed through the works of Lubac. And then I took the precaution of discussing the question in detail with Puech, Quispel, and Bultmann, that is, with the foremost living authorities on Gnosis and Christianity. They all agreed that this was indeed *the* issue.[31]

The latter part of this statement is somewhat misleading, because Bultmann, for example, had made it quite clear to Voegelin that he disapproved of Voegelin's characterization of *gnosis*. Bultmann accused Voegelin of a "secularization" of the term and doubted whether this gesture was "admissible." And again later, after the publication of *Wissenschaft, Politik und Gnosis*, Bultmann criticized Voegelin's use of the terms *gnosis* and gnostic. [32] But there is little reason to doubt the accuracy of the letter's first claim, that it was the reading of von Balthasar and Jonas that triggered the "gnosticism thesis" in Voegelin's mind. In a letter written to von Balthasar in May 1950, Voegelin expressed his gratitude because the *Prometheus* not only helped him to understand the history of thought (*Geistesgeschichte*) of the nineteenth century but also established "principles" (*Prinzipien*) that, we may infer, served as a model for his own enterprise in *NSP*.[33] Republished in 1947, just in time for Voegelin's Walgreen Lectures, von Balthasar's *Prometheus* is the first volume of *Die Apokalypse der deutschen Seele: Studien zu einer Lehre von letzten Handlungen* (3 volumes, 1937–1939). In this important work, von Balthasar considered *gnosis* next to chiliasm as one of the two important challenges to the "unity" (*Einheit*) and balance of Christian eschatology since the Middle Ages.[34] The affinity between the Prometheus motif (*Prinzip*), which von Balthasar found fully articulated in Goethe's 1773 Prometheus fragment, and what he understood as gnostic mythology was explored in key sections of the book. According to von Balthasar, German idealism found its unity in the fact that its representatives offered mere variations of the Prometheus motif and thereby continued a "geistesgeschichtliche Ahnenreihe," which included *gnosis*, Plotinus, Scotus Eriugena, Boehme, and the Kabbalah.[35] Joachim of Fiore is identified as the key figure in the tradition of chiliastic eschatology, which in turn contributed to certain variations in the history of the Prometheus theme.[36] As far as Voegelin's appropriation of *gnosis* is concerned, we can easily see that the combination of von Balthasar and Jonas accounts for both the idea of an uninterrupted chain of gnostic thought (von Balthasar) and the idea of a gnostic "spirit" or "essence" (Jonas).[37]

Some of the oddities of *NSP* can easily be explained as soon as we appreciate von Balthasar's *Prometheus* as a key influence. For example, the fact that *NSP* considered Gnosticism as an ancient religious movement "that accompanied Christianity from its very beginnings" and then failed to engage with the Gnosticism of late antiquity is unsurprising, because von Balthasar, too, excluded ancient *gnosis* from the analysis. Instead, Voegelin begins his historical investigation with Joachim of Fiore, while Scotus Eriugena is mentioned in passing as a major contributor in the "activation of ancient gnosticism" during the ninth century; von Balthasar, too, highlights the significance of both figures. Given that Voegelin acknowledged his debt to von Balthasar in letters—even in a letter to von Balthasar—it is astonishing that *NSP* fails to refer to the latter as a key inspiration.[38]

In fact, in some aspects of the argument, the transition from von Balthasar's *Prometheus* to Voegelin's *New Science* entails a *loss* of conceptual precision. Where von Balthasar more or less carefully distinguishes between chiliasm and *gnosis*, Voegelin speaks of "apocalyptic-gnostic movements" as if the two adjectives could easily sit together—which they cannot.[39] This confusion distorted Voegelin's work on Gnosticism from the start. As Gregor Sebba pointed out in 1978 in a letter to Voegelin, the term "Gnostic immanentization of the eschaton," which occurs in *NSP*, is an oxymoron:

> from the sources *that were available to you at the time,* it follows *without doubt* that not a single one of the features that are thought to characterize classical gnosis fits without problems. . . . Nevertheless the whole phenomenon of

> gnosis has a sharp profile. One motive applies throughout: *the radical rejection of any immanentization of transcendence.*[40]

It was von Balthasar's work rather than the ancient primary sources that grounded Voegelin's discussion of Gnosticism and modernity. Very much contrary to his usual insistence on "letting the principles of the analysis emerge from the material," he never studied the ancient gnostic material in any depth. In his defense one could point out that at the time when *NSP* was conceived, the primary sources were not easily available. By 1951 neither the findings from Nag Hammadi nor those from Qumran were publicly available, and precisely in order to make up for the unavailability of primary sources, Voegelin consulted the acknowledged experts in the field—Bultmann, Puech, Quispel, and others. Still, few of these experts failed to distance themselves from the interpretation that Voegelin imposed on whatever materials they shared with him.[41] Moreover, as Sebba noted, even on the basis of the limited primary and secondary sources that were available at the time, Voegelin's "modern *gnosis*" emerges as the very opposite of "the whole phenomenon of *gnosis*." Indeed, Voegelin *never* managed to clarify the nature of the historical link suggested in *NSP*. As late as December 1977, while working on "Wisdom and the Magic of the Extreme," Voegelin was still trying to work out the "distinction between ancient and modern gnosis."[42] The very idea that brought his work to public attention turned out to be, at least for Voegelin himself, a crucial loose end.

We are left with the conclusion that in his Chicago Lectures of 1951, Voegelin made a public commitment to a set of ideas that was borrowed, confused, wrong, and clearly violated the (paradoxical) rules of analysis he had outlined in earlier works and, importantly, in *NSP* itself.[43] Unsurprisingly, Voegelin's readers debate whether, in light of these oddities, *NSP* should be considered a mere aberration in Voegelin's lifework, for example, as a rare descent into Cold War rhetoric.[44] But these suggestions do not square with Voegelin's own assessment of the ideas first espoused in *NSP*. It is true, of course, that he later qualified these ideas, *but the qualification never amounted to an outright dismissal.* Rather, Voegelin eventually came to acknowledge that Gnosticism was but one element in the modern compound and that a more complete analysis would have to include other factors such as apocalypticism, neo-platonism, hermeticism, alchemy, magic, theurgy, and scientism. The analysis was incomplete, according to Voegelin, but not wrong. For example, at a symposium on "20 Years of The New Science of Politics" held at the University of Notre Dame in 1971, Voegelin noted that "there is nothing about *The New Science of Politics*, as I wrote it twenty years ago, that has to be retracted. It fits on the whole, still, but a lot has to be added."[45] As late as 1973, around the time of the publication of *The Ecumenic Age*, Voegelin insisted that "[t]he application of the category of Gnosticism to modern ideology, of course, stands";[46] but Voegelin never distanced himself from *NSP* and in fact continued to work on the loose ends of his Chicago Lectures, in particular on the crucial distinction between ancient and modern *gnosis*.[47] And although he apparently never gave up hope that he would eventually find a solution to the problem, he never considered filling the gaps by doing his homework, that is, by returning to the primary sources.

Voegelin described *The New Science of Politics* as a "livre de circonstance" —a title that seems well chosen for many reasons.[48] The sudden, unexpected but hoped-for recognition implied in the invitation to deliver the prestigious Walgreen Lectures, the publicity of the lectures, the time pressure that comes with the immovable deadlines provided by lectures, the strong sense of discovery sparked by the reading of von Balthasar and then Jonas, together with what appears to have been a critical state in his reflections on his *History of Political Ideas* project—all these liminal conditions might have led to a premature conceptual closure, with overconfidence compensating for gaps and obvious weaknesses. In his letters, Voegelin confirmed that "the framework of the lectures"—and the "limitations of the lecture form"—"compelled [him] to leave numerous loose end[s]";[49] but once the book was out, and the success was there, Voegelin's life had changed and he was burdened with the expectations of a growing audience.

The fact that it is not easy for any thinker to question and undermine the basis of his or her success does not exhaustively explain Voegelin's lifelong persistence in the pursuit of *NSP*'s loose ends. There were other situations in which he demonstrated a remarkable indifference toward opportunities to become something like a public intellectual. Rather, the continuous significance of Gnosticism in Voegelin's thought is most persuasively explained in terms of its relationship to the central concerns of his mystic philosophy—dissolutions of order, immunity, and the *via negativa*. Voegelin assigns such great importance to Gnosticism because, to him, it represents the countermovement to the movement of the *via negativa*. In light of our earlier discussion of Voegelin's understanding of Reality—as a continuous movement beyond its own structure, echoed in the soul's mystical inner movement—it is clear that the search for finality and absolutes at the level of symbols effectively appears as an artificial truncation of reality. For Voegelin, there is no shortcut to the infinite depth of the Divine, but the false appeal of Gnosticism rests precisely on the empty promise that the arduous labors of the negative way were superfluous and illusory, to be eclipsed by the immediacy and finality of *gnosis*. Gregor Sebba's perceptive review of Voegelin's treatment of Gnosticism reaches the same conclusion:

> In the final analysis you call Gnostic everything that reflects a truncation of reality, and this goes far beyond the narrow concept of gnosis.[50]

At the center of Voegelin's mystic philosophy, therefore, we find a pair, a dynamic relationship—the relationship between the reflective distance of the *via negativa* and the truncation of reality through *gnosis*; between infinite movement and dead end. In his late work, Voegelin began to reflect on this relationship in abstract terms. Historically, he explained, the meditative quest—"noetic exegesis"—does not "arise independently of the conception of order of the surrounding society, but in a critical argument with the latter. Wherever noesis appears, it stands in a relation of tension to society's self-interpretation."[51] In other words, "the movement towards truth always resists an untruth."[52] In these terms, therefore, we can identify Gnosticism, both as a historical exemplar and as a type, as the target that initiated—and sustained—Voegelin's resistance to untruth. In the unfolding of his mystic philosophy, *his criticism of Gnosticism represented the initial exclusion that made everything else possible.* Voegelin's late efforts to master *NSP*'s loose ends testify to his awareness of the fact that his mystic philosophy was built on, and continued to be informed by, this initial exclusion. Inadvertently, it seems, the "livre de circonstance" had become a cornerstone.

V.

As we have seen from the quotations above, Voegelin's *via negativa* was a quest for immunity, a form of self-protection against the consequences of dissolutions of order and the concomitant death of reality. One important aspect of the reflective distance toward absolute coordinates is a form of humility that emphasizes that reality is unfathomable and that the Divine is unknown; it is the humility of an ignorance that is self-aware, that knows that it does not know. This humility permeates Voegelin's work.[53] It is implied in his refusal to subscribe to, and endorse, a position; it is explicit in his references to "the abyss extending beyond into the incommunicable substance of the Tetragrammaton," to the "tetragrammatic depth of the unfathomable divine reality that has not even the proper name 'God,'" and to the "paradoxic experience of not-experientiable reality."[54] This humility is built into the nonfinality and reflective distance of the in-between, of the *metaxy;* it is the foundation of the "Platonic restraints" that are evoked in *The Ecumenic Age* and exemplified, arguably, in the same volume's chapter on "The Pauline Vision of the Resurrected."[55] It is also implicit in Voegelin's self-limitation as a philosopher, who, *qua* philosopher, must answer the question of why "God create[d] the world which is in such disorder that one has then to be saved from its disorder" with a simple, modest "We just don't know."[56] Within Voegelin's framework, humility is also closely related to a form of silence, because, if the Divine is unknown, ineffable, and incommunicable, silence may well be the most appropriate form of reverence.[57]

But just like Voegelin's negative way, humility too acquires its meaning and its significance for Voegelin as one term in a dynamic pair of two terms. The negative way is the countermovement to the gnostic truncation of reality and vice versa. And opposed to Voegelin's humility we find the presumptuousness of those who claim to know reality in its totality, who map out reality as a closed system, thereby either immanentizing or denying the formative presence of the Beyond. Just like any other belief, these constructions will eventually fail under the pressure of a changing reality, but in the meantime, especially if critical resistance is socially and politically suppressed, they can cause considerable suffering and loss of life. Within this social and political context, *Voegelin's intellectualized humility is simply a manifestation of his via negativa* and as such its purpose, too, is to achieve and sustain one's immunity against spiritual disorder. Moreover, as a form of resistance, it also assumes a more positive role in that it can become a more or less open and public stance against the surrounding crisis.

The ambiguity of Voegelin's *via negativa*—and of humility—as a form of resistance stems from the fact that it attains its meaning and significance in a dynamic relationship with its opposite. In such a relationship, the quest for immunity is at the same time a form of self-assertion, an expression of a desire to be right when everything and everyone else is proven wrong. Seen from this angle, Voegelin's negative way turns into a manifestation of intellectual pride, which assumes that, as long as proper precaution is taken, the philosopher will indeed remain unaffected by the crisis of the very society to which he belongs. A historical "crisis," as Voegelin explained, only affects the "spirit of the time" as it infuses institutions, and we will be affected individually only if, quite unnecessarily, we "make the order of [our] own soul dependent on the institutions undergoing the crisis." In other words, there was no obligation to enter a period of personal crisis just because society was in crisis—even if occasionally that could mean that we would have to face the "deadly consequences" of living in such a society in crisis.[58] For Voegelin, crisis was always and exclusively a social phenomenon, and personal immunity was a distinct possibility if not an obligation. The pride we are referring to in this context corresponds to the philosopher's unwillingness/inability to contemplate the possibility that his own thought could be a symptom of the very disease he had diagnosed in his social environment. What is at stake here is the crucial relationship between the philosopher's analysis of crisis and the crisis itself: what is cure and what is disease?[59]

We are left, therefore, with two perspectives on Voegelin's reflective distance, which, if characterized by the terms humility and pride, appear to be diametrically opposed. Where, in this opposition, would Voegelin locate himself? As the quotations in the previous paragraph suggest, the language and tone of immunity clearly predominate in his writings. Yet, it is against this backdrop that a few late remarks, interspersed in his writings, suddenly seem to assume great significance. In his very late writings, published and unpublished, we find evidence of a new, more introspective awareness: the quest for immunity is not as straightforward as his earlier writings suggested. The very late work not only acknowledges that the relationship between movement and countermovement, between truth and untruth, is dialectical and may derail into a *mimetic* struggle between theologies, but the late work also alludes to the possibility that the target(s) of Voegelin's criticism—and the targeting itself—may have cast a shadow over the unfolding meditative quest:

> through the oppositional component of meaning something of the untruth opposed creeps into the symbolization of truth.[60]

Moreover, there is a sense in which the process of deformation—the differentiation of untruth—contributes to the formative quest for truth:

> a movement of resistance [against truth], if it achieves clarity about its experiential motivations and elaborates the story of its deformative quest, can contribute substantially to the understanding of the paradox in the formative structure it resists, while the defenders of the truth may fall into the various traps prepared by their own self-assertive resistance and thus contribute substantially to an understanding of the forces of deformation.[61]

As the quotation shows, Voegelin was quite aware of the fact that "resistance to untruth" and prideful self-assertion could well be indistinguishable. It follows that

> in the depth of the quest, formative truth and deformative untruth are more closely related than the language of "truth" and "resistance" would suggest.[62]

But the language of "truth" and "resistance," of course, is Voegelin's language. Thus, we find in these statements an acknowledgment not only that resistance may undermine immunity but also, and more strongly, that the language in which Voegelin had approached these problems was inadequate.

We know that there is continuity from these late confessions to his personal meditations shortly before his death. That the sin of pride was on his mind is obvious from the fact that he requested 1 John 2:15–17 as one of his two funeral readings—a text that again highlights the problem of pride:

> *Do not love the world or the things in the world.*
> *If any one loves the world, love for the Father is not in him.*
> *For all that is in the world, the lust of the flesh and the lust of the eyes and pride of life, is not of the Father but is of the world.*
> *And the world passes away, and the lust of it; but he who does the will of God abides forever.*

When his astonished wife asked why he had chosen those verses, Voegelin answered simply "for repentance."[63]

VI.

How are we to read these late statements? And how should they inform our reading of Voegelin's earlier work? The concluding chapter of René Girard's first book, *Deceit, Desire, and the Novel,* although it deals with novelists rather than scholars, suggests that such late introspective reflections may represent a crucial turning point in the author's self-understanding. According to Girard, many great novels were written in a two-stage process, with the author's self-demystification and conversion in between. The first draft of the novel is often a form of self-justification, with a clear distinction between good and evil, truth and untruth, but "if the writer has a potential for greatness," after writing the first draft, as he or she rereads it, the writer realizes that the self-justification "he had intended in his distinction between good and evil will not stand self-examination." The "novelist of genius" thus becomes able to see that "he and his enemy are truly indistinguishable" and henceforth can "describe the wickedness of the other from within himself, whereas before it was . . . completely artificial." To Girard, this experience of conversion is "shattering to the vanity and pride of the writer"; "it is an existential downfall."[64] At the same time, however, it signifies the origin of true insight.

The key moment in the novel where this insight will, or will not, find its place is the conclusion:

> Truth is active throughout the great novel but its primary location is in the conclusion. The conclusion is the temple of that truth. The conclusion is the site of the presence of truth, and therefore a place avoided by error.[65]

The novelistic conclusion "is a reconciliation between the individual and the world, between man and the sacred."[66] The hero, "when he renounces the deceptive divinity of pride . . . frees himself from slavery and finally grasps the truth about his unhappiness."[67] This moment of "belated lucidity" inspires not only the hero but also his creator and infuses the entire novel:

> The hero succumbs as he achieves truth and he entrusts his creator with the heritage of his clairvoyance. The title of hero of a novel must be reserved for the character who triumphs over metaphysical desire in a tragic conclusion and thus becomes *capable of writing the novel.* The hero and his creator are separated throughout the novel but come together in the conclusion.[68]

"Great novels," Girard explains, "always spring from an obsession that has been transcended"[69]—great novels are the evidence of a conversion. The "truly great novels are all born of that supreme moment and return to it the way a church radiates from the chancel and returns to it."[70]

> This moment is the expression of a new and more detached vision, which is the creator's own vision. This ascending movement must not be confused with pride. The aesthetic triumph of the author is one with the joy of the hero who has renounced desire.[71]

It is precisely the absence of desire in the vision that makes it possible to recapture past desires. In this sense, the vision is a "panoramic vision," a "revivification of the past," and thus a form of remembering. Indeed, "the inspiration always comes from memory and memory springs from the conclusion."[72] In the creative process, the conclusion is the true beginning of the novel, the moment of its possibility. Without the conclusion, there would be no beginning. Therefore, "the conclusion must be considered as a successful effort to overcome the inability to conclude." Girard agrees with Maurice Blanchot, who suggested that the "inability to conclude . . . is an inability to die in the work and to free oneself in death."[73] Girard also notes the significance of John 12:24–25, which reverberates at crucial moments in the great novels, because the "breadth and depth of vision" belong to "the new being who is literally born of the death."[74]

> *Truly, truly, I say to you, unless a grain of wheat*
> *falls into the earth and dies, it remains*
> *alone; but if it dies, it bears much fruit.*
>
> *He who loves his life loses it, and he*
> *who hates his life in this world will*
> *keep it for eternal life.*

Girard's suggestions are instructive in that they help us formulate what we perceive to be the central problem in Eric Voegelin's philosophy. The central problem concerns the relationship between the philosopher and the crisis he analyzes; between the resistance to untruth and the untruth resisted. To what extent was Voegelin's work contaminated by the very crisis that it claimed to have unveiled? The late reflections suggest that he became increasingly aware of this problem as a loose end, thereby introducing a third, possibly mediating, factor into this relationship: conversion (as understood by Girard).

It was not until those very late reflections that Voegelin contemplated the possibility that he and his enemies are truly indistinguishable; but there can be no doubt that in the self-examination performed in these late texts, this possibility is articulated in the clearest of terms. In this context, it appears significant that the second reading Voegelin requested for his funeral was John 12:24–25, exactly the two verses highlighted by Girard as the perfect expression of the distinction between a death that is an extinction of the spirit and a death that *is* spirit. Can we understand Voegelin's late statements, therefore, as conclusions, as temples of truth and thus as evidence of a conversion? Or are we "giving too much importance to a few forgotten lines?"[75]

VII.

That René Girard emphasizes the importance of conclusions as the "temple of truth" in the *concluding* chapter of his book is, of course, not a coincidence. In perfect accordance with its contents, "The Conclusion" of *Deceit, Desire, and the Novel* is evidence of Girard's own conversion:

> When I wrote the last chapter of my first book, I had had a vague idea of what I would do, but as the chapter took form I realized I was undergoing my own version of the experience I was describing. I was particularly attracted to the Christian elements, for example, Stepan Verkhovensky's final journey and turn to the Gospel before his death. So I began to read the Gospels and the rest of the Bible. And I turned into a Christian.[76]

This "intellectual-literary conversion," as he calls the experience, at first did not imply any change of life, but it prepared the way for a "definitive conversion" in which "the aesthetic gave way to the religious."[77]

For Girard, as well as for some of the novelists he studied in his first book, the experience of the successful overcoming "of the inability to conclude," which is an experience of conversion, finds an obvious spiritual home in the Christian Gospels. Girard's later work suggests that this affinity is due to the fact that in both contexts the underlying experiences signal a successful overcoming of scapegoating. If we are looking for answers to our questions about the significance of Eric Voegelin's late reflections, therefore, his encounters with the Gospels may provide a sensible starting point for our search.

For both sympathetic readers and critics alike, Voegelin's attitude toward Christianity is a highly sensitive issue.[78] Soon after the publication of the first three volumes of *Order and History*, Hannah Arendt predicted that Voegelin would be unable to complete the series, because "[h]e cannot cope with Christianity, it breaks his scheme."[79] When the fourth volume of *Order and History* finally appeared, 17 years after the previous volume, with only one chapter directly addressing the Gospels, sympathetic readers who wished to see Voegelin firmly established within a Christian camp found themselves on the defensive. Gerhart Niemeyer was only one among many critics who took volume 4 as evidence that "Voegelin [had] approached a great spiritual reality from a standpoint extraneous to it."[80] The fact that Christian critics such as Niemeyer expressed their disappointment with Voegelin's treatment of Christianity in the form of an excommunication had an unfortunate, lasting effect on the subsequent debate, which increasingly revolved around the question of whether or not Voegelin *was* a Christian. It is ironic that most readers of Voegelin have surprisingly firm views on the question, while Voegelin's self-understanding in relation to Christianity remained as unsettled as the debate overall.

The build up to volume 4 of *Order and History* provides ample evidence of Voegelin's struggle with "such ticklish questions as Christianity."[81] Especially in his letters to the Louisiana State University (LSU) Press editors, who were waiting for volume 4, Voegelin was honest enough to admit that the delay was caused by various "troublesome questions" concerning Christianity and its historical success—why should Christianity have been "victorious in rivalry with the mystery religions and Stoic philosophy"? The same letter from which these quotations were taken also announced that Voegelin had "all of a sudden" found an "obvious, simple solution" to the problem;[82] and yet, as so often, the sense of elation did not last. Almost ten years later, he confessed in a letter that he was (still) "paralyzed" by the very same problem—why did Jesus and the Gospels "have the historical success of forming a civilization"?[83]

While he was struggling with such fundamental questions, he remained painfully aware of the fact that his volume on Christianity would become the most scrutinized of all his books, partly because the earlier *Order and History* volumes, as well as *NSP,* had raised great expectations:

> We must consider that the volume on Christianity will attract particular attention, and come under fire from all sides. It must be impeccable—or else.[84]

In light of this awareness, the actual contents and shape of volume 4 of *Order and History* is all the more remarkable. Only one chapter in the book is devoted to a New Testament figure—Paul—and the chapter has only 32 pages. It is divided into two parts—§1, "The Pauline Theophany," and §2, "The Egophanic Revolt"—with the second part repeating the usual list of thinkers who, according to Voegelin, represented a "derailment" or, in the language of *The Ecumenic Age,* an "egophanic revolt": Fichte, Hegel, Comte, Nietzsche, Feuerbach, Marx. This reduces Voegelin's analysis of Paul to a mere 20 pages. Of course, Christianity is referred to in other parts of the volume and, indeed, of the entire series, but it is surprising, surely, that in an approximately 1,800-page treatise entitled *Order and History,* only 20 pages should be devoted to a more systematic analysis of Christian experiences and symbols. The brevity is indicative of deeper problems in Voegelin's analysis.

Burdened with the awareness of his readers' expectations, Voegelin seemed keen to emphasize that the Christian revelation (and Paul's account of it) represented a genuine advance in the differentiation of the truth of existence. The "Pauline myth," according to Voegelin, "is distinguished by its superior degree of differentiation" compared with "the more compact types," which presumably also included the Platonic type.[85] The chapter on Paul therefore continues the analysis of "The Gospel and Culture" essay, where Voegelin had already established that the Gospels "take the decisive step of making the experience of man's tension toward the Unknown God the truth to which all truth of reality must conform."[86] In contrast to these statements, however, the Paul chapter frequently returns to Plato as the key measure. In philosophy, Voegelin argued, "the noetic analysis of the *metaxy* has gone as far as in the Gospel movement, and in some points [it] is superior to anything we find in the Gospels." In fact, he finds the "Pauline analysis of existential order through man's tension toward the divine ground . . . not so clear as the Platonic-Aristotelian," although "the equivalence of the result is clear enough."[87] Somewhat later in the text Voegelin observes that "the mythopoetic genius of Paul was not controlled by the critical consciousness of a Plato," and he finds Paul's interpretation of his vision "analytically deficient."[88]

These contradictions are real, but they are eventually resolved—still within the same chapter—in an account that no longer emphasizes historical succession and increasing differentiation; rather, the difference between philosophy and the Pauline interpretation of the Christian revelation is one of "accent":

> The Pauline analysis of existential order closely parallels the Platonic-Aristotelian. That is to be expected, since both the saint and the philosophers articulate the order constituted by man's response to a theophany. The accent, however, has decisively shifted from the divinely noetic order incarnate in the world to the divinely pneumatic salvation from its disorder, from the paradox of reality to the abolition of the paradox, from the experience of the directional movement to its consummation.[89]

If, as Voegelin suggested, Reality is a continuous movement beyond its own structure, our observation of the movement can place the "accent" either on the "directional movement" (structure) or on "its consummation" (beyond structure, transfiguration). The relationship between philosophy and Christianity, therefore, ultimately appears as one of complementarity. Within Voegelin's framework, this is indeed a very elegant solution, but in a sense its very elegance is also its problem, because the solution is determined by the framework rather than by a careful consideration of Christian symbols and experiences. In other words, Voegelin's treatment of Christianity assumes the form of an application of a system of ideas that preexisted his scholarly encounter with Christianity. Thus, he could afford to be brief on Christianity, because all he needed to do was to "fit the materials into the pattern that is well established."[90] And once we understand the system—the pattern—the outcome of its application is fairly predictable.

The limitations of the system become particularly obvious whenever Voegelin appropriates elements of the history of Christian thought and dogma in support of the system. His interpretation of the Definition of Chalcedon (AD 451), concerning the union of the two natures, divine and human, in the one person of Christ, is a good example of Voegelin falling back on a well-established pattern:

> This valiant attempt of the *patres* to express the two-in-one reality of God's participation in man, without either compromising the separateness of the two or splitting the one, concerns the same structure of intermediate reality, of the *metaxy,* the philosopher encounters when he analyzes man's consciousness of participation in the divine ground of his existence.[91]

Voegelin returned to Chalcedon on a number of occasions, always in order to underline the same point, that in spite of the different accents, philosophy and Christianity are fundamentally equivalent.[92] His reading of Chalcedon, however, misses the essential point in a characteristic fashion. To say that Christ has both natures in one person implies that he is most certainly not "in-between." Indeed, if we continue to pursue the spatial metaphors, the definition achieved at Chalcedon implies that Christ is precisely not "in-between" but "outside." Voegelin did not ignore the radical core of Christianity but, from within his system, he could see the core only as a distortion, as a derailment.

However, the brevity of Voegelin's treatment of Christianity in volume 4 cannot be explained exclusively on the grounds that in his approach to Christian symbols he fell back on preexisting ideas; the *content* of these ideas needs to be considered as well. As we noted earlier, the pattern he applied was based on an initial exclusion—the exclusion of Gnosticism, of the truncation of reality as the countermovement to the movement of the *via negativa.* Thus, in his search for a Christianity that was free from Gnosticism, Voegelin had to argue—somehow—that the Incarnation, although a concretization of the divine, was nothing but a manifestation of the Unknown God, and that the Unknown God remained unknown even though "the divine Logos" had become "present in the world through the representative life and death of a man," of Christ. The argument is stretched but at least it is brief, because, if Jesus can do no more than remind us of the "presence" of an Unknown God, there can be "no message of Christ" and "no doctrine to be taught."[93] In other words, if Christianity is purged of Gnosticism (as understood by Voegelin), *nothing is left*.

Voegelin's system can render the Incarnation meaningful only as a manifestation of the *metaxy*. Any addition to this picture, to the extent that it creates absolute coordinates and truncates Reality, evokes the danger of the gnostic derailment. But as Voegelin knew very well, the history of Christianity is largely a history of such additions; indeed, it seems untenable to catalog Christian symbols as mere superimpositions on Voegelin's *metaxy*. For example, the notion that Christ was not just a revealer (for example, of the *metaxy*) but also an atoner appears to have been constitutive of the earliest Christian self-understanding. Voegelin, however, is struggling to find a place for these additions, and eventually is forced to conclude that the danger of a gnostic derailment was intrinsic to Christianity from its very beginnings:

> Considering the history of Gnosticism, with the great bulk of its manifestations belonging to, or deriving from, the Christian orbit, I am inclined to recognize in the epiphany of Christ the great catalyst that made eschatological consciousness an historical force, both in forming and deforming humanity.[94]

The "Gospel and Culture" essay, too, emphasizes the same danger:

> It will be necessary, therefore, to reflect on the danger that has given the Unknown God a bad name in Christianity and induced certain doctrinal developments as a protective measure, i.e., on the danger of the gospel movement derailing into gnosticism.[95]

Given his approach to Reality, therefore, it is not at all surprising that Voegelin should have placed Christianity and *gnosis* in such close proximity.[96] Under the pressure of his own framework, the "impeccable book" he wanted to write about Christianity shrank to a mere 20 pages. The brevity of the chapter is a measure of the extent to which Voegelin and his enemy had indeed become truly indistinguishable.

VIII.

Voegelin continued to struggle with the "ticklish problems" of Christianity after the publication of *The Ecumenic Age*. Though there were many loose ends that needed attending to, one example may suffice to demonstrate that Voegelin never succeeded in persuading himself that he had grasped the essence of the Christian truth. In 1977, Voegelin writes in a letter:

> As far as the theoretical issues are concerned, I am now fully occupied with clarifying the question of "What is a Vision," which turned out to be central to the understanding of Christianity.[97]

Because the term "vision" occurs in the very title of the chapter on Paul, Voegelin briefly discusses its meaning at the beginning of the chapter. The relevant passages refer to a vision as an "event in metaleptic reality which the philosopher can do no more than try to understand to the best of his ability." The event of the vision occurs in the *metaxy* and therefore "must not be split into 'object' and 'subject'":

> There is no "object" of the vision other than the vision as received; and there is no "subject" of the vision other than the response in a man's soul to divine presence.

However, the next sentence explains that "the vision emerges as a symbol from the Metaxy, and the symbol is both divine and human," leaving the reader to wonder in what ways the vision can be both event and symbol.[98] While the chapter uses the term, even in its title, it remained undertheorized and thus constituted an important loose end. There is, however, a further reason why Voegelin felt he had "to return to the problem of 'vision,'" and this reason is related to the overall framework of his thinking, especially to his unfolding theory of consciousness. In his contribution to the *festschrift* published on the occasion of Eric Voegelin's 80th birthday, Anibal Bueno subjected Voegelin's theory of consciousness to a detailed analysis and suggested that "the metaxy should be regarded as an index for the relation between the temporal and eternal poles of the experience."[99] Voegelin thanked Bueno for his paper in a letter dated 24 February 1981, adding:

> What I liked especially was your critical remark that the metaxy should be characterized as an "index." *It touches on a question that worries me all the*

> *time*. The term "index" was chosen in Anamnesis, in order to express the experience of a movement pointing towards the poles of the existential tension in the metaxy—but is the centre of the movements, the metaxy, itself the index of a movement?[100]

At the time of writing the letter, Voegelin had already taken steps to address the problem:

> At present, I am inclined to follow the course I have started in "Wisdom and the Magic of the Extreme": to follow Plato's analysis of this transition movement under the symbolism of the "vision." If this analysis of an experience of the visionary transition from compactness to differentiation is followed through to its implications, it would introduce the historical process of the "vision" as a further dimension into the structure of consciousness.[101]

What is at stake in these statements is indeed a key piece in the jigsaw that is Voegelin's theory of consciousness: the "location" and nature of the movement in which "a metaxy can become differentiated." This problem, then, was also the place where he wanted to anchor the term "vision." Written as a contribution to a conference on "the sense of imperfection," the "Wisdom and the Magic of the Extreme" essay provided the occasion to develop "vision" as a concept and thus to fill a crucial gap left in the Paul chapter of *The Ecumenic Age*. The "Wisdom" essay advances the notion that "the truth of reality, answering and questioning, arises in consciousness through the interaction of vision and noesis." The differentiation of "vision" allows Voegelin to present the philosopher's quest as a version of Anselm's *fides quaerens intellectum*, of faith seeking understanding, with "vision" corresponding to *fides* and "noesis" to *intellectus*. However, Plato remains the main reference throughout:

> In Plato's case, the *fides* has found its symbolic truth in the vision of love as the source of order in reality and by the vision of truth in human existence through participation in the movement of reality toward the divine Beyond; the *intellectus* is the noetic action of exploring the structures in a process of reality whose fundamental order and direction are revealed by the visions (*opsis*).[102]

The essay then proceeds to explore the implications of these ideas, culminating in the presentation of "Vision," now capitalized, as a "structure" with a number of "facets" (six altogether). Vision, then, is "man's participatory experience of 'seeing' the paradox of . . . reality"; it is also the "experienced possibility of raising the 'seeing' . . . from compactness to a state of reflective differentiation"; and it is "the body of language symbols which express the truth of reality and the stages of its emergence," including the symbol/index *metaxy* with "its human movements of questioning and seeking in response to the divine drawing." On the surface, therefore, Voegelin's "vision" achieved what it was meant to achieve, to present the *metaxy* as an index of the movement from compactness to differentation.

However, the "Wisdom" essay can hardly be considered an advance in clarity. It is three times as long as the Paul chapter and thus adds much depth to Voegelin's analysis, but its inflationary use of terms such as vision, Vision, visionary, and so on does not inspire confidence that the author has managed to clarify the issues at stake. The term "vision" (singular or plural) occurs 77 times; the capitalized "Vision" occurs 27 times; we find the adjective "visionary" 14 times, and the noun "visionary" (singular or plural) occurs 9 times.[103] Apart from the frequent juxtaposition of "Plato's Vision" (capitalized, singular) and "Christian visions" (not capitalized, plural), it seems impossible to identify any insight or pattern underlying the variations in the terms used, almost suggesting a stream of consciousness method of writing. We know that the essay, subtitled "A Meditation," developed "as the result of an ongoing thought process"; there was no outline that Voegelin followed. As he explained to Thomas Hollweck,

> Transitions are good places to check whether what one has done so far can stand. . . . It does not matter what I happen to be thinking about this or that, but what emerges as the process of thought [*Gedankengang*].[104]

Toward the end of the essay, Voegelin repeats the insights from *The Ecumenic Age,* but now in the language of "visions." Visions come "with" or "in" different modalities, noetic and pneumatic, with the former emphasizing "the structure in the movement" of reality and the latter emphasizing "the movement in the structure."[105] A new term was added, and earlier insights were transferred to it. But was clarity gained or lost?

The configuration of the "Wisdom" essay, with its emphasis on the interaction of vision and noesis, was not stable. In later writings, the language of visions, though present, is far less prominent. For Voegelin, the meditation on visions represented a late transitional stage toward the configuration that finds its clearest articulation in volume 5 of *Order and History.* After the "Wisdom" essay, Voegelin turns his attention to the "site" of the vision and locates it in "the mysterious It-reality." Because he was unable to finish the volume, it is impossible to say whether Voegelin would have continued to consider the new configuration a stable and satisfactory resolution "of the problems" as he perceived them. Within his framework, the resolution is strikingly elegant, but the original purpose of the meditation on visions—the understanding of Christianity—was somehow dropped along the way. The fragment of volume 5 that we have does not include a serious discussion of Christian experiences or symbols. It is true, of course, that such a discussion might have been included in later sections of the work if Voegelin had had the time to complete it; but the material that we do have allows us to conclude that any future discussion of Christianity would again have assumed the form of an application of—and a falling back on—a given set of ideas.

The "problem" of Christianity, however, imposed itself again on Voegelin's mind during the last months and weeks of his life as plans had to be made for his funeral. He requested a Lutheran order of service with the two short readings cited above (1 John 2:15–17 and John 12:24–25); but the planning of the service was preceded by a more fundamental discussion between Eric Voegelin and Robert Hamerton-Kelly, then dean of the Stanford Memorial Chapel, on whether Voegelin qualified for a Christian burial. *This discussion was initiated by Voegelin,* very much to Hamerton-Kelly's surprise:

> he summoned me when he was in the hospital. It was about a month before he died, and I talked to him one on one. . . . And he said, "I wanted to ask you whether I qualify for a Christian burial." And I said, "Well, of course, you do." And he said, "No, no, no, not at all." . . . Well, and then we went from there, and I in retrospect realized once again I was quite out of my depth. . . . Here obviously was a person who was conscientious about these things, and wanted to discuss really whether he was a Christian or not. . . . But what does stand in my mind was that I felt I had to persuade him that he was entitled to a Christian burial.[106]

On another occasion in the same context, Voegelin asked Hamerton-Kelly about the meaning of a key expression in the first verse of the Letter to the Romans—"being set apart for the Gospel of God." We know enough about Voegelin's last weeks and days to be able to conclude that the very question "Am I a Christian?" was one of the central concerns of his final meditations.[107]

There is, then, no conclusion in Voegelin's encounters with Christianity. His written work on the subject, published and unpublished, suggests that he never came to terms with "the ticklish questions" posed by Christian experiences and symbols. The "never coming to terms" means, in this context, that he failed to reassure himself that he had grasped the essence of Christianity—of the experiences, the symbols, and the historical "success." The few pages he wrote on the subject, as we noted above, always assumed the form of an application of—and a falling back on—the paradoxical language of the Unknown God and the "paradoxic experience of not-experientiable reality." Voegelin's insistence on the ultimate mystery of Reality and its divine ground does *not* reflect the "humble access" of meditative prayer but the assertion of a system that has a paradox at its center. When Voegelin had the occasion to observe this falling back in other authors, he would speak of a "failure of transcendence."[108]

It is ironic, and also revealing, that one of the key notions of the system—the in-between or *metaxy*—was itself the result of a hypostatization, because, contrary to Voegelin's claims, *metaxy* is *not* a technical term in Plato. *Metaxy* is a common term; it is not a noun but a mere preposition or adverb. The wide range of meaning covered by *metaxy* makes it simply unsuitable as a technical term. As Zdravko Planinc observed, the term occurs about 100 times in the Dialogues, and "by no stretch of the imagination can the substantive matters of all the passages in the dialogues be related by the fact that the word 'metaxy' appears in them."[109] Even more important than the grammatical and semantic properties of *metaxy* is the fact that *Plato's philosophical language does not have "technical" terms*—a fact that is highly significant for any serious appreciation of Plato's philosophy.[110]

But Voegelin's restlessness in these matters also suggests that he was never quite satisfied with his own appropriations of Christian symbols. For a short while after the publication of the "Gospel and Culture" essay, and then later after the publication of *The Ecumenic Age,* Voegelin felt that he had found a solution to the problems, only for the loose ends to crop up again as he tried to move on.

What, then, is the significance of those late statements—of those "few forgotten lines"—in which resistance to untruth and prideful self-assertion appear as twins? The concluding chapter of René Girard's first book invited us to look at these statements in Voegelin's late meditations as expressions of a moment of belated lucidity, of a "turning around" and of the overcoming of an obsession. Girard's chapter also implied that for him as well as for the novelists he studied, Christianity became the obvious spiritual home for their experiences. Voegelin's encounters with Christianity, in contrast, remained inconclusive. The final volume of *Order and History* finds him *in search of order,* perfecting his system. In her foreword to the volume, Lissy Voegelin remembers:

> In his last months I saw him, almost every day, reading and rereading the manuscript, making slight corrections occasionally, and always pointing out to me: This will be Volume 5. He liked his work and often talked about it, and he let me know that he knew very well that these pages are the key to all his other works and that in these pages he has gone as far as he could go in analysis, saying what he wanted to say as clearly as it possibly could be said.[111]

We conclude, therefore, that Voegelin's late admissions do not point beyond his system; they are the result of the system turning inward, applying itself to itself, radicalizing itself. The initial exclusion—Gnosticism—remained excluded.

IX.

This essay set out to reflect on Eric Voegelin's contribution as a whole and thus on the unity of his work. In my search for this unity, I decided early on that I would follow the loose ends of the work in the hope that they would lead us to a center in the overall configuration of loose ends—that is, to the central problem that sustained Voegelin's lifelong quest. I found this center in the ambiguous relationship between the philosopher's analysis of crisis and the crisis itself. Using Girard's essay on conclusions, I looked at Eric Voegelin's late meditations, in order to establish whether the late confessions provide evidence of a successful resolution of the problem. In the previous section, however, I concluded that the central loose end remained a loose end throughout, making it all the more plausible to present it as the key index of the unity of his lifework.

In the following, I want to explicate my analysis further by confronting directly Eric Voegelin's late suggestion that his work continued the meditative tradition of St. Augustine and St. Anselm of Canterbury. As noted above, the "Wisdom and the Magic of the Extreme" essay is subtitled "A Meditation"; similarly, the fragment "The Beginning and the Beyond" bears the subtitle "A Meditation on Truth." In these two essays, Voegelin commits himself to the literary form of the meditation as the proper format for his attempt "to clarify the formative center of existence, the *metaxy,* and to protect this noetic center against the deformative forces prevalent at the time."[112] Voegelin refers to Augustine and Anselm as his predecessors:

> I have taken special care . . . to conduct the analysis in such a manner that its abstractness would not hide its close relation to Saint Anselm of Canterbury's language, in the Augustinian tradition, of the *fides quaerens intellectum* and the correlative *credo ut intelligam*.[113]

That Voegelin should make such a commitment is surprising, considering that one of Anselm's two major meditations, the *Proslogion*, assumed the form of a proof for the existence of God. Without qualifications and modifications, such a proof cannot be integrated into Voegelin's framework, because, as he observed, "the cardinal problem of the logical proof for the existence of God is an attempt at constructing the Unknown God."[114]

Accordingly, Voegelin's analysis of Anselm's *Proslogion* had to qualify its character as a proof and emphasize its meaning as a "prayer of love by the creature to the Creator to grant a more perfect vision of His divinity."[115] Most importantly, Voegelin had to present Anselm's prayer as a movement in, and exploration of, the *metaxy*. Unfortunately, the language of the *Proslogion* does not explicitly refer to an in-between of any kind, and thus Voegelin had to look elsewhere for a term that at least in his reading became a reference to the *metaxy*. Not without a sense of triumph—and relief?—Voegelin's search succeeded in unearthing an expression that was close enough for his purposes:

> in the preface to *De Fide Trinitatis*, Anselm can speak of the understanding possible in this life as a *medium inter fidem et speciem*, as something between plain faith and the vision granted through grace in death. The *medium*, the In-Between, thus appears as a concept after all.[116]

Voegelin concludes that Anselm "clearly understood the cognitive structure [of the prayer] as internal to the Metaxy."[117] A second qualification still assumes that it is wrong to consider the prayer as a proof but accepts that there is a context in which this misunderstanding would be eminently plausible. The context in question is the "struggle" that unfolds with the arrival of the "fool" from Psalm 14:1, who says "in his heart, 'There is no God.'" The fool expects the "explorer of faith" to be engaged in a proof for the assertion that God exists, and it is in response to the fool that the "noetic reflection of the spiritualist acquires the character of an affirmative proposition concerning the existence of God."[118] In other words, without the fool, Anselm's prayer has no need to present itself as a proof. In support of this observation, Voegelin points out that the noun *probatio* does not occur in the *Proslogion* but "only" in the appendix, in Anselm's response to Gaunilo, a monk of Marmoutier, who speaks "in behalf of the fool."[119]

In addition to these two qualifications of Anselm's meditation, Voegelin also introduces two modifications. The first one consists in a deliberate "expansion of the *fides quaerens intellectum* beyond Anselm's Christian horizon to the manifold of non- and pre-Christian theophanic events."[120] Every *fides*, not only the Christian, is to be included in the quest for understanding by reason.[121] The second modification concerns the somewhat inconvenient fact that for Anselm, "the finality of the [Christian] Creed is absolute":

> Although a search for the better understanding of the *fides* by means of the philosopher's reason implies a critical distance to the symbolism explored, no such distance is sensed in the Anselmian reflections. . . . There is no attempt to establish, or question, the truth of the concepts in the light of the experiences that have engendered them. Hence, the Anselmian language cannot be taken over *telquel*, because it lacks the stratum of reflection that is our present concern.[122]

Many sympathetic readers of Voegelin have concurred that the *fides quaerens intellectum* was the "essence of his method."[123] Still, his reading of Anselm's *Proslogion* is characteristically far-fetched. In the preface to the text, Anselm makes his purpose very clear, and the fact that the noun *probatio* does not occur—although *probandum* is there—seems fairly insignificant:

> I began to wonder if perhaps it might be possible to find one single argument that for its proof required no other save itself [*quod nullo alio ad se probandum quam se solo indigeret*], and that by itself would suffice to prove that God really exists, that He is the supreme good needing no other and is He whom all things have need of for their being and well-being, and also to prove whatever we believe about the Divine Being.[124]

The quotation also makes clear that what is at stake in Anselm's prayer is not only the existence of God but his attributes—what is to be shown is that God exists *as we believe in him*. A more detailed analysis of Anselm's actual *argumentum* reveals that it was meant to offer a proof "that the essences of Goodness, Truth, Justice, etc., which he had shown in the *Monologion* to be the necessary attributes of God, must cohere in a single Being, and that this Being, properly understood, cannot be thought of as non-existent."[125] Anselm's God is not Unknown.

Furthermore, Anselm's text involves the fool from the beginning, long before the exchange with Gaunilo. That the fool is the target of the *Proslogion* is made clear as early as in chapter 2. In fact, in his response to Gaunilo, Anselm leaves the fool behind:

> Since it is not the Fool, against whom I spoke in my tract, who takes me up, but one who, though speaking on the Fool's behalf, is an orthodox Christian and no fool, it will suffice if I reply to the Christian.[126]

But the key problem with Voegelin's appropriation of Anselm is the fact that he misunderstands and/or misrepresents the experience underlying Anselm's meditation. Having outlined his concern—finding *that* single argument—with great clarity, Anselm proceeds to tell the story of its discovery:

> But as often and as diligently as I turned my thoughts to this, sometimes it seemed to me that I had almost reached what I was seeking, sometimes it eluded my acutest thinking completely, so that finally, in desperation, I was about to give up what I was looking for as something impossible to find. However, when I had decided to put aside this idea altogether, lest by uselessly occupying my mind it might prevent other ideas with which I could make some progress, then, in spite of my unwillingness and my resistance to it, it began to force itself upon me more and more pressingly. So it was that one day when I was quite worn out with resisting its importunacy, there came to me, in the very conflict of my thoughts, what I had despaired of finding, so that I eagerly grasped the notion which in my distraction I had been rejecting. Judging, then, that what had given me such joy to discover would afford pleasure, if it were written down, to anyone who might read it, I have written the following short tract dealing with this question as well as several others, from the point of view of one trying to raise his mind to contemplate God and seeking to understand what he believes.[127]

In this report Anselm makes it very clear that the text of the *Proslogion* was written *after a meditative process had reached its conclusion*. Just as in the "great novels" studied by Girard, the "conclusion is the true beginning" of the *Proslogion*, the "moment of its possibility."[128] The *Proslogion* was written "under the impulse of an original insight," in a state of excitement caused by a genuine sense of discovery and illumination.[129] The "finality" of Anselm's language is "the finality of one who has swept the floor to find a coin which was lost, and has found it."[130] In all his texts, Anselm aimed at "precision of language, of argument, of definition: but only when prolonged meditation had already brought him to see the truth with instantaneous clarity":

> If ever Anselm had a moment of hesitation between two conflicting conclusions, we are not allowed to see it: in all his writings, he appears on the field already a victor, ready to explain, perhaps to demonstrate, but not to fight.[131]

Voegelin states the obvious, therefore, when he notices a lack of "critical distance" in Anselm, for the nature of Anselm's experience was precisely such that the distance was overcome. If Voegelin wants to add this distance—reflective distance—to the meditation, he profoundly changes its character. Moreover, there *is* distance in Anselm's work—namely, the distance between the meditation and the subsequent articulation of its conclusions in language, argument, and definition. Voegelin's writings, in contrast, lack *this* distance.

Voegelin's meditative essays were not written after the conclusion of the meditation; they *are meditations in search of a conclusion*—reason in quest of faith. In light of this observation, it is not at all surprising that the problem of endings—and of conclusions—continued to haunt Voegelin's essays from the very first to the last volume of *Order and History.* One of the greatest problems that plagued Voegelin while he was working on the *Order and History* volumes was the fact that a beginning had to be made "without knowing how the story will end."[132] The problem becomes thematic in the opening reflection of volume 5, *In Search of Order,* where he explains that "the story has no beginning before it has come to its end."[133] The unfinished character of Voegelin's lifework is not due to the fact that he died while still working on key texts; rather, it is due to the fact that in his case, and contrary to that of Anselm, the articulation of the meditative process *is* the meditative process.

X.

In the *Proslogion,* Anselm pours out his heart in prayer:

> Come then, Lord my God, teach me where and how to seek You, where and how to find You. Lord, if you are not present here, where, since You are absent, shall I look for You? On the other hand, if You are everywhere why

> then, since You are absent, do I not see You? But surely You dwell in "light inaccessible" [1 Tim. 6:16]. . . . Never have I seen You, Lord my God, I do not know Your face.[134]

There are two main reasons why Anselm cannot "see" God's "face." The first one is the "light inaccessible" of God's presence, God's immensity, and his overwhelming splendor and fullness.[135] The second reason does not refer to God's attributes, however, but to the limitations of Anselm's soul:

> Lord my God, You who have formed and reformed me, tell my desiring soul what You are besides what it has seen so that it may see clearly that which it desires. It strives so that it may see more, and it sees nothing beyond what it has seen save darkness.[136]

Voegelin too considers the previous quotation important because he reads it as a comment on the "limits of the noetic quest"; with this quotation, Anselm "acknowledges that the God found by the truth of reason is not yet the God whom the seeker has experienced as present in the formation and re-formation of his existence."[137] But Anselm's text continues along different lines: the darkness he sees is not the darkness of the Unknown God but the darkness of his own soul:

> Or rather it does not see darkness, which is not in You in any way; but it sees that it cannot see more *because of its own darkness.*[138]

Anselm takes for granted what Girard's "novelist of genius" realizes in a moment of "existential downfall": that self-justification through externalization is a sign of vanity and pride. He knows that the soul's darkness does not represent the limit of the noetic conceptual analysis but its affliction with sin:

> I acknowledge, Lord, and I give thanks that You have created Your image in me, so that I may remember You, love You. But this image is so effaced and worn away by vice, *so darkened by the smoke of sin,* that it cannot do what it was made to do unless You renew it and reform it.[139]

The problem of sin, therefore, is crucial to Anselm's meditation. His *fides quaerens intellectum* responds to the Lord's command that we should have faith, which requires the overcoming not just of ignorance but also of sin.[140] In this respect, Anselm simply follows the model of Augustine's *Confessions:*

> Who will give me help, so that I may rest in you? . . . What am I myself to you, that you, that you command me to love you, and grow angry and threaten me with mighty woes unless I do? . . . Too narrow is the house of my soul for you to enter it: let it be enlarged by you. It lies in ruins; build it up again. I confess and I know that it contains things that offend your eyes. Yet who will cleanse it? Or upon what other than you shall I call? From my secret sins cleanse me, O Lord.[141]

The notion of sin does not occur in Voegelin's meditations, which claim to use Anselm's *Proslogion* and Augustine's *Confessions* as models. Is this incongruence a mere result of "abstractness," as Voegelin thought?

We can envision an alternative meditative quest that in many ways would appear to be equivalent to Voegelin's. This quest would begin, not with resistance to untruth, but with resistance to sin. And for every term evoked in Voegelin's quest, there would be an equivalent term in our quest. Some terms may be common to both meditations. And yet, although the "processes of thought"—Voegelin's *Gedankengang*, cited above—in the two movements may well appear equivalent in the sense of a structural correspondence of terms, the *meaning* of the meditative movements would diverge.[142] The main reason for this divergence is closely related to the central problem in Eric Voegelin's philosophy as identified in this essay: while we may be able to define ourselves in opposition to untruth, the peculiar nature of the category "sin" makes it very difficult for us to resist sin without having to meditate our own sinful afflictions. The notion of sin, much more than untruth, can hardly be evoked without introspection, because sin, in its personal and transpersonal dimension, always includes pride as a component.[143]

NOTES

1. At the time of writing this essay, only the two correspondence volumes—volumes 29 and 30—were still awaiting publication. For an insightful review of the *History of Political Ideals* volumes in the collected works, see Arpad Szakolczai, "Eric Voegelin's History of Political Ideas: A Review Essay," *European Journal of Social Theory* 4, no. 3 (2001): 351–68.

2. Charles R. Embry, ed., *Robert B. Heilman and Eric Voegelin: A Friendship in Letters 1944–1984* (Columbia: University of Missouri Press, 2004); Peter Emberley and Barry Cooper, eds., *Faith and Political Philosophy: The Correspondence between Leo Strauss and Eric Voegelin 1934–1964* (University Park, PA: Penn State University Press, 1993); Gerhard Wagner and Gilbert Weiss, eds., *Alfred Schütz, Eric Voegelin—Eine Freundschaft, die ein Leben ausgehalten hat. Briefwechsel 1938–1959* (Konstanz: UVK, 2004).

3. Geoffrey L. Price, *Eric Voegelin: International Bibliography 1921–2000* (Munich: Fink, 2000).

4. Eric Voegelin, *On the Form of the American Mind,* ed. Juergen Gebhardt and Barry Cooper, trans. Ruth Hein (Baton Rouge: Louisiana State University Press, 1995), 5.

5. Voegelin, *On the Form of the American Mind,* 3.

6. Eric Voegelin, "Autobiographical Statement at Age 82," in *The Beginning and the Beyond: Papers from the Gadamer and Voegelin Conferences,* Supplementary Issue of the *Lonergan Workshop,* volume 4, ed. Fred Lawrence (Chico, CA: Scholars Press, 1984), 111–31 (127).

7. Michel Foucault, *The Archaeology of Knowledge* (London: Tavistock, 1974), 17.

8. Eric Voegelin to Peter E. Berger, Editor of Social Research, 19 December 1967, Box 36, File 36.29. All box and file numbers in this essay refer to the Eric Voegelin Papers at the Hoover Institution Archives, Stanford University, California.

9. Eric Voegelin to John East, 18 July 1977, Box 10, File 10.23. Numerous letters in the Eric Voegelin Papers testify to Voegelin's impatience and frustration. See, for example, Eric Voegelin to Robert Schuettinger, 13 October 1969, Box 43, File 43.4; Eric Voegelin to Stephen J. Tonsor, 3 April 1969, Box 37, File 37.27; Eric Voegelin to Peter E. Berger, Editor of Social Research, 19 December 1967, Box 36, File 36.29; Eric Voegelin to George H. Nash, 9 December 1974, Box 26, File 26.13. Voegelin concluded his letter to Nash with an appeal: "I can only hope that you have not written too much nonsense about the work I am doing."

10. Eric Voegelin to Dante Germino, 13 May 1970, Box 14, File 14.14.

11. Gregor Sebba, "Prelude and Variations on the Theme Of Eric Voegelin," *Southern Review* 13 (1977): 646–76 (665). The exchange of letters between Voegelin and Sebba, which includes this discussion of the "mystic philosopher," is from 1973.

12. Eric Voegelin, *Autobiographical Reflections,* ed. Ellis Sandoz (Baton Rouge: Louisiana State University Press, 1989), 113.

13. Voegelin, *Autobiographical Reflections,* 113.

14. Eric Voegelin to Friedrich Engel-Janosi, 31 March 1943, Box 11, File 11.7.

15. Voegelin, *Autobiographical Reflections,* 113.

16. Voegelin, *Autobiographical Reflections,* 114.

17. See the notes on mysticism dated 3 December 1970, Box 84, File 84.9. Volume 5 of *Order and History* was meant to include a chapter on mysticism. See, for example, the plans and outlines in "For the beginning of Volume 5," dated 6 November 1979, p. 2, Box 84, File 84.9. On mysticism and "freedom," see Eric Voegelin to Manfred Henningsen, 17 May 1969, Box 17, File 17.15.

18. Voegelin, *Autobiographical Reflections,* 114.

19. Eric Voegelin to Karl Löwith, 17 December 1944, Box 24, File 24.4. All translations from letters written in German are my translations.

20. Eric Voegelin to Elizabeth de Waal, 28 August 1966, Box 39, File 39.17.

21. Eric Voegelin to Carl W. Ernst, 9 October 1977, Box 12, File 12.1, EVP.

22. Friedrich Nietzsche, quoted in Paul Mendes-Flohr, "Editor's Introduction," in Martin

Buber, *Ecstatic Confessions: The Heart of Mysticism* (Syracuse, NY: Syracuse University Press, 1996), xiv.

23. Eric Voegelin, *The Ecumenic Age*, vol. 4, *Order and History* (Baton Rouge: Louisiana State University Press, 1974), 19.

24. Voegelin, *The Ecumenic Age*, 269.

25. Voegelin, *The Ecumenic Age*, 133–34.

26. Eric Voegelin, *The New Science of Politics*, in *Collected Works of Eric Voegelin*, vol. 5, *Modernity without Restraint: The Political Religions; The New Science of Politics; and Science, Politics, and Gnosticism*, ed. Manfred Henningsen (Columbia: University of Missouri Press), 75–241 (190); the list of modern "Gnostic movements" is from Eric Voegelin, "Ersatz Religion: The Gnostic Mass Movements of Our Time," in *Modernity without Restraint*, 293–313 (295).

27. Max Ways, "Journalism and Joachim's Children," *Time*, 9 March 1953.

28. Eugene Webb, "Voegelin's 'Gnosticism' Reconsidered," in *Political Science Reviewer* 34 (2005): 48–76 (48).

29. Murray Jardine, "Eric Voegelin's Interpretation(s) of Modernity: A Reconsideration of the Spiritual and Political Implications of Voegelin's Therapeutic Analysis," *Review of Politics* 7, no. 4 (Fall 1995): 581–605 (581).

30. Voegelin, *Autobiographical Reflections*, 64.

31. Eric Voegelin to Carl J. Friedrich, 12 April 1959, Box 13, File 13.16.

32. Rudolf Bultmann to Eric Voegelin, 19 July 1957 and 4 March 1960, both in Box 8, File 8.55.

33. Eric Voegelin to Von Balthasar, May 20, 1950, Box 7, File 7.8. In a Marketing Questionnaire for *The New Science of Politics*, then still entitled "Beyond Modernity," Voegelin wrote: "The idea that modern politics is essentially a Gnostic movement is quite new. It is probably not known to anybody except one or two specialists like Hans Urs von Balthasar." Box 38, File 38.21. The introduction to part 1 of *Science, Politics, and Gnosticism* and the preface to the American edition of the same text do refer to Jonas and Von Balthasar as key authors on "ancient" and "modern" gnosticism respectively. See Voegelin, *Modernity without Restraint*, 247 and 253. In a lecture entitled "The Remergence [*sic*] of Gnosticism in Modern Times," delivered on 18 March 1972, Voegelin again confirmed that it was the reading of *Prometheus* that drew his attention to gnosis. Box 77, File 77.7, 2.

34. Hans Urs von Balthasar, *Prometheus: Studien zur Geschichte des deutschen Idealismus* (Heidelberg, Germany: Kerle Verlag, 1947), 21, 26, 37.

35. Von Balthasar, *Prometheus*, 139–57 (146).

36. Von Balthasar, *Prometheus*, 25–26.

37. The first volume of Hans Jonas's *Gnosis und Spaetantiker Geist* was published in 1934. In 1957, Jonas explained that discerning "an essence of Gnosticism as a whole" was indeed the key objective of the 1934 work. See Jonas, *The Gnostic Religion: The Message of the Alien God and the Beginnings of Christianity*, 2nd ed. (Boston: Beacon Press, 1963), xvii.

38. *The New Science of Politics* refers to the *Prometheus* in footnotes 23 and 26 in the chapter on "Gnosticism: The Nature of Modernity," but neither footnote reveals Voegelin's debt to von Balthasar. See *The New Science of Politics*, in *Modernity without Restraint*, 186, 189.

39. This term still appears in *The Ecumenic Age*, 237–38, and refers to modern movements, suggesting that modernity adds the apocalyptic element to an underlying gnostic core.

40. Gregor Sebba to Eric Voegelin, 20 October 1978, Box 35, File 35.7, my emphasis. Sebba was a personal friend and a sympathetic reader of Voegelin. In turn, Voegelin trusted him as a reliable interpreter of his work. "I always like Sebba writing about my work." See Eric Voegelin to Donald E. Stanford, 24 January 1975, Box 36, File 36.34; see also Eric Voegelin to Robert Heilman, 19 June 1966, Box 17, File 17.9; also Eric Voegelin to Gregor Sebba, 21 April 1966, Box 35, File 35.5. Sebba's review of Voegelin's work on gnosticism was published as "History, Modernity, Gnosticism," in *The Philosophy of Order: Essays on History, Consciousness and Politics*, ed. Peter J. Opitz and Gregor Sebba (Stuttgart: Klett-Cotta, 1981), 190–241. The expression "Gnostic immanentization of the eschaton" is from *The New Science of Politics*, 234 and 240–41.

41. For Bultmann's reservations, see above. Manfred Henningsen notes that Gilles Quispel considered "Voegelin's symbolic transfer of meaning from ancient Gnostic religion to modern ideological movements with some reservation." See his "Editor's Introduction" in *Modernity without Restraints*, 16. Finally, in 1987, Hans Jonas told Eugene Webb that Voegelin had not understood his conception of gnosticism. See Eugene Webb, "Voegelin's 'Gnosticism' Reconsidered," 72, n. 13.

42. Eric Voegelin to Arno Baruzzi, 30 December 1977, Box 7, File 7.15.

43. The rules outlined in *The New Science of Politics*, in *Modernity without Restraint*, 109–12, are a more sophisticated version of the rules from *On the Form of the American Mind*, referred to above.

44. See Michael G. Franz, *Eric Voegelin and the Politics of Spiritual Revolt: The Roots of Modern Ideology* (Baton Rouge: Louisiana State University Press, 1993); Eugene Webb, "Eric Voegelin at the End of an Era: Differentiations of Consciousness and the Search for the Universal," in *International and Interdisciplinary Perspectives on Eric Voegelin*, ed. Stephen A. McKnight and Geoffrey L. Price (Columbia: University of Missouri Press, 1997), 159–88; Eugene Webb, "Review of Michael G. Franz, *Eric Voegelin and the Politics of Spiritual Revolt*," in *Eric Voegelin Research News* 3 (1997), archived at *http://vax2.concordia.ca/~vorenews*; and Geoffrey L. Price, "Recovery from Metastatic Consciousness: Voegelin and Jeremiah," in *Politics, Order and History: Essays on the Work of Eric Voegelin*, ed. Glenn Hughes, Stephen A. McKnight, and Geoffrey L. Price (Sheffield, UK: Sheffield Academic Press, 2001), 185–207 (185–86).

45. Transcript of a paper delivered by Eric Voegelin at the Eric Voegelin Symposium on "20 Years of *The New Science of Politics*," University of Notre Dame, Spring 1971, 2, Box 77, File 77.6.

46. Voegelin, *Autobiographical Reflections*, 66–67.

47. As noted above, the issue was still on his mind while he was working on what became his last published major essay. See Eric Voegelin, "Wisdom and the Magic of the Extreme," in *Collected Works of Eric Voegelin*, vol. 12, *Published Essays 1966–1985*, ed. Ellis Sandoz (Baton Rouge: Louisiana State University Press, 1990), 315–75 (338–39). It is present also in the unfinished *In Search of Order*, vol. 5, *Order and History* (Baton Rouge: Louisiana State University Press, 1987), 37.

48. The "livre de circonstance" is from a letter to Elizabeth Scott, 17 December 1959, Box 38, File 38.1.

49. Eric Voegelin to John H. Hallowell, 28 January 1953, Box 63, File 63.11; see also Eric Voegelin to Thomas H. Clancy, 26 April 1953, Box 63, File 63.11.

50. Gregor Sebba to Eric Voegelin, 30 September 1978, Box 35, File 35.7.

51. Eric Voegelin, "What is Political Reality?" in Voegelin, *Anamnesis: On the Theory of History and Politics* (Columbia: University of Missouri Press, 2002), 341–412 (343).

52. Voegelin, *In Search of Order,* 39.

53. See especially Paul Caringella, "Voegelin: Philosopher of Divine Presence," in *Eric Voegelin's Significance for the Modern Mind,* ed. Ellis Sandoz (Baton Rouge: Louisiana State University Press, 1991), 174–205.

54. See Eric Voegelin, *Israel and Revelation,* vol. 1, *Order and History* (Baton Rouge: Louisiana State University Press, 1956), 411; *The Ecumenic Age,* 264; *In Search of Order,* 103. All these passages are referred to in Caringella's article, "Voegelin: Philosopher of Divine Presence," 176–77.

55. For the "Platonic restraints," see Voegelin, *The Ecumenic Age,* 234.

56. Eric Voegelin, transcript of a lecture entitled "The Beyond and Its Parousia," given at Santa Clara University, 16 October 1982, at a conference on "The Meaning of History," Box 85, File 85.10, p. 25. See also Voegelin, "Wisdom and the Magic of the Extreme: A Meditation," 337. See Plato, *Laws,* trans. A. E. Taylor, in *The Collected Dialogues of Plato,* ed. Edith Hamilton and Huntington Cairns (Princeton, NJ: Princeton University Press, 19th printing, 2005), 1225–1513 (1244), 644d-e: "We may imagine that each of us living creatures is a puppet made by gods, possibly as a plaything, or possibly with some more serious purpose. That, indeed, is more than we can tell."

57. Paul Caringella introduced Voegelin to Josef Pieper's *The Silence of St Thomas,* first published in English by Pantheon Books in 1957. It is obvious why Pieper's discussion of the "negative element" in St. Thomas would have appealed to Voegelin, who in 1944 had called for a "new Thomas." See Eric Voegelin to Friedrich Engel-Janosi, 6 January 1944, Box 11, File 11.7. For Voegelin, humility is also central to "tolerance," which he, again following Bodin, conceives of "as a balance between the realms of silence and symbolic expression." See Voegelin, "What is Political Reality?" 396.

58. See, for example, letter to Herr Schüddekopf, 27 February 1953, Box 34, File 34.6. My translation.

59. In some of Voegelin's notes we find formulations that seem to suggest that Voegelin occasionally saw glimpses of the problem. See, for example, the notes dated 3 December 1970, Box 84, File 84.9, where Voegelin explains that mysticism arose as a "revolt of personal experience" against dogma and then adds, in parentheses and capitals, "TO WHAT EXTENT IS THE 'PERSONAL RESPONSE' BOUND TO THE 'SOCIAL FIELD'?"

60. The term *mimesis* is used in Eric Voegelin, "The Beginning and the Beyond: A Meditation on Truth," in *Collected Works of Eric Voegelin,* vol. 28, *What Is History? And Other Late Unpublished Writings,* ed. Thomas A. Hollweck and Paul Caringella (Baton Rouge: Louisiana State University Press, 1990), 173–232 (203), and in "Quod Deus Dicitur," *Collected Works of Eric Voegelin,* vol. 12, *Published Essays 1966–1985,* 376–94 (389). The quotation is from "Wisdom and the Magic of the Extreme," 349.

61. Voegelin, *In Search of Order,* 39.

62. Voegelin, *In Search of Order,* 37.

63. Paul Caringella shared this information concerning Voegelin's funeral plans with the "evforum" Yahoo group on 6 September 2005. See *http://groups.yahoo.com/group/evforum/message/4014* (accessed 10 August 2006).

64. René Girard, in James Williams and René Girard, "The Anthropology of the Cross: A Conversation with René Girard," in *The Girard Reader,* ed. James G. Williams (New York: Crossroad, 1996), 262–88 (284).

65. René Girard, *Deceit, Desire, and the Novel: Self and Other in Literary Structure,* trans. Yvonne Freccero (Baltimore: The Johns Hopkins University Press, 1965; reprinted 1988), 307.

66. Girard, *Deceit, Desire, and the Novel,* 308.

67. Girard, *Deceit, Desire, and the Novel,* 307.

68. Girard, *Deceit, Desire, and the Novel,* 296–97.

69. Girard, *Deceit, Desire, and the Novel,* 300.

70. Girard, *Deceit, Desire, and the Novel,* 310.

71. Girard, *Deceit, Desire, and the Novel,* 297.

72. Girard, *Deceit, Desire, and the Novel,* 297.

73. Girard, *Deceit, Desire, and the Novel,* 308–9.

74. Girard, *Deceit, Desire, and the Novel,* 311.

75. Girard, *Deceit, Desire, and the Novel,* 302.

76. Girard in "The Anthropology of the Cross," 285.

77. Girard in "The Anthropology of the Cross," 285–86.

78. Key titles in a growing list of publications include Thomas J. J. Altizer, "A New History and a New but Ancient God? A Review-Essay," in *Journal of the American Academy of Religion* 43 (1975): 757–64, reprinted in *Eric Voegelin's Thought: A Critical Appraisal,* ed. Ellis Sandoz (Durham, NC: Duke University Press, 1982), 179–88; Thomas J. J. Altizer, "The Theological Conflict between Strauss and Voegelin," in *Faith and Political Philosophy: The Correspondence between Leo Strauss and Eric Voegelin,* ed. Peter Emberley and Barry Cooper (University Park, PA: Penn State University Press, 1993), 267–77; Bernhard W. Anderson, "Politics and the Transcendent: Voegelin's Philosophical and Theological Exposition of the Old Testament in the Context of the Ancient Near East," in *Eric Voegelin's Search for Order in History,* ed. Stephen A. McKnight (Lanham, MD: University Press of America, 1987), 62–100; Bruce Douglass, "The Gospel and Political Order: Eric Voegelin on the Political Role of Christianity," *Journal of Politics* 38 (1976): 25–45; Bruce Douglass, "A Diminished Gospel: A Critique of Voegelin's Interpretation of Christianity," in *Eric Voegelin's Search for Order in History,* ed. Stephen A. McKnight (Lanham, MD: University Press of America, 1987), 139–54; Michael P. Frederici, *Eric Voegelin: The Restoration of Order* (Wilmington, DE: ISI Books, 2002), 166–205; Michael P. Morrissey, *Consciousness and Transcendence: The Theology of Eric Voegelin* (Notre Dame, IN: University of Notre Dame Press, 1994); Gerhart Niemeyer, "Eric Voegelin's Philosophy and the Drama of Mankind," *Modern Age* 20 (Winter 1976): 22–39; Gerhart Niemeyer, "Christian Faith, and Religion, in Eric Voegelin's Work," *Review of Politics* 57 (1995): 91–104; John J. Ranieri, "What Voegelin Missed in the Gospel," in *Contagion: Journal of Violence, Mimesis, and Culture* 7 (Spring 2000): 125–59; William M. Thompson, "Voegelin on Jesus Christ," in *Voegelin and the Theologian: Ten Studies in Interpretation,* ed. John Kirby and William M. Thompson, Toronto Studies in Theology

vol.10 (Toronto: Edwin Mellen Press, 1983), 178–221; William M. Thompson, "Christ and Christianity in *Israel and Revelation*," in *Voegelin's Israel and Revelation: An Interdisciplinary Debate and Anthology,* ed. William M. Thompson and David L. Morse (Milwaukee: Marquette University Press, 2000), 215–41; William M. Thompson, "'The Gospel Movement': Pulls and Counterpulls in Voegelin's Interpretation of Christ and Christianity," in *Politics, Order and History: Essays on the Work of Eric Voegelin,* ed. Glenn Hughes, Stephen A. McKnight, and Geoffrey L. Price (Sheffield, UK: Sheffield University Press, 2001), 440–61; Fritz Wagner, "Voegelin and Christianity," paper delivered at a panel organized by the Eric Voegelin Society at the annual conference of the American Political Science Association, Boston 2002, *http://www.artsci.lsu.edu/voegelin/EVS/panel82002.htm#Wagner* (accessed 18 August 2006); David Walsh, "The Reason-Revelation Tension in Strauss and Voegelin," in *Faith and Political Philosophy,* ed. Emberley and Cooper, 349–68; Harold L. Weatherby, "Myth, Fact, and History: Voegelin on Christianity," *Modern Age* 12 (1978): 144–50; Eugene Webb, "Eric Voegelin's Theory of Revelation," in *Thomist* 42 (1978): 95–110; Frederick D. Wilhelmsen, "Professor Voegelin and the Christian Tradition," in Wilhelmsen, *Christianity and Political Philosophy* (Athens: University of Georgia Press, 1978), 193–208.

79. Hannah Arendt is quoted in Sebba's "Prelude and Variations," 648.

80. Niemeyer, "Eric Voegelin's Philosophy and the Drama of Mankind," 35.

81. Eric Voegelin to Donald. R. Ellegood, 15 January 1961, Box 23, File 23.28.

82. Eric Voegelin to Donald. R. Ellegood, 22 January 1961, Box 23, File 23.28.

83. Eric Voegelin to Hans Sedlmayer, 31 May 1970, Box 35, File 35.8.

84. Eric Voegelin to Donald R. Ellegood, 9 March 1959, Box 23, File 23.28. In his responses to readers who inquired about the fate of volume 4, Voegelin was eager to defuse the impression that the delay had anything to do with Christianity "breaking his scheme," to use Arendt's formulation. The problem, he insisted on those occasions, was not Christianity but modernity. See, for example, Eric Voegelin to David A. Nordquest, 19 August 1969, Box 27, File 27.17.

85. Voegelin, *The Ecumenic Age,* 250.

86. Eric Voegelin, "The Gospel and Culture," in *Collected Works of Eric Voegelin,* vol. 12, *Published Essays 1966–1985,* 172–212 (208).

87. Voegelin, *The Ecumenic Age,* 246.

88. Voegelin, *The Ecumenic Age,* 267.

89. Voegelin, *The Ecumenic Age,* 241.

90. Eric Voegelin to Donald R. Ellegood, 22 January 1961, Box 23, File 23.28.

91. Eric Voegelin, "Immortality: Experience and Symbol," in *Collected Works of Eric Voegelin,* vol. 12, *Published Essays 1966–1985,* 52–94 (79).

92. A further reference to Chalcedon is in Voegelin, "Wisdom and the Magic of the Extreme," 370.

93. Voegelin, "The Gospel and Culture," 189–90.

94. Voegelin, *The Ecumenic Age,* 20.

95. See Voegelin, "The Gospel and Culture," 200.

96. In the earliest plans for volume 4 of *Order and History*, "Apocalypse, Christianity and Gnosis" was to be treated as *one* complex of religions. See, for example, Eric Voegelin to Donald R. Ellegood, 22 February 1963, Box 24, File 24.1. Also in Voegelin, "Political Science and the Intellectuals," unpublished essay, Box 62, File 62.17, p. 12.

97. Eric Voegelin to R. J. Bishirjian, 20 July 1977, Box 8, File 8.18.

98. All quotations from Voegelin, *The Ecumenic Age*, 242–43.

99. Anibal A. Bueno, "Consciousness, Time and Transcendence in Eric Voegelin's Philosophy," in *The Philosophy of Order: Essays on History, Consciousness and Politics*, ed. Peter J. Opitz and Gregor Sebba (Stuttgart: Klett-Cotta, 1981), 91–109 (106).

100. Eric Voegelin to Anibal A. Bueno, 24 February 1981, Box 8, File 8.52. My emphasis.

101. Voegelin to Bueno, 24 February 1981.

102. Voegelin, "Wisdom and the Magic of the Extreme," 337.

103. I am assuming that the editors of the volume preserved the capitalization of the original manuscript/typescript.

104. From Thomas Hollweck, "Reading, Not Deconstructing Voegelin After All," *http://www.artsci.lsu.edu/voegelin/EVS/Panel32002.htm#Hollweck* (accessed 14 August 2006).

105. Voegelin, "Wisdom and the Magic of the Extreme," 369.

106. Robert Hamerton-Kelly, quoted from the transcript of a session of the "Politics and Apocalypse" Workshop, Stanford, California, July 2004, session with Paul Caringella, Tape #1, 2, p. 36.

107. Ellis Sandoz, in the second edition of *The Voegelinian Revolution* (New Brunswick, NJ: Transaction, 2000), tells the story of a late exchange between Voegelin and his wife, Lissy, just days before he died, in which he exclaimed, "At last I understand Christianity!" She replied: "Yes, Eric, but you're going to take it with you!" The evidence for Voegelin's late exclamation is unknown, but the statement as such, if authentic, implies that he felt that, until that very moment, he had been unable to understand Christianity.

108. Eric Voegelin to Donald E. Stanford, 15 September 1970, Box 43, File 43.15.

109. Zdravko Planinc, "The Uses of Plato in Voegelin's Philosophy of Consciousness," *Voegelin Research News* 2, no. 3 (September 1996), *http://vax2.concordia.ca/~vorenews/v-rnII3.html*.

110. Lothar Kramm drew Voegelin's attention to this fact in a letter of 7 July 1982, Box 22, File 22.4. However, Voegelin did not reconsider his position. *In Search of Order* repeats again that the Greek word *metaxy* was "developed by Plato as the technical term in his analysis of the structure [of consciousness]" (16). Voegelin's analysis of the term drew on Liddell-Scott's Greek-English lexicon. See Eric Voegelin to Manfred Henningsen, 26 December 1964, Box 17, File 17.14, p.2.

111. Lissy Voegelin, foreword to *In Search of Order*, xv.

112. Voegelin, "Wisdom and the Magic of the Extreme," 317.

113. Voegelin, "The Beginning and the Beyond," 191.

114. Eric Voegelin to Gregor Sebba, 16 November 1970, Box 35, File 35.6.

115. Voegelin, "The Beginning and the Beyond," 193.

116. Voegelin, "The Beginning and the Beyond," 194.

117. Voegelin, "The Beginning and the Beyond," 196.

118. Voegelin, "The Beginning and the Beyond," 199.

119. Voegelin, "The Beginning and the Beyond," 197.

120. Voegelin, "The Beginning and the Beyond," 191.

121. See also "Response to Professor Altizer's 'A New History and a New but Ancient God?'" in *Collected Works of Eric Voegelin,* vol. 12, *Published Essays 1966–1985,* 292–303 (294).

122. Voegelin, "The Beginning and the Beyond," 193.

123. See, for example, Morrissey, *Consciousness and Transcendence,* 14 and 16.

124. Anselm of Canterbury, preface to *Proslogion,* trans. M. J. Charlesworth, in Anselm of Canterbury, *The Major Works,* ed. Brian Davies and G. R. Evans (Oxford: Oxford University Press, 1998), 82–104 (82).

125. From R. W. Southern, *Saint Anselm: A Portrait in a Landscape* (Cambridge: Cambridge University Press, 1990), 128.

126. Anselm, "Reply to Gaunilo," trans. M. J. Charlesworth, in Anselm of Canterbury, *The Major Works,* 111.

127. Anselm, preface to *Proslogion,* 82–83.

128. Girard, *Deceit, Desire and the Novel,* 308–9.

129. See Southern, *Saint Anselm,* 129.

130. Southern, *Saint Anselm,* 117.

131. Southern, *Saint Anselm,* 114–15.

132. Eric Voegelin to Donald R. Ellegood, 22 February 1963, Box 24, File 24.1.

133. Voegelin, *In Search of Order,* 13.

134. Anselm, *Proslogion,* 1, 84.

135. Anselm, *Proslogion,* 14, 95–96; on this theme, see especially *Proslogion,* 16.

136. Anselm, *Proslogion,* 14, 96.

137. Voegelin, "Quod Deus Dicitur," 383; the section is also quoted, with less analysis, in "The Beginning and the Beyond," 195.

138. Anselm, *Proslogion,* 14, 96. My emphasis.

139. Anselm, *Proslogion,* 1, 87. My emphasis.

140. See the helpful discussion by Montague Brown, "Faith and Reason in Anselm: Two Models," in *The Saint Anselm Journal* 2, no. 1 (Fall 2004): 10–21.

141. Augustine, *Confessions,* 1.1, trans. John K. Ryan (Garden City, NY: Image Books, 1960), 43.

142. Those who claim that the two meditations—Voegelin's and Augustine's/Anselm's—are the same not only in terms of their structure but also in terms of their meaning already operate from within Voegelin's framework.

143. See also Josef Pieper, *The Concept of Sin,* trans. Edward T. Oakes, S.J. (South Bend, IN: St. Augustine's Press, 2001), especially chapter 5: "Pride and Desire."

Contributors

ROBERT HAMERTON-KELLY was educated at the University of Cape Town and Rhodes University (BA, 1958) in South Africa, at Gonville and Caius College, Cambridge University in the UK (BA, 1961; MA 1966) and Union Theological Seminary, New York City (Th D 1966). He was a fellow of the Alexander von Humboldt Foundation at the University of Münster (Westfalen) in 1972 and at the University of Munich in 1977. He was an Assistant Professor of Religion at Scripps College in Claremont, California, (1966–70), an Associate Professor of the New Testament at McCormick Theological Seminary, Chicago, (1970–72) and Dean of Chapel, Senior Minister of Memorial Church and Consulting Professor of Religious Studies and, by courtesy, Classics (1972–86) at Stanford University in California. He was also Senior Research Scholar in Ethics in the Center for International Security and Arms Control and the Institute for International Studies at Stanford (1986–1997).

As Dean of Chapel and Consulting Professor he was a full member of the Stanford Faculty (Member of the Academic Council) and as a Research Scholar, a member of the Academic Staff. He lectured in Religious Studies, in the Greek section of Classics, and in the Ethics of International Security in general (Just War Theory and the proper use of military force) and the ethics of nuclear weapons in particular (Deterrence), in the department of Political Science: Program in International Relations. He retired early from Stanford in

1997 to become the Senior Minister of the Woodside Village Church in the vicinity of Stanford, and retired from there in 2004. Since retirement he continues to host a biweekly seminar at the university with René Girard on the theme of Religion and Violence, and to lecture and publish in that field. He is one of three founding members of the Colloquium on Violence and Religion, organized in 1990 and now a flourishing international scholarly group whose journal, *Contagion*, is a leading publication in the field.

RENÉ GIRARD is Andrew B. Hammond Professor of French Language, Literature and Civilization and Professor of Comparative Literature, Emeritus at Stanford University and a member of the Académie française. He was born in the southern French city of Avignon on Christmas day in 1923. Between 1943 and 1947, he studied in Paris at the École des Chartres, an institution for the training of archivists and historians, where he specialized in medieval history. In 1947 he went to Indiana University on a year's fellowship and eventually made almost his entire career in the United States. He completed a PhD in history at Indiana University in 1950 but also began to teach literature, the field in which he would first make his reputation. He taught at Duke University and at Bryn Mawr before becoming a professor at Johns Hopkins in Baltimore. In 1971 he went to the State University of New York at Buffalo for five years, returned to Johns Hopkins, and then finished his academic career at Stanford University where he taught between 1981 and his retirement in 1995.

Girard continues to lecture and write and still offers a seminar at Stanford, where he and his wife Martha make their home. In 1990, friends and colleagues of Girard's established the Colloquium on Violence and Religion to further research and discussion about the themes of Girard's work.

FRED LAWRENCE is Associate Professor of Theology at Boston College. He is the founder and director of the Lonergan Workshop, an annual workshop held at Boston College where Lonergan scholars share their research. He also edits the *Lonergan Workshop* journal, an annual publication of the papers presented at the previous year's workshop.

JÓZEF NIEWIADOMSKI was born in 1951 (in Poland). He studied Philosophy and Theology at the Catholic University in Lublin/Poland and at the Theological Faculty of the University of Innsbruck. He was Lecturer in Theology and Philosophy in Innsbruck and Salzburg. From 1991 to 1996 he served as Professor in Linz, Austria. Since 1996 he has been Professor for Dogmatic Theology at the Theological Faculty of the University of Innsbruck, where, since 2004, he has been Dean of the Faculty. Niewiadomski has been Guest-Professor in Jerusalem and is a member of the European Academy of Science and Arts.

WOLFGANG PALAVER was born in 1958 in Zell am Ziller (Austria). He is professor of Catholic social thought at the Institute for Systematic Theology and chair of the interdisciplinary research platform "World Order–Religion–Violence" of the University of Innsbruck. Since 2003 he is also executive secretary of the Colloquium on Violence and Religion. He has written articles and books on Thomas Hobbes, Carl Schmitt, and on the relationship between religion and violence. His most recent books are *René Girards mimetische Theorie* (2004) and *Passions in Economy, Politics, and the Media: In Discussion with Christian Theology* (Edited with Petra Steinmair-Pösel; 2005).

JOHN RANIERI is Associate Professor of Philosophy at Seton Hall University, South Orange, New Jersey. He is the author of *Eric Voegelin and the Good Society* (1995), as well as a number of articles dealing with the work of René Girard, Bernard Lonergan, and Leo Strauss. He is currently working on a book focusing on the ways in which Eric Voegelin and Leo Strauss make use of the Bible in their political philosophies. This is part of his overall interest in the relationship between biblical traditions and contemporary cultural/political theory.

STEFAN ROSSBACH received his doctorate from the European University Institute, Florence, and is now Lecturer in Political Theory and Methodology in the Department of Politics and International Relations at the University of Kent at Canterbury. He is the founding director of the Centre for the Study of Politics and Spirituality (CSPS), also based in Canterbury. His research focuses on the spiritual dimension of politics and political philosophy. Among his publications is *Gnostic Wars: The Cold War in the Context of a History of Western Spirituality* (Edinburgh University Press).

PETER THIEL is an American financier, entrepreneur and philanthropist. In 1998, Thiel founded PayPal where, in four years as CEO, he led the electronic payments company to profitability and an IPO. Today, PayPal's 133 million customers (in 103 countries) transfer $50 billion annually. After selling PayPal to eBay, Thiel launched Clarium Capital Management, a global macro fund, where he invests $2 billion as the firm's CEO and portfolio manager. In 2004, Thiel became a founding investor and board member of Facebook, now one of the ten most trafficked Internet sites in the United States, with 30 billion page views per month. Also in 2004, Thiel founded and became Chairman of Palantir Technologies, a national security software company that allows governments and businesses to detect subtle relationships hidden in large amounts of data.

Thiel earned a BA in Philosophy from Stanford University in 1989 and a JD from Stanford Law School in 1992. He sits on the Board of Overseers of the Hoover Institution and has taught on issues of globalization and sovereignty at Stanford Law School.

Printed and bound by CPI Group (UK) Ltd, Croydon, CR0 4YY

09/06/2025

14685842-0001